W9-AFO-794

Jean Rhys at "World's End"

Jean Rhys at "World's End"

Novels of Colonial and Sexual Exile

by Mary Lou Emery

 University of Texas Press, Austin

First Edition, 1990

Requests for permission to reproduce material from this work
should be sent to Permissions, University of Texas Press, Box 7819,
Austin, Texas 78713-7819.

⊛ The paper used in this publication meets the minimum
requirements of American National Standard for Information
Sciences—Permanence of Paper for Printed Library Materials,
ANSI Z39.48-1984.

Library of Congress Cataloging-in-Publication Data

Emery, Mary Lou.
    Jean Rhys at "World's End" : novels of colonial and sexual exile /
by Mary Lou Emery. — 1st ed.
       p.   cm.
    Includes bibliographical references.
    ISBN 0-292-71126-3
    1. Rhys, Jean—Criticism and interpretation.   2. West Indies in
literature.   3. Colonies in literature.   4. Sex role in literature.
5. Exiles in literature.   6. Women in literature.   I. Title.
PR6035.H96Z64   1990
823'.912—dc20   90-31402
                                                               CIP

To Stephen Paul Wootton
and Claire Elizabeth Emery-Wootton

Contents

Acknowledgments

*F*or incomparable cooking and conversation that nourished my thinking throughout the writing of this book, I would like to thank my friends and colleagues of the Food for Thought Feminist/Critical Theory Reading Group. I am especially grateful to Adalaide Morris, whose thoughtful and attentive responses to sometimes several drafts of at least half of the book's chapters helped me to clarify concepts, more purposefully direct arguments, and make this study much better than it might have been; to Katherine Hayles, whose responses to drafts of several chapters brought to my attention further implications of my arguments; and to Huston Diehl, whose suggestions allowed me to envision alternate ways of presenting and organizing material. I want to thank Peter Nazareth for carefully reading an early draft of Part One and, perhaps most important, for aiding my continuing education in Caribbean and Third World literatures.

Students are most often the ones who educate the educators, and I have had the good fortune of reading the writings of Jean Rhys and Wilson Harris with an especially thoughtful group of graduate students just as this book entered the copy-editing stage. I am grateful to all of the members of the Fall 1989 course Modernist Crosscurrents for allowing me to test my ideas in discussions with them and for questions and suggestions that helped me to refine particular points of my arguments.

Thanks to Laura Mumford for questions concerning an early draft of Part One, to Don Marshall for responses to Chapter 3, to Cheryl Herr for comments on a version of Part One, and to Rebecca Faery for encouraging remarks about brief but important sections of the manuscript. Lucio P. Ruotolo first encouraged my interest in Jean Rhys, and I am thankful for his continuing enthusiasm.

I am grateful to the University of Iowa for awarding me an Old Gold Award and a Developmental Assignment and to the Department of English for granting me a semester's leave of absence so that I might begin and continue work on this study. While on Developmental Assignment, I worked at University House on the University of Iowa's Oakdale Campus, where the collegial atmosphere organized by Jay Semel and the computing facilities and other essentials of current scholarship managed by Lorna Olson aided in the manuscript's completion. The Office of the Dean of Arts and Letters at Stanford University provided funds for some initial research on Jean Rhys at the McFarlin Library at the University of Tulsa. I would like to thank Thomas F. Staley, David Farmer, and the staff of Rare Books and Special Collections at the University of Tulsa for their helpful cooperation.

Portions of Chapter 2 first appeared in *Twentieth Century Literature* 28, no. 4 (Winter 1982): 418–430, and portions of Chapter 8 first appeared in *The Review of Contemporary Fiction* 5, no. 2 (Summer 1985): 145–150.

Introduction

*I*n silences and the spaces in between words, sounds, shapes, and colors, we have learned to find much of significance in twentieth-century art and literature. Such spaces can be social as well as aesthetic. In Jean Rhys's novels, silenced "foreign" and female voices, inhabiting marginalized and usually urban social spaces, speak and signify their lives in ways that have profoundly engaged and disturbed the novels' readers. Outsiders among outsiders, characters such as Anna Morgan in *Voyage in the Dark* (1934) and Sasha Jansen in *Good Morning, Midnight* (1939) find expression in narratives that also remain marginal to even alternate modernist canons of women's and West Indian literature. Perhaps the best way to understand the powerful yet disconcerting effects of reading Rhys's fiction is to understand more fully the nature of the in-between spaces it explores.

They are the spaces, discovered by trespassing and then traversed repeatedly, of colonial and sexual exile: the streets of London in 1914 where a young Creole woman attempts to support herself after the death of her West Indian father, the bars of Paris in 1937 where a somewhat older woman of vague nationality attempts to improvise an identity, and the rooming houses in either city that both shelter and isolate most of Rhys's solitary protagonists. The dates and places are not insignificant. The fact that London was on the verge of war in 1914, that the Purity Crusades patrolled its streets suspicious of the activities of working-class women, that fascist bombs exploded in the streets in 1937 in Paris, and that thousands of Jews were made homeless as the Nazis marched through Europe—all contribute to our understanding of the nature of the in-between spaces in Rhys's novels.

These marginalized spaces and the characters who make their lives in them find representation in narratives that are also difficult to place securely. From a feminist perspective, Rhys's protagonists can be read sympathetically as victims of "the social structure" or of "patriarchal oppression." Nevertheless, their apparent complicity in their own oppression remains to disturb readers, and psychological diagnoses of passivity, masochism, and even schizophrenia have become a critical commonplace. Reading Rhys's fiction as West Indian literature suggests a cultural and historical context outside of the strictly European and offers possibilities for interpretation that go beyond the psychological. However, feminist and Third World perspectives rarely combine in readings of Rhys's work. When they do, the resulting analysis usually depends upon a structural analogy between colonial hierarchies and sexual oppression that still positions the protagonist as a victim who lacks agency and offers little or no resistance.

In this study, I am interested in the tension between the two spaces or contexts of Rhys's writing—the West Indian colonial context and the modernist European—as it is inscribed in terms of sex/gender relations in her novels. I wish to direct critical attention away from the mainly European aesthetic, moral, and psychological standards that I believe have operated to misread and, at times, to devalue Rhys's writing, writing that, in fact, challenges those standards. This move away from the European and toward Caribbean cultural values complicates feminist perspectives on Rhys that view her works in terms of sexual difference only. I argue that the Caribbean cultures that emerge fully in *Wide Sargasso Sea* shift the moral ground of critical judgment by presenting an alternative to European concepts of character and identity. From the vision of this alternative, evaluations of Rhys's protagonists as passive or masochistic victims no longer hold; instead, we can perceive their efforts at dialogue, plural identities, and community. We can also attempt to understand the reasons for the successes and failures of their efforts within a historical framework that takes into account the ideologies of a male-dominated colonial system and its decline in the early twentieth century.

Decolonization meant (and means still) the end of a world governed by empire. In the dismantling of empire, old identities based on cultural, racial, gender, and class hierarchies fracture; new identities and nations emerge. With these shifts, the very concepts of identity and patriarchal nationhood are challenged. In the title of this study, "World's End" refers to this historical and conceptual rupture as the context of Jean Rhys's writing. The endings referred to are not truly final; they open new ways of seeing the world, of constituting identity in the previously occluded, marginalized, or in-between social spaces inhabited by Jean Rhys's protagonists.

As title, "World's End" works in an overdetermined way since Rhys associated it with the London district where she first began to write, and medieval Europeans used it to describe the islands from which she came. It aptly describes what European "discovery" brought to the natives of those islands and also, in a historical turnabout, the ending of the world of empire, four hundred years later, that decolonization brought and that European modernism signified.

"World's End" refers most particularly to the signs on the buses that Jean Rhys notes in her autobiography *Smile Please*. In the chapter titled "World's End and a Beginning," Rhys writes: "The room she got me was not in Chelsea but in Fulham. 'World's End' was on the buses. The first morning I woke up there it seemed to me the furniture was so like that in the room I had just left that moving hardly made any difference" (*Smile Please*, p. 128). The move did make a difference, however. Rhys was suffering then from what felt to her like the end of the world in the humiliating aftereffects of a love affair terminated by her lover, an older and wealthy man who continued to send her money through his attorneys. Nevertheless, alone in a boardinghouse room on the margins of London, she began to write her first novel, which became *Voyage in the Dark*, her third novel to be published: "It was after supper that night—as usual a glass of milk and some bread and cheese—that it happened. My fingers tingled, and the palms of my hands. I pulled a chair up to the table, opened an exercise book, and wrote *This is my Diary*. But it wasn't a diary. . . . I filled three exercise books and half another . . . ." (*Smile Please*, pp. 129, 130). Presumably, the manuscript recounted "everything that had happened to me in the last year and a half . . . what he'd said, what I'd felt" (*Smile Please*, p. 129); but by the time it had been revised and published in 1934, it had become what critics would later recognize as "our first Negritude novel," a remarkable and prototypical novel of a West Indian in exile.[1]

That a humiliating romance in which the older man speaks while the young woman can only feel[2] can also shape and be shaped by the experience of colonial exile tells us much about Jean Rhys's fiction and its place at the intersection of several kinds of modernism. One of these modernist crosscurrents is that of an emerging West Indian literature that develops from a strong sense of its own place in the Caribbean and of its plural histories and cultures. Hence, the title of this study refers also to the site at which Christopher Columbus disembarked in 1492 and on subsequent voyages, islands considered by

European geographers to be "an unknown land" located where "a part of our habitable earth ends."[3]

Columbus's "discovery" of the West Indies, his inability to call them by their proper names, and the ensuing colonization with its accompanying slave trade and brutal exploitation of the lands and their peoples launched a renaissance for Europe and a catastrophe for the native peoples of the Caribbean. The "New Heaven and World" which Columbus claimed for Spain was truly the world's end for its original inhabitants and for the African slaves brought there to labor. From within that catastrophe, however, developed historically the conditions for a new West Indies and the beginning of a new twentieth-century literature of which Jean Rhys is a major contributor, even originator.

Keeping in mind the locations represented in the several connotations of "World's End"—urban spaces marginalized by the appearance of solitary women in public, the Caribbean islands invaded and possessed by Europeans, and the islands and urban Europe upset in the process of decolonization—we can read the fiction categorized as Rhys's early "continental novels"[4] as, instead, beginning experiments in female and Third World modernism written in dialogue with European modernism. In the early novels, for example, the characters' attempts at resistance and community falter for specific social reasons and result in a narrative style of female irony that registers both the attempt and the failure, the expectation and the disillusionment. This irony, companion of an isolated and alienated female protagonist, vies in *Voyage in the Dark* with a more communal satirical laughter that derives from the Caribbean carnival. The tension between the two intonations, muted in the three other early novels, partakes also of an exploration of subjectivity that seeks an alternative to that of the European novel.

With the term "modernism," I include the process of social modernization, and my discussions of the novels move from close readings of particular passages to broader delineations of the social spaces in between cultures and in between what the Victorians perceived as public (masculine) and private (feminine) spheres. Within European discourse, these two different kinds of in-between spaces are linked through codings of mass culture as feminine, associations of the feminine with the "primitive," and perceptions of the colonial native as always part of a mass or crowd. Rhys's fiction responds to the constitution of the colonial woman as overdetermined Other through experimental narrative styles that question colonial and sexual ideologies and explore the political implications of modernism.

The following chronology marks major events in Rhys's life; it should also aid the reader in identifying and dating the various published and unpublished versions of Rhys's novels and in discerning the periods in which they were composed.[5]

1890	Ella Gwendolen Rees Williams born in Roseau Dominica.
1907	Leaves Dominica for England, where she attends Perse School for girls in Cambridge.
1908	Leaves Perse School for the Academy of Dramatic Art (now Royal Academy of Dramatic Art); her father dies; she joins traveling chorus troupe.
1909	Has love affair with wealthy older man who leaves her after eighteen months.
1911–1913(?)	Writes manuscript that later becomes *Voyage in the Dark*.
1917	Meets Jean Lenglet, a.k.a. Edward de Nève.
1919	Travels to Holland to marry Lenglet.
1920	Gives birth in Paris to son William, who dies three weeks later.
1922	Gives birth to daughter Maryvonne in Brussels. Assembles some stories or sketches titled "Triple Sec" (which later appear in *The Left Bank* [1927]) at the request of Pearl Adam, who introduces Rhys to Ford Madox Ford.
1923	Jean Lenglet is arrested for illegally entering France, sentenced to prison, and afterward extradited to Holland.
1924	Lives with Ford Madox Ford and Stella Bowen in Paris. Becomes Ford's mistress and protégée.
1927	Publication of *The Left Bank and Other Stories*.
1928	Publication of Rhys's first novel, *Postures* (originally titled *Masquerade* by Rhys, titled *Postures* by Chatto and Windus, then retitled and published in 1928 in England and 1929 in the United States as *Quartet*), which draws on her experiences with Ford and Bowen. Appearance of her translation of Francis Carco's *Perversity* under Ford Madox Ford's name.
1929–1932	Lives in England with Leslie Tilden Smith; visits Paris several times, while composing *After Leav-*

ing Mr. Mackenzie and after, until outbreak of World War II in Europe.

1930   Publication of *After Leaving Mr. Mackenzie.*

1932   Divorces Jean Lenglet and marries Leslie Tilden Smith. Publication of her translation of Edward de Nève's *Barred* (based on events that also appear in *Quartet*).

1934   Publication of *Voyage in the Dark* following revision of the concluding scenes at the publisher's request. The original version is published in Nancy Hemond Brown, "Jean Rhys and *Voyage in the Dark*," *London Magazine* 25, nos. 1 and 2.

1936   Spends four months in the West Indies, where she begins work on *Good Morning, Midnight.*

1939   Publication of *Good Morning, Midnight.*

1945   Works on early version of *Wide Sargasso Sea.* Death of Leslie Tilden Smith.

1947   Marries Smith's cousin, Max Hamer, and lives with him in London.

1952   Max Hamer imprisoned for six months for misappropriating check forms from his company.

1953   Moves with Hamer to Cornwall.

1956   Moves to Cheriton FitzPaine in Devon.

1957   BBC production of radio play based on *Good Morning, Midnight.* An ad is placed asking for Rhys's whereabouts; she answers and is "rediscovered" after years of obscurity. She announces she is working on a novel, which becomes *Wide Sargasso Sea.*

1964   Max Hamer dies; Rhys suffers a heart attack.

1966   Publication of *Wide Sargasso Sea,* which wins the W. H. Smith Award, the Arts Council of Great Britain Award for Writers, and the Heinemann Award of the Royal Society of Literature.

1968   Publication of *Tigers Are Better-Looking.*

1975   Publication of *My Day.*

1976   Publication of *Sleep It Off, Lady.*

1978   Receives the Commander of the Order of the British Empire for her contributions to literature.

1979   Dies on May 14. Posthumous publication of *Smile Please: An Unfinished Autobiography.*

Masquerades

One

Modernist Crosscurrents

*L*ike other West Indian writers of the pre– and post–World War I generations, Jean Rhys left the Caribbean island of her birth for the metropolitan centers of England and Europe. Uprooted from a closed community, she had to survive in what Bruce King has called "the chaos of western freedom."[1] However, unlike her fellow exiles, Claude McKay and V. S. Naipaul, whom King discusses, Rhys experienced a specifically female alienation and sexual vulnerability that intensified when her father's death forced her in 1908, a year after her arrival, to leave London's Academy of Dramatic Arts to earn her own living.

It is not surprising that Rhys, then called Gwendolyn Williams, changed her name to Vivien or Ella or Emma Gray and found work in a traveling chorus troupe.[2] At the turn of the twentieth century, the theater attracted women of almost every class—to its audiences with promises of glamor, sentiment, and romance and to its stages with promises of work, creativity, and independence. As a space in between what the Victorians perceived as the feminine domestic sphere and the masculine public realm, the theater institutionalizes female marginality. It seems to operate in two contradictory ways at once in giving meaning to working women's lives. The theater can make legitimate and pleasurable the fractured identities of socially displaced women, yet it cannot give them the "solid" class background they may lack or have lost by entering the theater. It disguises women whose social status might be questioned, and yet it immediately renders questionable their social status, especially their sexual respectability. Like the Caribbean carnivals of Rhys's homeland, it can turn the masks imposed upon social "others" into potentially subversive masquerades.[3] Yet the theater exposes "otherness" to view and consumption and, as an institution of European culture, perhaps contains it.

The writer now known as Jean Rhys relished the theatrical, and she felt vulnerable without the feminine costumes of fashion, makeup, and a married name. The West Indian carnival of her home in Dominica inspired similarly mixed feelings of pleasure and fear. It seemed to her that from the carnival parades "life surged up to us"; yet she "was very afraid of the masks."[4] Perhaps more than the European theater, the Caribbean carnival can claim a revolutionary history since its masquerades have triggered mass rebellions against colonial rule. Nevertheless, sociologists and critical theorists have debated whether the turnabouts of Carnival reinforce the hierarchies they repeat in reverse so that they, too, ultimately only contain revolutionary action.[5] Rhys's novels raise the question of the political force of masquerade and of the masses, whether colonial natives or twentieth-century women, who enact it.

The West Indian carnival and the European theater share similar political ambiguities as a result of the colonial history that connects them. The planters brought to the West Indies traditions of medieval European festivals which natives of the islands and imported Africans adapted to slave culture in celebrations that mimicked and satirized colonial masters just as they had ridiculed feudal and church authorities in Europe.[6] Both dramatic celebrations take place in marginal spaces that open the way for sexual, political, and imaginative license; the street and the stage become sites of illusion and fantastic transformations. These in-between spaces are neither properly public nor respectably private, and in them illusion manifests as reality. In the twentieth century, however, the European theater becomes an established institution even in its working-class vaudeville and intellectual avant-garde forms. Rhys's novels place carnival scenes and allusions to the carnival alongside events and metaphors of European theater as a challenge to the colonizing culture, as an alternate vision of community, and as a counter-worldview, often eclipsed by what Mikhail Bakhtin might call the "official feast" of early twentieth-century Europe.[7]

In the early novels, published between 1928 and 1939, carnival tropes express both the connections to European culture and the ambiguities of Carnival itself through the different possible meanings of "mask" and "masquerade." The explicit theme of masquerade is not confined to novels with a Caribbean setting.[8] For instance, Sasha Jansen, the protagonist in *Good Morning, Midnight* (1939), which takes place entirely in Europe, becomes a mistress of disguise in two senses of the word "mistress": she both manages disguise and submits to it sexually: "Another Pernod in the bar next door to the cinema. I sit at a corner table and sip it respectably, with lowered eyes. Je suis une femme convenable, just come out of the nearest cinema . . ."[9] Sasha attempts desperately to wear with success the masks that she believes others will perceive as respectable femininity. The French phrase and the reference to cinema suggest that European culture demands such feminine artifice. Disguise imprisons her in two ways: as a mask that is imposed by others, or that she believes others demand in order to treat her humanely, and as the perpetual masquerade, or masking of the lack of identity, that seems to constitute her "femininity":[10] "Besides, it isn't my face, this tortured and tormented mask. I can take it off whenever I like and hang it up on a nail. Or shall I place on it a tall hat with a green feather, hang a veil over the lot, and walk about the dark streets so merrily?" (*Midnight*, p. 43). Sasha first claims choice in this passage—more specifically, the right to refuse the mask that is the tortured face of femininity. She does not continue, however, to describe what she implies lies beneath the mask—"my face." Instead, she slips beyond an either-it-is-false/or-it-is-real set of choices into the realm of imaginative transformation. Hats, sometimes veiled, and new dresses, shoes, and gloves signify for all of Rhys's characters the respectable costume of a lady. Yet here Sasha imagines the hat as fantastically tall and feathered in green so that the mask becomes a deliberate masquerade and brings her the freedom to "walk about the dark streets," precisely the sites of her anxieties, "so merrily."

This dynamic between the notion of mask as imposed—a constraining simulation—and of masquerade as playful overacting that threatens to expose the mask works throughout Jean Rhys's fiction. The passage is edged with irony, and so are others that reveal Sasha's knowledge of the masquerade:

> I am in the middle of a long article by a lady who has had her breasts lifted when he takes the dryer off my head.
> "Voilà," he says . . . . "Yes," he says, "a very good blond cendré. A success." (*Midnight*, p. 62)

With such irony, the narrative continually liberates Sasha, if only for a moment. In this moment and others like it, she comes close to the carnivalesque.[11] That she cannot achieve its communal laughter results more from the context in which she makes the attempt than from any deficiency in her character, for throughout the novel, she attempts the playfulness of Carnival; at one point she yearns, "I've never been really young. I've never played . . ." (*Midnight*, p. 155).

The allusions to Carnival in *Good Morning, Midnight* perform as signs of protest and countercommunity that find expression in the play of "femininity" and questions of personal and, ultimately, literary style. However, Sasha's attempts at subversive play falter dangerously in Paris in 1937, where impending war and the rise of fascism figure far more powerfully than retracings, from Europe to the Caribbean and back again, of the carnivalesque.

The overwhelming danger facing Sasha, represented in an "exhibition" that is both actual and metaphorical, is a political threat made personal due to her sexual vulnerability. Commenting on the "female transgressor as public spectacle," Mary Russo states, ". . . in the everyday indicative world, women and their bodies, certain bodies, in certain public framings, in certain public spaces, are always already transgressive—dangerous, and in danger."[12] Rhys's protagonists find that their longings for adventure have made them transgressors of public spaces, and they fear making spectacles of themselves. Carnival emerges as a memory and a discourse that allows them to rescript the meaning of the spectacle so that they do indeed make it themselves and so that it gains the potential for ritual resistance. Nevertheless, while their presence on the streets, in bars, and in cafes becomes disturbing to others, they feel exposed and threatened. Even their efforts at alliance with other marginalized people bring great risk. Russo cites the point made by Victor Turner and Emmanuel Le Roy that the marginal position of women, Jews, and others in the "indicative" world makes their presence in the "subjunctive" or possible world of the carnival "quintessentially" dangerous; Jews have been stoned and women raped.[13] The carnival metaphors in Rhys's novels resonate with this contradictory potential freedom and inevitable risk, a sometimes exhilarating yet frightening slide between playful pleasures and the play between life and death. They motivate narrative experiment, unsettling readers' expectations of female protagonists and shaping new dimensions in the modernist novel and in West Indian literature.

In *Voyage in the Dark* (1934), masquerade is explicitly tied to actual carnival scenes so that "carnival as semiotic performance" and "carnival as historical performance" engage simultaneously.[14] *Voyage in the Dark* portrays a young Creole woman who tours the small towns of England with a music hall company. This version of the European theater plunges Anna Morgan into poverty and sexual vulnerability from which she never recovers. At the novel's end, in a fever from a crudely induced abortion, she hallucinates scenes of a carnival celebration in which masks become overdetermined signs of her eclipsed West Indian identity, her sexual exploitation in England, the false authority of white Europeans, and also, as they did historically, parodies of such authority.

> He laughed and it sounded funny. "Les émotions fortes," he said. I said, "Stop, please stop." "I knew you'd say that," he said. His face was white.
> *A pretty useful mask that white one watch it and the slobbering tongue of an idiot will stick out—* . . .
> *I was watching them from between the slats of the jalousies dancing along dressed in red and blue and yellow the women with their dark necks and arms covered with white powder . . . and I knew why they were laughing . . .* (*Voyage*, pp. 158–159)

Masks, ritual inversion, unruliness, the grotesque body, communal and satirical laughter conjoin the "primitive" or colonial outsider with "the feminine" as socially constructed Other—and conversely, as the Other attempts to constitute her subjectivity in the face, so to speak, of her otherness.

Through the theater, carnival, masks, and masquerade, Rhys's novels place twentieth-century European social and literary values into narrative tension with an emerging Caribbean vision. In her fifth novel, *Wide Sargasso Sea* (1966), published twenty-seven years after the publication of the last of her "continental novels," the Caribbean vision finds full expression and redirects our readings of the earlier novels as beginning experiments in West Indian literature. The carnival tropes in Rhys's novels express the three contexts of her writing that I will discuss in Part One: the Caribbean culture in which she grew up and its literary naissance in the mid–twentieth century, the modernist celebration of style in which she apprenticed her writing in Paris of the 1920s, and the "spectacle" of femininity or of women transgressing masculine public space that her characters enact in desperate alienation. My discussion circulates among several critical discourses, including the history and criticism of West Indian literature, analyses of European modernism, and the social history of women in the modern period. Rhys's novels invite us to see the connections, made invisible through colonial ideology and literary specialization, among these contexts. They urge us to weave these discourses together even, or especially, with their rough edges showing, for the connections expose histories of tension and violence.

*T*o view Jean Rhys as a woman writer only or to discuss her as a West Indian author or a European modernist exclusively limits our understanding of her work. For in each context, her writing remains outside the main current by virtue of its participation in the other two. I see her novels as textual sites both in between and intersecting these three important currents of twentieth-century cultural history and literature. My interest in the events of her life, therefore, does not lie in building a psychological portrait or even in constructing a unified narrative that ties the events together. Rather, I am interested in her plural and often conflicting outsider identities as West Indian writer, European modernist, and woman writer at the closing of the era of empire, and the ways in which she occupied the spaces in between such identities.

In the in-between social spaces that display and expose Rhys's characters, they discover that "it's in what you think is a distorting mirror that you see the truth" (*Midnight*, p. 24). To play with such mirrors, as at a fair, can prompt hilarious and subversive "reimagings" of self. Rhys's writing is rich with ironies, parodies, and satires that distort conventions of the everyday for the sake of truths that cannot be verified except through the logic of carnival masquerade and turnabout.

The statement also implies its opposite—that it's in what we think are clear reflections that we miss the truth. If we take such logic seriously, questions posed by masquerade and the distortions of carnival mirrors can guide our thinking about the always problematic relation between the author and her writing. Commentators on Rhys's novels speak of their protagonists as if they are all reflections of one another, as if "the heroines are basically interchangeable."[15] The novels are also commonly read as almost unwavering mirrors of Jean Rhys's life. Some critics rearrange the chronological order of the novels' publication in their discussions to follow the life of what becomes a single protagonist at different ages, and then describe or imply the ways the protagonist is Jean Rhys.[16] Autobiographical readings persist in spite of the arguments of several critics, such as Veronica Marie Gregg, concerning the differences among author, character, and text. Gregg has distinguished convincingly between the "truths" that Rhys sought to express in her writing, pressuring the raw materials of language and literary tradition, and the "facts" or "events" of her life.[17] We have much evidence in Rhys's letters and the drafts of her manuscripts to demonstrate her dedication to what might be considered the distorting craft of writing fiction.[18]

The pressures of language and literary tradition from three emerging canons—the female, European modernist, and the West Indian— reshape the biographical facts as literary truths in Rhys's novels.

The larger social context of these literary movements gives meaning to both the distorting mirror of the text and the truths we may see in it, and a sociocritical perspective can give us the wide focus we need to see the multiple contexts of Rhys's writing. We can distinguish then between an approach that views her characters as psychological types or reflections of Jean Rhys and one that sees connections among the social forces shaping the author and the novels. The first approach draws upon and develops European literary and psychological notions of "character" and "self" and so misses the implications of the Caribbean context of Rhys's writing and her identity as a West Indian writer critical of the colonizing countries' concepts and values even if governed by them. The second approach views the events of Rhys's life as indicators of the conflicting values, ideologies, and social circumstances in which she wrote. It allows us to perceive in the same mirror competing cultural visions and to understand them within a larger gendered colonial system as it declines.

Primary materials are available to tell us about Rhys's life, including her incomplete autobiography *Smile Please* (1979), *The Letters of Jean Rhys* (1984), and the unpublished notebooks that Teresa O'Connor has incorporated into her recent study.[19] Many of the "facts" are now well known: her upbringing in Dominica, various jobs in England with traveling theatrical companies followed by a disastrous love affair, a marriage, and a period spent wandering in Europe.

Many critics view her mentorship with Ford Madox Ford in Paris during the 1920s as the most important influence of her writing career, and certainly he must have helped her along. Their relation seems all the more significant since she also became Ford's mistress.[20] However, I think that such influences as Ford's on Rhys's writing are similar to those of European modernism on other West Indian writers who found in it techniques and aesthetic values that they adapted to express the concerns of an emerging Third World literature. Edward Brathwaite, Derek Walcott, and Wilson Harris, for example, found formal models in T. S. Eliot and in Joseph Conrad that helped them to shape the materials of Caribbean culture, its multiracial societies, folk dialects, and the historical conflicts of colonialism.[21]

Viewing Rhys as a Third World writer as well as a woman in exile in Paris helps us to better understand her outsider status there. In her study *Women of the Left Bank*, Shari Benstock has described Rhys as "an outsider among outsiders," who never found a community of writers or of women who might nurture and stimulate her talent.[22] Isolated from women and taken up by men as a protégée or mistress, Rhys experienced exile differently, by virtue of her colonial background, from someone like Gertrude Stein and, by virtue of her sex, from someone like Claude McKay. She married three times and gave birth to two children, one of whom died three weeks after its birth. She suffered from illness, poverty, and dependence on alcohol. In these "facts" are the traces of social forces that denied poor women proper medical and child care and denied unmarried women live-lihoods and respectability. Our understanding of Rhys's novels de-pends upon an understanding of the local nature of such social forces, particularly their ideological and actual operations in specific places and times, operations I will discuss later in this chapter and through-out the book.

In 1927, Rhys returned to England, where she eventually settled even though she said she hated its climate and values. To readers of her fiction-as-her-life, such contrariness, along with passivity, mas-ochism, victimage—drifting aimlessly, feeling fated to suffer help-lessly—characterize Rhys and her protagonists as if they mirrored one another clearly.[23] While we can find similarities between Rhys, as she and others present her life and psyche, and critics' interpreta-tions of her characters, the texts themselves question the evaluation of psychological and moral character in terms like "helpless," "pas-sive," and "masochistic." The themes of masquerade, along with other narrative elements, challenge such psychological essential-ism. What does it mean to describe, diagnose, and judge "character," especially female Caribbean character?

To explore the question further, we should consider the doubled homelessness of Rhys's characters. In North American and Euro-pean psychology, character begins at home, in interaction with a specific family in a particular culture. Yet the characters in Rhys's early novels lack homes and homelands. Circumstances and their own actions have isolated them from families, husbands, and friends. How dispossessed women constitute and know themselves becomes the question the novels explore. They do so in the in-between spaces, both physical and psychological, inhabited by the homeless.

*I*f all women by virtue of their sexual positioning as Other are mar-ginalized, as many feminists have argued, the female protagonists of Rhys's early novels experience a doubled marginality in their exile from the homes of men who could grant them lives of feminine do-mesticity and sexual respectability. Bereft of husbands and fathers, the heroines of Rhys's novels contend with the violence of femi-nized poverty and sexual barter. They do not stay at home; nor do they go home at night. They climb the stairs to a room somewhere on the Left Bank or in Bloomsbury, perhaps alone, perhaps not. They inhabit, for the most part, the streets, cafes, bars, and, if they can afford it, dress shops of European cities where no one knows where they come from or even their names. In this sense they participate in the anonymity of mass culture as they consume its manufactured clothes, movies, and world exhibitions. But their participation is specifically female; they constitute members of the crowds of women that Andreas Huyssen argues threatened the precarious masculine order of modernity.[24] Huyssen refers to the first wave of the feminist movement and the deliberate efforts made by women to enter public life, but in the case of Rhys's characters, we encounter women who entertain no ambitions; they simply find themselves thrust by circumstance outside the protections and constraints of the family. They wander almost aimlessly, living in between the gendered urban spaces of early twentieth-century England and Europe.

While Rhys's novels inscribe specifically female experiences and differ markedly from the works of male modernists in their point of view, even among works by women they are, as Benstock says of Rhys herself, marginal. The characters walk the streets of Paris and London without money, friends, or family. Unlike the narrator of Virginia Woolf's essay *Street Haunting*, they never return from their twilight wanderings to "their own doorstep again . . . to feel the old possessions, the old prejudices, fold us round; and the self which has been blown about at so many street corners . . . sheltered and enclosed."[25] We have only to compare Rhys's homeless protagonists to May Sinclair's Mary Olivier or to Woolf's Clarissa Dalloway or even Lily Brisco, with her nearby father and ties to upper-middle-class gentility, to see the differences in class and kinship that isolate them and that prohibit even the illusion of an enclosed and sheltered self.

Without such illusions, it becomes difficult in Rhys's novels to distinguish the mask from the masquerade; the play between these aspects of disguise, rather than a discovery of authentic selfhood, shapes the narrative and characterizations. Lacking authentic selfhood in European terms, Rhys's characters do not appear capable of overcoming difficulties; they seem weak, lacking in courage, and willingly exploited. They continually miss opportunities for epiphany or self-awareness. Perhaps for these reasons, unlike Virginia Woolf or H. D., Rhys has remained a disturbing presence on the edges of current feminist criticism.

If sexual difference is the major screen of interpretation, the characters and their fates (for they always seem "fated") conform to clichés of the feminine rather than expectations for the feminist.

Obsessions with makeup, clothes, and men mark the novels, perhaps even stigmatize them. Especially the early novels remain disturbing to feminist readers who sometimes prefer to exclude all but
the "West Indian" novels, *Wide Sargasso Sea* and *Voyage in the
Dark*, from their discussions.[26] Even so, they do not treat them as
West Indian literature. Instead they attribute the novels' merits to
their status as exemplary women's texts or to Jean Rhys's superior
technique,[27] not recognizing their Caribbean values and aesthetics.
Another kind of homelessness, that of colonial exile, brings to the
novels this alternate aesthetic.

Through colonial exile, the marginality of Rhys's female characters multiplies. Anna Morgan of *Voyage in the Dark* lives in England
in exile from her place of birth on the island of Dominica. However,
she never felt truly at home on her native island because of her
status as a white Creole woman. Elizabeth Nunez-Harrell has described this status as that of "an outcast, a sort of freak rejected by
both Europe and England, whose blood she shares, and by the black
West Indian people, whose culture and home have been hers for two
generations or more."[28] In *Wide Sargasso Sea*, the young blacks call
Antoinette "white cockroach" and "white nigger," epithets for the
Euro-Creole woman who, as Nunez-Harrell points out, bears the
brunt of guilt for the history of slavery and the cruelties perpetrated
by her ancestors. At the same time, she identifies and is identified
with the lowest social castes. Anna longs, then, for a lost home, but
one in which she could never feel at ease. Thus, she envies what she
perceives as the ease, warmth, and gaiety of black culture and longs
also to be black. For these reasons, we can understand why, though
the character and the author of the novel are of European descent,
Kenneth Ramchand has called it "our first Negritude novel."[29]

In some ways white Creoles experience a double dose of a quintessential aspect of Caribbean experience, the marginality of living
in between cultures. Derek Walcott expresses the pain of this division as experienced by black West Indians when he asks in "A Far
Cry from Africa": "Where shall I turn, divided to the vein?"[30] Black
West Indians must construct their identities as always divided by
the history of slave trading; if educated, they have learned to admire
English language and culture while detesting British colonial rule.
The search for a lost identity through Africa becomes complicated,
as it does in Walcott's poem, by the current realities of an Africa
which the West Indian has not personally known but made into a
metaphor, or, as Louis James puts it, "an area of the mind."[31] Living
in between two cultures, belonging to neither completely, characterizes what sociologists have called the "marginal man": "one who

is poised in psychological uncertainty between two (or more) social worlds; reflecting in his soul the discords and harmonies, repulsions and attractions of these worlds, one of which is often 'dominant' over the other . . ."[32] James feels that West Indian writers, living between Africa and Europe, find a moment of self-discovery when they reject possession by either. In this simultaneous acknowledgment and rejection, writers find new forms for a West Indian literature unique to its own location, history, and cultural plurality.

But white Creoles are divided precisely within the context of the islands' histories and cultures. They descend from a class that no longer exists and whose history is morally shameful. They feel close to a black culture that they cannot be part of and that can only resent them, and they may still look to a "mother" country that long ago abandoned them and still considers them inferior. Discussing the colonial motifs in Rhys's novels, Helen Tiffin explains, "The white Creole is, as a double outsider, condemned to self-consciousness, a sense of inescapable difference and even deformity in the two societies by whose judgements she always condemns herself."[33] As Tiffin points out, following African-American and Caribbean writers such as W. E. B. Du Bois and Frantz Fanon, cultural marginality divides the psyche, makes it Other to itself, and permits no unified—even if illusory—sense of self.

Rhys's identity as a white Creole West Indian writer, then, is an unstable one—although that instability may make her all the more a part of the heterogeneity of Caribbean cultures. Among the West Indian writers who command our attention today, such as Derek Walcott, Edward Brathwaite, Samuel Selvon, Earl Lovelace, and Michelle Cliff, to name a few, Rhys remains an odd one out, a Euro-Creole woman who, in fifty-six years, returned to her native Dominica for only one brief visit. Hence, to some readers, only *Voyage in the Dark* of her four early novels seems to be influenced by her West Indian background. Since the other three take place, for the most part, on the continent, they appear to chronicle an almost generic expatriate's down-and-out bohemian life. Yet, as Benstock points out, even among the expatriates, Rhys remained an outsider. The specific and multiple nature of her exile stems from the difference of the place from which she came—not England, not originally anyway, nor an increasingly powerful United States, but a tiny colony wherein her identity was always divided.

Rhys once asked, "Am I an expatriate? Expatriate from where?"[34] Her question repeats the European attitude toward the Caribbean as a "background of nothing" or, at best, an "antique romance," but it also alludes to a background of plural, unconsolidated cultures and a divided national identity of rich potential that the European eye could only perceive as disorganized or simply "nothing."[35] Her question states implicitly the discovery of West Indian writers that identity depends upon place even as it questions the identity of that place. Living as an outcast even among expatriates, Rhys writes novels that reinscribe the colonial divisions of a Caribbean heritage displaced once more.

It is not surprising then that a passage from the novel considered her most European, *Good Morning, Midnight,* is quoted in the introductions to two studies of Caribbean literature as expressing "the concerns that pervade West Indian writing."[36] One editor states that when the narrator of the novel remarks, "I have no pride—no name, no face, no country. I don't belong anywhere," she conveys the West Indian "uncertainty of cultural identity" and "sense of estrangement." But it is important to understand the specific difference of this estrangement, that as outsiders among already eccentric texts, Rhys's novels portray an absence rather than loss of identity and the homelessness of one who never had a home.

*B*ecause of the always-divided identity of the white Creole, we cannot view Rhys's most well-received and widely read novel as taking either its protagonist or its author "home." *Wide Sargasso Sea* does take place in Jamaica and Dominica, making explicit a colonial background referred to or suggested in the earlier novels. But the setting in itself cannot give the protagonist a home; rather it places her divided identity within the cultural and historical context of its division, enabling a reconceptualization of the very concept of identity. Reading *Wide Sargasso Sea,* we find named the specific historical and social forces of the female homelessness and exile it chronicles. And we come closer to answering the question of what it means to diagnose and judge female Caribbean "character."

Since *Wide Sargasso Sea* comprises a "prequel" to what may be every woman's favorite novel, *Jane Eyre,* it invites rereadings of Brontë's novel and comparisons between the protagonists. *Wide Sargasso Sea* has challenged readers of *Jane Eyre* to reconsider the monstrous figure of the madwoman in the attic so that some feminist critics recognize Rhys's subversion of the good woman/bad woman dichotomy, viewing Jane and Antoinette as parts of the same psyche, and some perceive the parallels Rhys draws between the madwoman and the woman of reason, making them sisters rather than rivals.[37] The deliberate intertextuality of *Wide Sargasso Sea* with *Jane Eyre* sets *Wide Sargasso Sea* apart from Rhys's earlier novels by more than its date of publication and lends it greater interest to most readers. However, while all readers recognize the difference in setting between this novel, placed in nineteenth-century Jamaica and Dominica, and Rhys's earlier novels, set in early twentieth-century England and Europe, few feminist readers actually approach the novel as Caribbean or Third World literature. This is an odd oversight, due I think to its connection to the earlier English novel but also to the extreme specialization within literary studies. Of all her novels, it is the only one set in the West Indies, and it is the novel that established her reputation among critics of Caribbean literature as a West Indian writer. The novel seems to have found two communities of readers, those who take a feminist approach and those who take a West Indian approach, and the two groups rarely converse with one another.[38]

In *Wide Sargasso Sea,* the madwoman silenced in *Jane Eyre* speaks, and her voice exposes and turns upside down the values, patriarchal and colonialist, upon which the plot and characters of Brontë's novel depend. Perhaps one reason this novel attracts feminist critics more strongly than Rhys's earlier novels is that in it a forced and exploitative marriage provides a context missing in the early novels for understanding the uniquely female vulnerability of the protagonist and her specifically feminine defense of beauty, a defense her husband perceives as deceit. Overwhelmed by what he thinks of as her alien beauty and that of the island she loves, Antoinette's husband feels he has been tricked and seeks revenge by appropriating the mechanisms of illusion and beauty on which she depends. Thus, he gives her another name, diagnoses her as mad, and speaks of her as his "marionette." She seems all the more passive and victimized, but clearly driven to enact this quintessential femininity.

However, understanding the dynamics of masquerade in Rhys's novels as part of the carnivalesque as well as "the feminine" helps us to revise purely gendered readings of the characters' obsessions with the magic of appearance, gesture, and playacting. The carnivalesque also suggests something more profound concerning our tendencies to "read" and judge individual character. Rhys's novels remain outsiders to the major concern of what Gayatri Spivak has termed "high feminism": the individual woman as subject.[39] *Wide Sargasso Sea* not only confronts the good woman/bad woman dichotomy, it also challenges the notions of an inviolable self and integrity of character, and it disrupts the unitary point of view that crafts character in concert with moral authority.

Much of European modernist writing by authors such as Joyce,

Woolf, Conrad, and Ford explores and reconceptualizes the self, and we can also read Rhys's novels as texts of ironic alienation or portrayals of divided consciousness. But Rhys's characters are not just divided through the unconscious or alienated by what Perry Meisel calls the "myth of the modern," the loss of a natural self: they fragment most importantly through suppressed histories and eclipsed geo-cultural locations. Though European psychological concepts of the privatized and autonomous self may be available, both within the text and "outside" it to readers, they do not adequately explain protagonists whose psyches find expression and meaning through interdependence with their social-historical context, a context "foreign" to Europeans.

Read as Caribbean fiction that also turns on (in both senses of revolving on and turning against) a classic "woman's novel," *Wide Sargasso Sea* requires a feminist reading that takes into account more than sexual difference and that recognizes the formal ruptures of convention that cultural difference may introduce to modernism. In this way, treating *Wide Sargasso Sea* as Caribbean fiction directs our readings of Rhys's earlier "continental" novels. The numerous allusions in these early novels to cultures and places other than the European are more than incidental or autobiographical. They place alongside the narratives made possible by European modernism a difference of place and identity that alters the structure of even modernist narrative conventions. The alterations may appear as stutterings, interruptions, or silences.

In *Good Morning, Midnight,* for example, which takes place entirely in Paris, Sasha finds a rare moment of peaceful contentment in an artist's studio surrounded by West African masks and listening to beguine music from Martinique. A solitary, nearly derelict outsider in Paris, she identifies with a mistreated mulatto woman in a story the artist tells her. The scene offers an appropriate conclusion—or the beginning of a satisfactory end—to a quest/romance plot, yet it appears in the middle of the novel and is dropped, undeveloped.[40] Julia Martin, in *After Leaving Mr. Mackenzie* (1930), returns from Paris to her family in England to find her mother dying. The loss of her Brazilian mother represents all the losses of warmth and love in Julia's life. At her funeral, Julia almost finds a moment of profound self-knowledge, but the moment skews somehow and the narrative continues in a deliberately disconnected manner. Anna Morgan, the protagonist in *Voyage in the Dark,* a novel that takes place in London, recalls her childhood home in the Caribbean and says she always wished she were black. She gains understanding of what it means to be black through the hallucinated visions of a feverish delirium presented in an italicized interior monologue that ends the novel, but does so inconclusively. Even in *Quartet* (1928), Rhys's first novel to be published in which no references to another country or race appear, carnival images and the zombie motifs of possession and dispossession structure the plot and characterization through experiments with voice and shifting point of view. As if alluding to an absent, hidden, or disguised cultural setting, Rhys first titled the novel *Masquerade*.[41]

The alterations of conventional narrative that we find in Rhys's early novels may appear as silences, inactions, or even formal flaws; however, they record a double displacement, colonial and sexual, that the conventional narrative and even European modernist narratives, with their presumption of a self to be displaced, divided, or lost, cannot adequately express. Rhys's narrative strategies and the masquerade that in her novels *is* character, expose the limits of novelistic convention and give us glimpses of other possibilities. Once we take masquerade seriously to question "character" in all of its meanings as literary convention, individual personality, and moral integrity, other qualities of the fiction move into focus.

An early passage in *Wide Sargasso Sea* narrates the child Antoinette's ability to mentally visit a place "somewhere else" where she becomes "something else. Not myself any longer" (*Sea*, p. 28). The protagonists in all of Rhys's novels struggle to inhabit a mental or imaginative world view that comes from "somewhere else" and counters negative judgments of their characters which they are always in danger of internalizing. The notion of "elsewhere" figures in feminists such as Luce Irigaray's theories of women's divided position within masculine discourse,[42] but it also derives from the creative turnabout of Carnival, the magic of obeah, the lore of the zombie, and the Arawak concept of *zemi*. Sandra Drake explains this concept in her study of Wilson Harris's fiction: "For the Arawak, the *zemi* existed not only in itself, as it could be experienced in the physical world as a stone or a shell, but it also contained and generated other possibilities of itself. These might be other shapes, other forms, other existences in parallel universes of possibility."[43] All of Rhys's novels offer glimpses of possibilities conjured by the *zemi*. Through dreams and what Mikhail Bakhtin has called "internal dialogization," the narratives dispel the hegemony of prevailing ideologies, including that of the consolidated and privatized self, and counter them with "other shapes," "other forms" that have their sources in West Indian history and culture.

In the ways that Rhys's writing subverts the European concept of character, it closely resembles that of Third World modernists such as Wilson Harris.[44] A Caribbean writer from Guyana, Harris has commented on the traditional realist convention of character "consolidation" which he rejects in favor of the idea of "fulfillment." In his novels, dreamlike narratives trace fulfillments of the person in which dichotomies of past and present, inner and outer, individual and collective blur as identities double and multiply in a palimpsest of history and plurality of cultures. It is no accident that Harris's *Palace of the Peacock* and Rhys's *Wide Sargasso Sea* both appeared in the 1960s and share similar textual qualities.

The 1960s mark a culmination of a West Indian literary naissance that began tentatively in the 1930s and became established in the 1950s. Reading *Wide Sargasso Sea* alongside Rhys's earlier novels suggests connections between European modernism of the 1920s and 1930s and the birth and development of West Indian literature from the 1930s through the present. Both the European and Third World modernist movements in which Rhys played an outsider role took, or are taking, place within a context of social conflict and change that we have come to describe as modernization. The conditions of modernization in Third World countries, such as the adoption of new technologies, have joined with the forces of nationalism and revolution at varying moments from the 1930s until the present, creating the context for the emergence of new literatures in Africa, India, and other former colonies, including those of the Caribbean.[45] In the 1920s and 1930s, these movements overlapped with movements for social change in Europe. As Rhys wandered the streets of Montparnasse during her visits to the continent, labor strikes, political riots, and factionalist bombs exploded in Paris. And during her visit to the West Indies in 1936, unemployment marches and movements for racial pride and national independence were shaking the Caribbean. Though she found the life of a tourist in Dominica a bit dull, Rhys's personal papers indicate that she was aware of the agitation among black people of the islands for better working and living conditions and for cultural pride.[46] Not coincidentally, she began writing *Good Morning, Midnight* with its threatening Parisian setting punctuated by allusions to Martinique, West Africa, masquerade, and masks while on her stay in the Caribbean.[47] Because of Rhys's upbringing in a plural and divided colonial culture, she could give modernism a distinctly different cast, reshaping what she learned from people like Ford in light of her uniquely eccentric experience and within a larger context of social and literary change.

The movements of negritude in Africa and the Caribbean and the transition of many former colonies to self-governing independent states gave rise to the new literatures in English which are at once connected to the traditions of English literature and also break radically from them. New literary journals emerged in the 1930s in Trinidad, Barbados, British Guiana, and Jamaica that provided an audience to native writers. In 1949 Hogarth Press published Edgar Mittelholzer's novel *A Morning at the Office*. Also in the 1940s a BBC program called *Caribbean Voices* introduced Caribbean writers to the English public, of which Rhys, then living in London, was a member.[48]

Rhys kept in touch with the struggles of her native island for self-governance through a friendship with her sister Dominican Phyllis Shand Allfrey. Allfrey was politically active in the effort to form the short-lived West Indian Federation and thus partly responsible for the developing sense of community among West Indian countries. She regularly sent Rhys issues of the *Dominican Herald*, which she and her husband edited, and later their opposition paper the *Star*, both of which chronicled the struggles of the island for independence. Through Allfrey, Rhys remained informed about a new West Indies and a West Indian literature marked by pride in its heterogeneous cultural past.[49] Writers such as Edward Brathwaite, Derek Walcott, and Wilson Harris were finding poetic and fictional forms through which to express a plurality of Caribbean histories and voices: Arawak, Carib, Maroon, black African, Creole. Following her marginalized participation in European modernism, Jean Rhys enriched this chorus of voices in *Wide Sargasso Sea* with that of a white Creole woman in a specific historical moment of dispossession. The tracing in her early "continental novels" of colonial difference is retraced and replaced in the explicitly West Indian novel of the 1960s.

Edward Brathwaite has asserted that the term "West Indian" refers to "someone of African descent" who shares "a common history of slavery."[50] Through writings by Caribbean women, the term gains an expanded, though no less precise, meaning. Simone Schwarz-Bart, a novelist from Guadeloupe, connects the historical period of slavery to which Brathwaite refers to the dynamics of sexual slavery. In her novel *The Bridge of Beyond*, the character Telumee descends from slaves but does not fully understand "the curse of being a master, the curse of being a slave" that the blacks of Guadeloupe "carry in [their] veins" until she emerges, with the help of a community of women, from the spell of an abusive sexual relationship. Only then can she go "beyond" her inheritance of slavery to discover a new magic and power.[51] The protagonist of *Wide Sargasso Sea*, Antoinette (Bertha) Cosway Mason (Rochester), undergoes sexual and class enslavement as a white Creole woman that positions her, too, within

multiplicitous West Indian histories of possession and dispossession. Even her names, acquired through her mother's marriages, her
own, and reference to an earlier English novel record the layering of
identities within the history and literature of colonialism. The in-
terconnecting dynamics of sexual and colonial slavery in *Wide Sargasso Sea* cast a new light on the early novels and their seemingly
passive and masochistic "victims." We can see in them instead a
quest for identity that is also a quest for "elsewhere" as an alternate
history and community. Reviewing Rhys's novels in this light, it
soon becomes difficult to maintain the categories dividing British or
even English, European, and Commonwealth, Third World, or West
Indian literatures. Rhys's writing lies somewhere between them and
thus enables us to see again the social conflicts and histories that
the categories and their oppositions sometimes obscure.

Two

Countertexts, Countercommunities

*T*he West Indian writer, according to Wilson Harris, embarks on a series of beginnings to journeys that explore specific geo-political, spiritual, and aesthetic space: "It is as if within his work he sets out again and again across a certain territory of primordial but broken recollection in search of a community or species of fiction whose existence he begins to discern."[1] Across the "certain territory" of the Caribbean region, which is also the psychic territory of "primordial but broken recollection," its writers seek a "community or species of fiction." The phrase "community or species of fiction" makes its two elements seem equivalent in value and perhaps in kind; that is, to seek community *is* to discover a kind of fiction—the conditions for a story and also its form. The repetition of setting out, "again and again," describes the sense shared by many readers and critics of Rhys's early novels that they portray the same character repeatedly but at different stages in her life. However, if we consider the novels as West Indian literature, we see the novels' repetitions not in repeated character "types," but in repeated tracings and retracings of a "territory" of memory, of a psyche that is placed geopolitically and shared. The emphasis is spatial rather than temporal and results, as Harris states, in breaking "the spell of the self-sufficient social animal . . . the one-sidedness of self-sufficient social character."[2]

What emerges in place of the consolidated or self-sufficient character is the "obscure person," the person not counted by European colonizers as an individual but seen only as part of "an underprivileged crowd, a happy-go-lucky crowd, a political or a cricketing crowd, a calypso crowd."[3] Harris's description of the conventional (European) perception of the West Indian matches the rhetoric of nineteenth-century travel narratives. One subgenre of these narratives omits mention of native inhabitants except as a distanced, generalized "they." "They" do not appear at all as individuals but as a timeless, uncontextualized group or mass. The process of constituting a racial Other by perceiving natives as groups allows Western individuals to constitute themselves as sovereign subjects.[4]

In the context of European modernism and the social processes of modernization, the problem of the Western individual is doubly hinged: upon perceptions of the "primitive" and upon the simultaneous constitution and deconstruction of the feminine Other. Late nineteenth- and early twentieth-century European texts ranging from popular fictions of exploration to social and medical treatises linked the "savage" and the feminine in numerous ways. Evolutionary theory made it possible to establish a three-dimensional hierarchical scale that registered gradations in human value according to gender, class, and race. The English male aristocrat reigned at the top of the ladder, while the female "Hottentot" occupied its lowest rung, "at the nadir of human degeneration before the species left off its human form and turned bestial."[5] "Observation" and measurement of physiological characteristics such as skull size, ear shape, hair texture, and calf formation provided evidence for linking "degenerates" within the European races to those races considered inferior. The epithet "white nigger" for white Creole makes this association in a colonial setting in which the economic and political decline of the white planter class qualifies as degeneracy. Ironically, the emancipated blacks in *Wide Sargasso Sea* who call Antoinette "white nigger" draw upon the discourse that dehumanizes them to denigrate the declassed white women.

Economic and sexual power figure significantly in lining up the evolutionary scale. The positioning of white prostitutes on the scale is especially relevant to understanding the dynamics of racial and sexual colonization in Rhys's novels. The white working-class prostitute occupied a mobile position, on the threshold rung between white and black races and therefore dangerously liminal, or identified with the "Hottentot" at the very bottom of the hierarchy of moral and physical values, and therefore unredeemedly degenerate.[6]

Anna Morgan in *Voyage in the Dark* occupies at first a threshold position between black and white races. In England, she is considered white, though foreign; her aunt, however, suspects her of black lineage and so justifies depriving her of an inheritance. Declassed economically, she is exploited sexually while her co-workers in the chorus troupe dismiss her stories of Dominican life, calling her the "Hottentot." Although they also refer to her initially as "the Virgin," by the middle of the second chapter her landlady has labeled her a "tart," and by the novel's end she has entered into prostitution. The novel keys into the complex of associations that position one character as the simultaneous target of xenophobia, racism, and deeply institutionalized sexism. Anna shifts from a racially marginal social position that associates her with prostitution to what an English doctor in the novel's conclusion diagnoses as an innate pathological (and incurable) condition of prostitution.

The associations operating to cast Anna Morgan in the role of overdetermined Other include two additional and related elements—that of disease and that of the masses. We have already seen how a racial Other consolidates through the image of a crowd of natives. Andreas Huyssen has argued that European high modernism "constituted itself by a conscious strategy of exclusion, an anxiety of contamination by its other: an increasingly consuming and engulfing mass culture."[7] Fearful of the crowds of a newly emerging consumer culture and the threat they implied to individual identity, European artists and intellectuals went to great lengths to avoid contamination by the masses. In doing so, they identified the masses with women. Huyssen quotes Gustave Le Bon, author of the widely read sociological treatise *The Crowd*: "Crowds are everywhere distinguished by feminine characteristics."[8] The feminine characteristics that Le Bon and others such as Freud and Nietzsche saw in the masses included simplicity and extreme emotionality. These excesses seemed about to devour the individual bourgeois.

The fear of contamination and dread of disease operate both literally and metaphorically in the code that associates colonial natives/the crowd/women/mass culture in the constitution of an Other that takes many forms, all of which threaten to infect bourgeois individuals and weaken their hold on a precious property, the sense of a self. Writers slightly to the outside of this code, by virtue of divided nationality, write most eloquently about its motivating fears. As Joseph Conrad confessed in the "Familiar Preface" to *A Personal Record*: ". . . I have a positive horror of losing even for one moving moment that full possession of myself . . ."[9] It is not a coincidence that Conrad's fictional characters discover "the horror" in the heart of colonial Africa or that, in *Heart of Darkness*, the phrase becomes exchangeable with the (unspeakable) name of a European woman.

The moral disease that Marlow barely escapes in the Congo haunts the cities of Europe in the guise of womanhood. The Contagious Diseases Acts, the hygiene movement, and the social purity crusades all targeted working-class women and especially prostitutes, depriving them of their civil liberties and livelihoods ostensibly to control the spread of venereal disease. Under the Contagious Diseases Acts, police in certain areas of Britain could detain, arrest, and submit to forced medical examination any woman even suspected of prostitution.

Feminists then and now have argued that such "reforms" regulated working-class and female sexuality through the control of women's bodies.[10] The women in Rhys's fiction experience the harassment legitimated by the Contagious Diseases Acts even after the acts were no longer in force. Landladies evict Rhys's protagonists, police prod them, and they live in fear of some nameless exposure. Perceived as potential carriers of "social" disease, they themselves become ill. Anna, Marya, and Julia suffer actual illnesses; Sasha becomes alcoholic; and Antoinette endures the pain and punishment of "madness." It is as if they have been made sick by a culture that perceives them so. Illness and disease become tropes and actualities in Rhys's fiction that enable an exploration of otherness. But rather than countering the dominant perceptions of working-class women as diseased with assertions of health and morality-after-all, the narratives use illness to criticize, satirize, and even move out of the discourse that marginalizes the characters. The reverse logic of carnival enables this move when, for example, the narrator in *Quartet* describes a woman who has just made a mean remark about another woman as "very healthy looking . . . with long, very sharp teeth" (*Quartet*, p. 70). The morality of health and the rightness of the well-fed no longer hold as illness opens the way for new perceptions and socially critical visions. While medical authorities, such as the doctor in *Voyage*, exercise their power over women's bodies and identities, they do not do so without challenge, even if it is a silent challenge of the imagination. Such authorities are themselves reacting to the "horror" of masses of women's bodies, suddenly visible.

As Huyssen and, more recently, Sandra M. Gilbert and Susan Gubar point out, "hordes" of women's bodies seemed to flow into the streets during the early part of the century.[11] They stormed the gates of colleges, the professions, and of politics, but they also simply worked, as typists, clerks, shop "girls," sales "ladies," mannequins, artists' models, actresses, and prostitutes. Like Rhys's geographically and spatially displaced heroines, they appeared without escort in business offices, matinee audiences, cafes, and bars. They trespassed on territory traditionally reserved for men, or at least for male control, and threatened to disprove, visibly, the lingering nineteenth-century ideology of separate spheres.

Feminist historians such as Judith Walkowitz and Mary Poovey have shown that Victorian patriarchal practices and ideologies did not operate monolithically but in divided and contradictory ways.[12] In their work, what appears singular is seen to result from contest among competing interests rather than concert among conspirators. Nevertheless, we can speak in retrospect of governing and influential ideologies. Michelle Rosaldo argued convincingly that feminist scholars' perceptions of a domestic/public split in many cultures derives from ideologies we have inherited from the Victorian period concerning the family and its relation to the marketplace.[13] The ideology of separate spheres—one, a domestic, feminine sphere and a haven from the other, public, masculine sphere—governed the social organization of gendered labor and of gendered identity. Though many women worked during the nineteenth century at home and in factories, they did not participate in public life as citizens. The term "public woman" retained its older meaning and operated to make sexually suspect the "mobs" of middle-class women who agitated for reforms and women's rights.

Rhys's characters hardly become feminists in active opposition to their oppression. But the exploitation, actual illnesses, poverty, and illegal abortions they suffer reveal the limitations of feminist reforms enacted just before World War I and the misogynist reaction against them during the period between the two world wars. They also disclose a social space, no longer confidently masculine and not ever respectably feminine, in which the tensions of sexual conflict and erotic ambiguity tighten.

Medical and police authorities were force-feeding feminists in prison when World War I began. The war itself interrupted the feminist movement with calls for women's loyalty to its cause and with opportunities for women to engage in sometimes challenging and often exhilarating public action. However, such opportunities closed with the war's end. Sandra M. Gilbert has described the misogyny characteristic of the war's aftermath when men reacted against the power and freedom some women had enjoyed on the home front.[14] Married women and dutiful daughters returned to their domestic labors. Single women or women who wished to prolong their adventures encountered the renewed misogyny with few defenses. True, single women alone on the streets could no longer be arrested as suspected prostitutes; but they were not granted the rights and privileges of men or even the respected status of an obviously married woman. They became sexually marginal, threats to an already besieged social morality. Condemned and harassed by purity crusaders, exploited by sexually adventurous men, denied job opportunities after the war that had demanded women's labor, they experienced a specific kind of female displacement and alienation.

Sexual marginality coextends with colonial exile in an overdetermined otherness that Jean Rhys's narratives explore in formal excursions that "set out again and again," in Wilson Harris's words, to undo the dichotomy of public/private that encodes as well dualities of civilized/foreign, reason/emotion, white/black, masculine/feminine, outer/inner, and citizen/mass. The narrative methods vary, but they usually follow a strategy of turning inward to excavate multiply displaced voices within the consciousnesses of single protagonists, then directing us outward again to the social forces of displacement and to possibilities for the reconstruction of community and consciousness.

Tone, narrative structure, and what Mikhail Bakhtin calls "dialogization" transform the psychological crisis of Rhys's marginal women into simultaneously private and social problems. One of the more explicit examples of this transformation occurs in *Good Morning, Midnight* when Sasha, humiliated by her brutal employer and her own lack of spine, critically revises a seemingly psychological defeat:

> Well, let's argue this out, Mr. Blank. You, who represent Society, have the right to pay me four hundred francs a month. That's my market value, for I am an inefficient member of Society, slow in the uptake, uncertain, slightly damaged in the fray, there's no denying it. So you have the right to pay me four hundred francs a month, to lodge me in a small, dark room, to clothe me shabbily, to harass me with worry and monotony and unsatisfied longings till you get me to the point when I blush at a look, cry at a word. We can't all be lucky—and it would be so much less fun if we were. Isn't this so, Mr. Blank? ... Let's say that you have this mystical right to cut my legs off. But the right to ridicule me afterwards because I am a cripple—no, that I think you haven't got. And that's the right you hold most dearly, isn't it? You must be able to despise the people you exploit. . . . Did I say all this? Of course I didn't. I didn't even think it. (*Midnight*, p. 29)

That the social mockery becomes self-mockery does not lessen, but heightens, the critical incisiveness of the passage. For though the narrator claims she did not think the words, much less say them, her inability to do so represents and proves the sex- and class-determined power imbalance she resists. Furthermore, the words are said, the dialogue engaged, even if in reflection, so that Sasha does not remain silenced by "Mr. Blank." Instead she achieves a kind of social or class consciousness by recognizing her commonality with "the people" he exploits.

Voyage in the Dark portrays the seemingly private tragedy of a young girl's seduction and abandonment in the London of 1914, her recourse to prostitution, subsequent pregnancy, and nearly fatal abortion. We read of these incidents through the voices of Anna Morgan's several fields of consciousness—fragmented voices, often in conflict with one another, that appear to speak with purely subjective irony, or even irrationality. In a monologue resembling Sasha's mockery of Mr. Blank, Anna parodies another representative of social control, her stepmother Hester, who has just cheated her of an inheritance. Parodying Hester's upper-class pretensions, Anna mimics her voice: ". . . an English lady's voice . . . Now that I've spoken, you can hear that I'm a lady . . . I have my doubts about you. Speak up, for I fear the worst . . . that sort of voice" (*Voyage*, p. 49). Later, she concentrates her desires for class revenge on the word that Hester claims for herself and denies Anna: "A lady—some words have a long, thin neck that you'd like to strangle" (*Voyage*, p. 120).

Such ironies and parodies allude to class affiliations that might aid the characters in their resistance. Other narrative strategies demonstrate similar efforts at alternate communities and alliances even when the characters become most solitary, most apparently passive and victimized.

In a depression following her lover's final departure, Anna withdraws into herself, shut up in a room with the curtains pulled tight. Her mind wanders and she remembers the lines from a song:

> *"And drift, drift*
> *Legions away from despair."*
> It can't be "legions." "Oceans," perhaps. "Oceans away from despair." But it's the sea, I thought. The Caribbean Sea. "The Caribs indigenous to this island were a warlike tribe and their resistance to white domination, though spasmodic, was fierce. As lately as the beginning of the nineteenth century they raided one of the neighbouring islands, under British rule, overpowered the garrison and kidnapped the governor, his wife and three children. They are now practically exterminated. The few hundreds that are left do not intermarry with the negroes. Their reservation, at the northern end of the island, is known as the Carib Quarter." They had, or used to have, a king. Mopo,

his name was. Here's to Mopo, King of the Caribs! But, they are now
practically exterminated. "Oceans away from despair . . ." (*Voyage*,
pp. 90–91)

The paragraph strikes the reader because of its improbability. It is
true that Anna, like Jean Rhys, is from the Caribbean island of Dominica. However, she is only nineteen and uneducated; here she
suddenly quotes at length and from memory a text concerning Caribbean history. This voice does not paraphrase the text but bounds
it definitively with quotation marks, signaling not a loose association in the character's stream of consciousness, but an excursion
outside of that consciousness into the realm of public discourse.
The quotation marks and the academic tone define both the excursion and its formal accuracy. What may appear to be subjective mus-
ings linking eccentrically one random thought to another actually
juxtaposes an intensely private memory to a public statement, point-
ing away from the self to the system of language and its formal conventions. This juxtaposition creates a dynamic movement and a
new symbol that bridges the gap between Anna's fragmented fields
of consciousness and the social world outside her drawn curtains.

The formal movement in the passage closely resembles the logic of
dreams, which juxtaposes seemingly arbitrary images to create new
stories and new meanings impossible in everyday conscious thought.
It traces the same dynamic Paul Ricoeur describes in his definition of
symbolic relations. Ricoeur proposes a dual hermeneutics in which
two dynamics work together to create a cultural symbol: an archae-
ological or regressive movement into the unconscious and a teleological or forward movement into social meaning.[15] Through language, the two processes unite. The movement into the unconscious
(Ricoeur calls it "the dispossession of consciousness") distorts or
conceals meaning while the teleological movement discloses meaning. The symbol contains both movements and is thus, in revised
Freudian dream language, overdetermined. The relations generating
the symbol take form, like metaphors or metonyms, within language;
the dream work represents these relations.

When the song lines "And drift, drift / Legions away from despair" first appear, they offer what Ricoeur refers to as a "sedimented"
symbol, one that is stereotypical and worn out, having its source in
nothing but the past. Anna remembers hearing the song at a music
hall matinee in Glasgow, so it originates in her personal past and
participation in a feminized mass cultural activity. According to
Ricoeur, sedimented symbols arise in the context of economically
derived alienation, an apt (if reductive) description of Anna's home-

lessness and poverty. But the act of articulating the song lines moves them outward, through language and into Anna's present life. This movement allows Anna to recreate their meaning in conjunction with other associations. Anna links her sexual exploitation and her despair to the exploitation of other oppressed people (other "masses")— the native Caribs—to their near extermination but also their fierce resistance. In fact, neither the Spanish in the sixteenth century nor the English in the seventeenth century ever entirely defeated the Dominican Caribs.[16] The associations Anna makes with this colonial history connect the song lines to structures and institutions of power and responsibility—the social context, in Ricoeur's schema, of "living" symbols. When Anna repeats the line at the end of the passage, it has acquired a meaning no longer concealed in the recesses of her memory or subconscious. Furthermore, she has changed the wording slightly to replace the military "legions" with "oceans," a word inclusive of the Caribbean Sea. As the lines have passed through the system of language and its conventions, they have acquired new significance from Anna's personal associations which, simultaneously, describe colonial history. She has transformed the meaning of native mobs and hordes of women to a shared struggle. The final meaning of the lines suggests that, though in private despair, she is also "oceans away" from that despair, linked to a history of fierce mass resistance in the Caribbean colonies. The "work" of dream logic creates this new meaning by integrating in Anna's monologue the conventions of public discourse with the private associations of the symbol. Through the formal techniques of Rhys's narrative, the lines of the song then become, for the reader, vehicles of meaning, or what Ricoeur would call "prospective" symbols, that consciously recognize other persons in a common human culture.

Ricoeur's hermeneutics are helpful in understanding this passage because they give us a way to interpret the movement between private and public language that shapes this modernist "interior monologue"; they also allow us to see how that movement and the style of interior monologue inscribe the dynamics of sexual and colonial relations in a search for community that is also an experiment in fiction.

The following passage from *Good Morning, Midnight* (1939) displays the same kind of narrative movement through the simultaneous sense and nonsense of phrases in different languages juxtaposed to one another:

I at once make up my mind that he wants to find out if I can speak German. All the little German I know flies out of my head. Jesus, help

me! Ja ja, nein, nein, was kostet es, Wien ist eine sehr schöne Stadt,
Buda-Pest auch ist sehr schön, ist schön, mein Herr, ich habe meinen
Blumen vergessen, aus meinen grossen Schmerzen, homo homini
lupus, aus meinen grossen Schmerzen mach ich die kleinen Lieder,
homo homini lupus (I've got that one, anyway), aus meinen grossen
Schmerzen homo homini doh ré mi fah soh la ti doh. (*Midnight*, p. 24)

Part first-person narration, part interior monologue, these lines first
describe then directly portray the character Sasha's private thoughts.
The passage moves beyond random subjectivism, however, through
point of view, sound patterns, and allusions that create social meaning in Sasha's madness.

The transition from first-person narration in "I at once make up
my mind . . ." to interior monologue in "Jesus, help me!" shifts our
attention away from the presumption of a shared public language
(the "I" narrator's assumption of an audience). We move into direct
presentation of private experience with no mediating voice to explain or visibly sequence the events of consciousness. The shift occurs simultaneously with the desperate appeal to Jesus for help (now
the only audience is a God who sees directly into one's heart, anyway); it then immediately turns from English sentences to German
fragments ("Ja ja, nein, nein . . ."), then to Latin phrases ("homo
homini lupus"), back to German ("aus meinen grossen Schmerzen"),
and finally to a recital of the musical scale. Like the passage from
Voyage in the Dark, this expression of interiority also creates a dual
movement: into Sasha's consciousness and a private language, but
with that private language the quest for another language, whether
German, Latin, or musical, any language that will allow her to com-
municate socially and to survive. For the man who wants to know if
she can speak German is her employer, and her job depends upon her
ability to perform. The shared language presumed by the "I" narrator of the first two sentences is a public one that he controls, one
that victimizes Sasha, or through which she enacts the role of victim. In response to this threatening social confrontation, she makes
her desperate appeal and then embarks on a search for the language
that will allow her to keep, if not her job, her dignity.

The search leads her to the repeated phrase "aus meinen grossen
Schmerzen mach ich die kleinen Lieder" (out of my great pains I
make the little songs). With the discovery of this line, Sasha does
find an alternative shared language, for the line is from a poem in
Heinrich Heine's "Lyrical Intermezzo."[17] It is not a German phrase
she can offer her employer or use to secure her job. And in that sense
it fails her. But it is a language that orders her apparently disordered

consciousness by linking her experience to the shared world of poetry and the common experiences of marginalized individuals.

Sound, more than sense, appears to pattern Sasha's monologues.[18] However, sound becomes sense in this passage, formalizing its theme of "little songs," a theme enhanced by the repetitive rhythm of the passage. Most important, the allusion to Heine's poem connects Sasha's isolated thoughts to those of a poet whom sociologists have named a "marginal man."[19] Like the Jewish Heine, Sasha faces homelessness and persecution that dehumanize her and those who oppress her ("homo homini lupus"—man is as a wolf to man). Through the line "out of my great pains I make the little songs," Sasha breaks through the enclosed privacy of the isolated self and joins the world of public, literary discourse. The private fragments of thought, image, sound, song—"doh ré mi fah soh la ti doh . . ."—make sense as she reorders them within a social and *inter*subjective world.

*T*he quest for community that I argue takes place in Rhys's novels requires a risky carnival space where social masks might become playful masquerade, false authorities objects of satirical mimicry, and the anonymous crowd a bonded gathering. When it works, it does so in the realm of the subjunctive, of the *zemi*, and of dream logic. If it succeeds, it brings together women of disparate and marginalized identities; if it fails, it usually fails to connect women or other marginalized individuals such as Jews or men displaced due to war and the shifting boundaries and politics of nation-states. The conditions of possibility are historical and social as much as psychological and involve, as I have argued, the histories of slavery and colonization, events of war, processes of modernization, and ideologies of sex and gender that have shaped twentieth-century literature.

Current debates over the definition of modernism and postmodernism in twentieth-century literature and their relation to one another involve a great deal of theoretical discussion about the nature of the subject—as now split, dissolved, or having always been a fiction. Fredric Jameson, like other Marxists such as Jürgen Habermas and Andreas Huyssen, insists on historicizing modernism and postmodernism rather than viewing them as simply changes in cultural styles. He identifies the period of modernism as one in which "the truth of [individual] experience . . . lies . . . in India or Jamaica or Hong Kong."[20] Jameson is not concerned with Caribbean or even Third World literature in this particular essay but rather refers to the stage of imperialism in European and North American history that precedes the later developments of postmodernism and multinational corporate capitalism. By "individual" Jameson means the Western individual who perceives his subjectivity in "a certain section of London or the countryside," in "privatized middle-class life," and who remains unaware of the colonial totality of which he is not only part but a determined part. What signals such absent awareness, Jameson argues, is modernist irony, the sense of a gap between authentic existence and actual experience. That gap stands in for knowledge of "the whole colonial system of the British Empire that determines the very quality of the individual's subjective life."[21]

Jean Rhys's novels offer us the opportunity to explore the gap from a perspective so marginalized through colonial and sexual exile that we must, with some discomfort, perceive dimensions of the system occluded by more canonical modernist texts. Within the crosscurrents of female, European, and Third World modernisms, her writing suggests reconceptualizing the subject beyond victimization in a way that no longer asserts Europe as the historical subject, but replaces it on a "certain territory," elsewhere.

Part Two

Marooned

Three

Wide Sargasso Sea

Obeah Nights

"So between you both I often wonder who I am and where is my country and where do I belong and why was I even born at all."[1] Questioning her nationality, birth, and personal identity, Antoinette (Bertha) Cosway Mason (Rochester) places herself as lost somewhere in between the two central figures of her life. One is her English husband, who has married Antoinette according to English law and custom, gaining all her property along with her person. The other is her black nurse, Christophine, a mysterious obeah woman exiled in Jamaica from her native Martinique. These two figures and the cultures they represent divide Antoinette, a white West Indian Creole. Her fate, however, is shaped by the patriarchal colonial authority vested in her husband and by the nineteenth-century romantic novel by Charlotte Brontë in which his character first appeared. From them, she receives a life of enslavement that parallels the history of the island's black people; from Christophine and the native Caribbeans, however, she learns to resist and transform their collective history.

"*(I lay awake all night long after they were asleep, and as soon as it was light I got up and dressed and saddled Preston. And I came to you. Oh Christophine. O Pheena, Pheena, help me)*" (*Sea*, p. 154). Encountering this passage in Part II of the novel, the reader is apt to echo Antoinette's earlier questions, especially about where she is. Antoinette's plea for Christophine's help startles the reader because Antoinette is not present. Her first-person narration in Part I has

Note: I take the title of this chapter from the title of a poem Rhys wrote while working on *Wide Sargasso Sea*. "Obeah Night" is reprinted in *The Letters of Jean Rhys*, ed. by Francis Wyndham and Diana Melly, pp. 264–266.

given way in Part II to that of her husband, unnamed in this novel, yet identified intertextually with Edward Rochester in *Jane Eyre*. This parenthetical passage interrupts a dialogue between the Englishman and the obeah woman that "Rochester" recounts. Furthermore, it comes from no identifiable place since Antoinette is absent, drugged and sleeping in another room, when the dialogue takes place. Antoinette's voice does not logically belong here, but not belonging is the condition that has defined her character from the novel's beginning.

The first two sentences of the first chapter identify Antoinette's narrating voice as excluded: "They say when trouble comes close ranks, and so the white people did. But we were not in their ranks" (*Sea*, p. 17). Antoinette and her mother, originally from French-dominated Martinique, do not belong to Jamaican white society. However, they are not black; they are white Creoles, descended from slave-owning men. Christophine explains to Rochester: "She is not *béké* like you, but she is *béké*, and not like us either" (*Sea*, p. 155). Nevertheless, it is to Christophine that Antoinette turns when she feels herself in most trouble.

Antoinette's identity, *who* she is, remains in question throughout the novel. The conflict of identity she faces and the novel's interest in madness as perception and experience make *Wide Sargasso Sea* an intense and finely tuned psychological novel. It also leads readers and critics to debate the quality of Antoinette's moral character according to their perceptions of whether and how she resolves her conflict of identities. The moral value at stake in these discussions derives from nineteenth-century realist novels, such as *Jane Eyre*, in which morality and integrity of character are conflated and in which both must be achieved through individual choice and action. By these criteria, Antoinette often fails to measure up. Her only act, the torching of Thornfield Hall, enables a morally ambiguous resolution, through suicide.

Wide Sargasso Sea, however, questions the moral values of the earlier *Jane Eyre*. As a twentieth-century novel by a West Indian writer that is, for the most part, set in Jamaica, it should be read and interpreted in a different cultural context—that of the Caribbean. In this context, the achievement of individual identity and the questions that prompt such a quest give way to different questions and a new concept of the individual, not measurable by nineteenth-century European moral standards. When Antoinette's disembodied voice pleads with Christophine to help her, the question of who she is gives way to the question of *where* she is. From what place does she speak?

The predetermined ending to *Wide Sargasso Sea* prompts the question in a slightly different way—from what place does she act? Although the conclusion repeats the fire in *Jane Eyre*, in *Wide Sargasso Sea* it occurs as a dream. In first-person narration, Antoinette describes a dream in which she wanders through the rooms of Thornfield Hall carrying a candle. "I dropped the candle I was carrying and it caught the end of a tablecloth and I saw flames shoot up" (*Sea*, p. 189). Through a wall of red fire, Antoinette sees visions of her past life; she screams and jumps. Then she awakens from her dream, steals the keys from Grace Poole, and unlocks the door of her attic prison room. The novel ends here with the dream foreshadowing its "real" conclusion.

We can begin to answer the question of Antoinette's location by observing that she inhabits a dream. Dream space is not "real" space, but, in this case, it is real literary space since we have seen those passageways and rooms in fiction before. The reader experiences an eerie sensation reading these final passages, because the dream is one we recognize; it seems very real to us as an explanation, from Bertha Mason's point of view, of the burning of Thornfield Hall. Then we read that Antoinette awoke. She unlocks the door again. We are returning to a previous place, in Thornfield Hall and in the narrative. It hasn't happened yet, and yet it has already happened, once in *Jane Eyre* and again in Antoinette's dream, and now it is going to happen again, for real—but where? The novel ends.

Rhys's writing here and its effect on the reader closely resemble the dreamlike narrative of another Caribbean novel, also published in the 1960s: Wilson Harris's *Palace of the Peacock*. In its beginning pages, the first-person narrator awakens from one dream into another dream: "I dreamt I awoke with one dead seeing eye and one living closed eye. I put my dreaming feet on the ground in a room that oppressed me as though I stood in an operating theatre, or a maternity ward, or I felt suddenly, the glaring cell of a prisoner who had been sentenced to die."[2] This "I" narrator shares with Antoinette a conflicted identity. His "I" (eye) moves between the imperialist landowner Donne and the mysterious, abused, and elusive "folk." He also recognizes his imprisoned and oppressed condition.

In Harris's novel, too, past and present encounter one another in the same space as a boat crew on a river journey become the doubles of men who made an earlier journey, enter the "straits of memory," and "die" just as their doubles did. In fact, Harris's novel and *Wide Sargasso Sea* share many common elements, similarities that support the idea that *Wide Sargasso Sea* belongs as much to a Third World modernist tradition as to a European.[3] I think that only in the context of African Caribbean history and culture can we solve the narrative puzzle of Antoinette's place. And by addressing the question "where," instead of "who," we can begin to understand how Rhys's modernism reconceptualizes our conventional notions of the individual.

In her book on Wilson Harris's fiction, Sandra Drake has made this important point:

> the crisis of Modernism is related to the Western colonial tradition. In fact, the Great War signaled not only the West's cultural crisis but also the incipient decline of the West's political and economic hegemony, although the fact was not widely recognized until later. That hegemony was based on the European empires first carved out, half a millennium before in . . . [the] Caribbean. Western economic development, which provided the basis for Western confidence, had in turn been based on the fruits of imperial possession.[4]

The waning of Western confidence opened new possibilities for the Third World's conception of itself. With the Treaty of Versailles arose nationalisms and the revaluing of native cultures and races. The movements of "negritude" and Pan-Africanism reversed the contempt with which blacks had been taught to view themselves. In Harris's view, however, such opposing systems of value reversed but still repeated the patterns of opposition generated by imperialist conquest and shaping the realist novel. As he puts it, "The narrow basis of realism . . . tends inevitably to polarise cultures or to reinforce . . . eclipses of otherness within legacies of conquest that rule the world."[5]

It would be a mistake to view Harris's position as a liberal withdrawal from conflict; instead it opens the way for entirely new concepts of culture and social and individual change, catalyzed by the victim's status but moving beyond the "victim/victor stasis." Revealing and empowering "otherness" becomes a central gesture in this cultural metamorphosis.

An entry into "otherness" opens early in *Wide Sargasso Sea*, and through it Antoinette's childhood takes a new direction. Rejected by her unhappy mother, Antoinette has turned for love and companionship to Christophine, Christophine's friend Maillotte, and Maillotte's daughter Tia, who is about Antoinette's age. She and Tia swim together in a garden pool, and one day Tia bets Antoinette three pennies that she can't turn a somersault underwater. Antoinette surfaces choking, but insists she has turned the somersault. Tia laughs and takes the money, taunting Antoinette: "Plenty white people in Jamaica. Real white people, they got gold money . . . . Old time white people nothing but white nigger now, and black nigger better than white nigger" (*Sea*, p. 24). When Antoinette emerges from the pool, she discovers that Tia has exchanged her dress for Antoinette's. In the black child's dress, Antoinette arrives home to meet a visitor from England, Mr. Mason, who eventually marries her mother and takes over their neglected estate. She has become Tia's double, by a forced exchange, and in that costume meets the man who will forcefully exchange her in marriage to another white Englishman.

Christophine tries to dress Antoinette in an old dress, and it tears as she pulls it over her head. Antoinette's previous identity no longer fits. She is becoming someone else, but she responds to the change by placing herself somewhere else. Leaving the house, she wanders through the wild and pathless parts of the Coulibri estate: "Watching the red and yellow flowers in the sun thinking of nothing, it was as if a door opened and I was somewhere else, something else. Not myself any longer" (*Sea*, p. 28). Rejected by her mother, betrayed by her black friend, and submitted to the neocolonialist Mason's plans, Antoinette cannot place herself among the island's people or her family. She resorts, in her pain, to a trick of her own imagination, recreating and replacing herself. Her response indicates that she has learned something about survival and internal resistance from the culture of slavery that preceded this period in the island's history. In this "trick," she opens a door onto otherness, "somewhere else." Antoinette's ability to be elsewhere, learned early in her childhood, gives her voice a formal power in the novel even as she becomes most socially powerless.

Antoinette's mother suggests to her inadvertently that "somewhere else" may be more than an imagined escape. In one of the first incidents of the novel, someone poisons Antoinette's mother's horse, and Annette despairs that now they are "marooned." With this word, which Antoinette later repeats, Annette suggests that her family has been wrecked and abandoned to their fates on a now strange and estranging island. However, in the context of Antoinette's imagination, the word takes on another possible meaning, one associated with Christophine and with the places on the island to which Antoinette escapes.

In Caribbean history, the term *Maroon* has come to refer primarily to the African and African American slaves who escaped from the plantations to hidden and nearly inaccessible parts of the islands. There they formed communities, defended themselves against soldiers, and carried out fierce and often successful guerilla warfare against the colonialists. The word *Maroon* derives from the Spanish *cimarron* and referred originally to domesticated cattle that had fled to the mountains around the summits or *cima*. Indians who escaped the genocidal tactics of the colonizers were then called Maroons. By the middle of the sixteenth century, the word had taken on connotations of being "wild," "fierce," and "unbroken." "Going to the Indians," "marronage," or flight was brutally punished by the colonialists whenever they captured a runaway slave. Yet *marronage* was practiced by the African and African American slaves on such a grand scale and with such success that colonialist governments of various islands were forced to negotiate and sign treaties with the Maroons.[6]

In Jamaica, the Maroons launched their attacks on the colonialists from the most inaccessible parts of the island—the "cockpit" country—and their heroic military feats are often attributed to the magical, spiritual powers of their leaders, especially those skilled in obeah. Oral history celebrates one obeah priestess in particular, Maroon Nanny, a woman who was skilled in the arts of camouflage and ambush and who was also capable of "catching the bullets of her foes and returning them with deadly effect."[7]

Annette, in her despair, has thus suggested to her daughter an alliance with another people who were formed as such politically and spiritually as much as racially or nationally. They included the original Amerindians, Africans brought to the islands, and Afro-Creoles born on the islands, all of whom became identified as Maroons through their desire for freedom, strategies of flight, and tactics of guerilla warfare. Inadvertently Annette alludes to places in the island's history that Antoinette might inhabit and the wild, unexplored parts of the island that may help her to survive. And she suggests possible kinship with Christophine, who, as an obeah woman, practices a magic that enables survival in dangerous and hostile environments.

The "elsewhere" Antoinette learns to inhabit is a geographical and historical space, real yet invisible in colonial Jamaica. It resembles the "elsewhere" described by some feminist critics as a psychological state of being in that it provides an alternate ground for subjectivity, but it differs from the notions of Luce Irigaray or Nancy K. Miller in its reference to the imaginative practices of real historical people and to the sites of their active resistance to slavery and colonialism.[8]

Through her dreams, Antoinette continues her exploration of the "otherness" eclipsed by European rationality. After meeting Mr. Mason, she dreams the first of three dreams that structure the novel: "I dreamed that I was walking in the forest. Not alone. Someone who hated me was with me, out of sight. I could hear heavy footsteps coming closer and though I struggled and screamed I could not move. I woke crying" (*Sea*, pp. 26–27). In this instance, "elsewhere" is no longer safe. Later, in Part II, which Edward Rochester narrates, we learn of his visit to a place in the forest and of events that recall Antoinette's dream. He has lost his way and come suddenly upon some stone ruins surrounded by tall rose trees and a wild orange tree: "Under the orange tree I noticed little bunches of flowers tied with grass . . . . Then I saw a little girl carrying a large basket on her head. I met her eyes and to my astonishment she screamed loudly, threw up her arms and ran . . . . She sobbed as she ran, a small frightened sound" (*Sea*, pp. 104–105). One critic has argued that in this scene Rochester has entered Antoinette's childhood dream, that the little girl is Antoinette, the dreaming child.[9] The ruins and bunches of flowers in Rochester's description suggest the remains of obeah rituals, still carried out in spite of the abandoned stone house and the long overgrown road. While in her dream Antoinette is terrified, in Rochester's visit to this "place," he too becomes lost and frightened by its alien magic. He asks a servant, "Is there a ghost, a zombi there?" And when he finally returns to the house, Rochester reads a chapter on obeah from a book about the Caribbean. The book defines *zombi* in this way: "*A zombi is a dead person who seems to be alive or a living person who is dead. A zombi can also be a spirit of a place, usually malignant but sometimes to be propitiated with sacrifices or offerings of flowers and fruit*" (*Sea*, p. 107).

With the arrival of Mason, who eventually marries Antoinette against her will to Rochester, her imagination begins its struggle against powerful forces. The struggle takes place elsewhere, in the space of dreams and magic, but we can also see that her imagination has become the ground of historical and political conflict.

Richard Mason has arrived on the island with plans to marry and acquire the estate that has fallen into decay following the Emancipation Act of 1834. "Marooned," Annette marries him. But Christophine sees the change in power relations more objectively: "No more slavery! She had to laugh! 'These new ones have Letter of the Law. Same thing. These new ones got magistrate. They got fine. They got jail house and chain gang. They got tread machine to mash up people's feet. New ones worse than old ones—more cunning, that's all'" (*Sea*, p. 26). The marriage does not save Annette, but leads instead to further ostracism from the suspicious white Jamaican society and eventually to the destruction of Coulibri, the death of her son Pierre, and her own madness and incarceration. Forced to barter herself in marriage, Annette betrays herself and her children. And in this sense, too, she has become like the legendary Maroons.

Unlike Annette, who does not even recognize her enemies until too late, the Maroons fought theirs fiercely. However, the history of their resistance is riddled with betrayals. In the sixteenth century in Dominica, where Rhys grew up, the Spanish offered the Maroons a truce on the condition that they leave the whites alone. Not trusting the Spaniards, the Maroons continued to fight and to terrorize the colonizers into more gentle treatment of the slaves. When their leader, Diego de Campo, was caught, however, he offered to lead expeditions against his former followers in exchange for his life. His betrayal resulted in curbing the threat of the Maroons and their power to win better treatment for the slaves.[10]

Annette's marriage solidifies the power of the neocolonialists; it also intensifies the conflict between blacks and whites. Mason knows nothing about the blacks and thinks of them as ignorant, harmless children. They, however, know of his wealth, his additional estates on Antigua, and, like Christophine, they recognize the power he holds. When a gathering of blacks sets fire to Coulibri, killing Antoinette's invalid younger brother, a prophetic incident with Tia dramatizes the contradictory relationship between Antoinette and her black friends. Fleeing from the burning house, Antoinette sees Tia in the crowd and runs to her: "As I ran, I thought, I will live with Tia and I will be like her . . . . When I was close I saw the jagged stone in her hand but I did not feel it either, only something wet, running down my face. I looked at her and I saw her face crumple up as she began to cry. We stared at each other, blood on my face, tears on hers. It was as if I saw myself. Like in a looking glass" (*Sea*, p. 45).

The doubling of Tia and Antoinette in this confrontation poses them simultaneously as Other and the same. The violent circumstances that divide them also bind them in imagined reflections of one another. Like the doublings in Wilson Harris's Guyanese novels, this differs from the traditional European concept of the double. Rather than opposing a "good" self and a "bad" self, both writers draw on Caribbean psychology and history for doublings and multiplications of character.[11] Rhys goes to the same sources to displace her characters so that doubling and displacing become twin methods for retrieving and reenvisioning the past, expanding character beyond the individual.

The confrontation between Tia and Antoinette recalls again the legendary Maroons, linking her to another historical scene of betrayal. Mason's residence on the island has turned the blacks violently against Antoinette's family. While Annette has argued with her husband about the threat posed to them by the black population, he has refused to listen. She has remained powerless within her marriage yet complicit with his ignorance and authority because of her marriage. A century earlier, the Maroons fought a successful battle against the British. Led by the famous Cudjoe and two of his brothers and joined by runaway slaves, the Maroons forced the British to sign a treaty on March 1, 1739, granting them freedom and 1,500 acres on which they could plant anything but sugar. In return for their freedom, they had to agree to return fugitive slaves, defend the island against foreign invaders, and accept two white residents. Eric Williams has described their paradoxical victory: "Given a special status within their respective societies, they challenged the slave system for themselves alone. They . . . were used to keep others in slavery."[12] Deprived of her earlier privilege as the wife and daughter of slave owners and excluded from white society, Annette attempts with her marriage to claim a special status and to keep her house and land. But to do this, she must "sell out" both herself and her property and enslave others, even those who, like Christophine, have helped her in the past.

Christophine and the power of obeah are central to our understanding of the historical conflicts in Jamaica and to the social and political battles fought on the ground of Antoinette's imagination. From the earliest days of slavery, the colonialists forbade any practice of religion among the slaves, whether Christian or African. Obeah, however, began in Africa as a secret religion and so was suited already to survival as an outlawed practice. In the colonies, it continued to thrive, and its practitioners gained a paradoxical power. They were vulnerable, as is Christophine, to discovery or betrayal, arrest, and imprisonment, yet they inspired respect and fear among believers.[13]

Obeah operated traditionally in two ways, one seemingly harmless, the other overtly political. Derived from West African witchcraft, obeah manipulated personal affairs, granting wishes, changing or catalyzing love affairs, securing revenge against enemies. Jamaican law identified the materials of obeah practice—"Blood, feather, parrots beaks, dogs teeth, alligators teeth, broken bottles, grave-dirt, rum, and egg shells"—and punished any slave on whose person or premises such materials were discovered.[14] When Antoinette runs to Christophine for help, she becomes momentarily frightened by the signs of obeah:

Her bedroom was large and dark. She still had her bright patchwork counterpane, the palm leaf from Palm Sunday and the prayer for a happy death. But after I noticed a heap of chicken feathers in one corner, I did not look round any more.

"So already you frightened eh?" (*Sea*, p. 117)

Though at first Antoinette resisted her marriage, it has awakened her sexual passion, a passion that then disgusts her husband. Rochester has turned against Antoinette and has been sleeping with her maid Amélie; in desperation, Antoinette solicits an aphrodisiac from Christophine. Christophine objects to this method and urges Antoinette to run away instead. Antoinette insists, but the potion succeeds only in making Rochester so ill that he believes Antoinette has poisoned him. The obeah fails for several reasons. Christophine gives the first: ". . . that is not for *béké*. Bad, bad trouble come when *béké* meddle with that" (*Sea*, p. 112). The second has to do with another betrayal, enacted when Antoinette turns her relationship with Christophine into another forced exchange: "Nearby a cock crew and I thought, 'That is for betrayal, but who is the traitor?' She did not want to do this. I forced her with my ugly money. And what does anyone know about traitors or why Judas did what he did?" (*Sea*, p. 118).

These reasons belong to the larger one of Antoinette's lack of place in this society. Neither *béké* nor black, her reliance on obeah for individual, personal matters cannot succeed, for as an individual she hardly exists. Indeed, she soon becomes a victim of the "magic" Rochester practices when he renames her Bertha: "Bertha is not my name. You are trying to make me into someone else, calling me by another name. I know, that's obeah too" (*Sea*, p. 147). The young woman Christophine sees at her cottage has changed: "Your face like dead woman and your eyes red like *soucriant*" (*Sea*, p. 116). Antoinette has become a zombie, a person dead while living.[15]

But obeah performed functions other than the manipulation of personal affairs. Obeah men and women maintained group cohesion and order by operating internally to detect and punish crimes among the slaves. They also worked their magic on behalf of slave rebellions and uprisings.[16] They provided leadership among the Maroons. They administered oaths and protection rituals to ensure group solidarity in resistance to the whites and were credited with the miraculous successes of several revolts including the "Tacky Rebellion" of 1760 in Jamaica.

While failing Antoinette in her personal wishes, Christophine's obeah power works in its social and political form, in ways that An-

toinette has not yet requested but makes use of continually throughout the novel and especially in the concluding scenes. We see these
successful workings of obeah, not in the plot, where it fails, but in
the novel's formal narrative elements and in its language. The first of
these elements to note is the central positioning of the scene in
which Antoinette runs to Christophine.

The novel divides into three parts, the first part narrated exclusively by Antoinette, the second narrated mostly by Rochester, and
the third, by Antoinette again. But Part II differs from the other two
sections in that Antoinette's voice interrupts Rochester's in order to
narrate her visit to Christophine's house. The interruption occupies
about eleven pages in the approximate center of Part II. The interruption is repeated once later in the section previously quoted when
Antoinette's voice, in italics and framed by parentheses, breaks in between the voices of Christophine and Rochester as they battle one
another in Rochester's interior dialogue. And this second interruption, as we have seen, returns to the scene of Christophine's house
and Antoinette's plea for the assistance of obeah. At the center of the
novel, then, and rupturing the "realism" of its narrative point of view,
appears the obeah scene. Only as a consequence of the narrative dis-
turbance afforded by the scene does Antoinette ever feel herself at
home on the island of Jamaica:

> [Christophine's] clothes smelled of clean cotton, starched and ironed.
> I had seen her so often standing knee deep in the river at Coulibri,
> her long skirt hitched up, washing her dresses and her white shifts,
> then beating them against the stones. Sometimes there would be
> other women all bringing their washing down on the stones again
> and again, a gay busy noise. At last they would spread the wet
> clothes in the sun, wipe their foreheads, start laughing and talking.
> She smelled too, of their smell, so warm and comforting to me (but
> he does not like it). The sky was dark blue through the dark green
> mango leaves, and I thought, "This is my place and this is where I
> belong and this is where I wish to stay." (*Sea*, p. 108)

Here Antoinette makes it clear that her quest involves place,
"where" rather than "who," and that her wish for Rochester's love
emerges only from her "real" situation, the fact of her marriage and
the limited options available to her. Her betrayal of Christophine
with her "ugly money" also betrays herself, but a self that cannot
even exist in the "reality" of the island's social and racial laws. She

cannot, realistically, stay in that place even if she does belong there. Her inability to do so makes her a zombie, and only the magic and irrational power of obeah will awaken her from this state to an "other," displaced reality.

It is at this point in the novel that many critics fault Antoinette's character, finding her now irrational, self-destructive, motivated by lust and the desire to please a man.[17] Why does she not take Christophine's advice to "pack up and go"? Rochester abuses her psychologically and physically; he openly sleeps with another woman. In spite of Christophine's urging that she "have spunks and do battle for yourself," Antoinette remains with Rochester, seeming to earn his other name for her, "Marionette." In contrast to Christophine, who has refused to marry in spite of having three children and has kept her own money, and in contrast to her English successor Jane Eyre, even in contrast to Amélie, the black servant girl who at least secures money from Rochester before she runs away, Antoinette lacks will and the power of moral choice. She seems to invite her victimization. Readers may sympathize with her plight, but they hardly admire her response.[18]

However, at precisely the point when Antoinette's character seems to fail, the ruptured realism of the novel's form finds a center and one to which it returns. The moment at which she becomes most enslaved to Rochester and therefore most slavish is the moment when the narrative opens, enters the realm of magic, and shows us and Antoinette the place where she, impossibly, belongs.

Rochester governs his wife as a master would a slave. He possesses her body, and as she explains to Christophine, ". . . I am not rich now, I have no money of my own at all, everything I had belongs to him" (*Sea*, p. 110). He claims her, as a new owner would claim a slave, by renaming her Bertha. He has from the beginning of their marriage considered her of a different species from his, "a stranger to me, a stranger who did not think or feel as I did" (*Sea*, p. 93). He sees her as irrational and promiscuous, and, charging her with madness, "breaks her up." Antoinette reacts to the conditions of her marriage in ways similar to the mechanisms of resistance typical of Jamaican slaves: laziness ("I'm very lazy you know. Like Christophine"), satire ("'Oh England, England,' she called back mockingly . . ."), plans for running away, and, eventually, suicide. These are all passive methods; the use of obeah is a more aggressive means, and possibly the potion Christophine gave her did not sicken Rochester accidentally. Obeah men and women often provided poisons for individually employed violent resistance. The destructive result of the "aphrodisiac" foreshadows the violent fire Antoinette sets to the master's house in the end. The only method not available to Antoinette is that of collective action, for she has been so isolated that she does not even know with whom she might find solidarity.

The sexual master-slave conflict between Rochester and Antoinette brings together several elements to the traditional romance plot. It lends the novel the aura and excitement of passion, exotic beauty, and the kind of tragedy that allows one paperback version of the novel to promise a "poisoned paradise" and "an heiress on the borderline between innocence and decadence." Rachel Blau DuPlessis has described the romance and its significance in Western culture: "Romance plots of various kinds, the iconography of love, the postures of yearning, pleasing, slipping, falling, and failing are, evidently, some of the deep, shared structures of our culture. . . . As a narrative pattern, the romance plot muffles the main female character, represses quest, valorizes heterosexual as opposed to homosexual ties, incorporates individuals within couples as a sign of their personal and narrative success."[19] Critics sometimes read *Wide Sargasso Sea* in this way, regretting the failure of the marriage and the reconciliation of opposites it might have secured.[20] In *Wide Sargasso Sea*, the historical and colonial setting amplifies oppositions: nature/civilization, female/male, black/white, inner/outer, madness/sanity, and dream/reality. Denied a place within this system, the heroine does not act as reconciler; rather she transgresses the boundaries of each opposition. Culturally exiled, she inhabits the margins of these culturally paired opposites. Antoinette longs to be black when she is white, asserts her sexual "nature" in an arranged marriage, shows us the logic in her madness, the reason in her magic, and finally transforms her dream into reality, her inner vision into an outer event. Had she made the "heroic" decisions some readers would prefer and become self-sufficient, her actions would maintain, rather than resolve, the oppositions. As in *Jane Eyre*, heterosexual romance could then prevail.

Wilson Harris recognizes this limit to the realistic novel when he contrasts the "self-sufficient character" of nineteenth-century realism to what he calls the "human person" whose character may be fulfilled but not consolidated. Harris finds a model for the human person in the West Indian slave, exactly the source, psychologically, of Rhys's "character" Antoinette. The slave is the person whose origins have been erased, who remains empty, without center, and therefore unconstrained and open. According to Harris, "An alteration needs to occur in the texture of the novel to allow these juxtapositions [of victor/victim] to play in such a manner that the creation of a vision through and beyond stasis, which I see as immensely pertinent to the late twentieth-century novel, may occur through an alteration in the settled fabric of realism that consolidates victor and victim . . . without that subjective alteration the community is doomed to perpetuate an endless reinforcement of conflict."[21] In *Wide Sargasso Sea,* the alteration occurs simultaneously with an obvious sexual enslavement, a failure of character essential to opening the possibility for a "human person."

The conflict, however, structures the overall pattern of the narrative in the intense opposition of voices and points of view. When Rochester's voice begins narrating Part II, he expresses his antagonism toward the islands and his new wife in metaphors of military conquest: "So it was all over, the advance and retreat, the doubts and hesitations. Everything finished, for better or for worse" (*Sea,* p. 65). They are honeymooning on another island estate called Granbois near a village with the foreboding name of Massacre. He feels menaced by the island's wild intensity of color and warmth, by what he perceives as malice and cunning in the natives, and by his new bride's beauty, her "long, sad, dark alien eyes . . . not English or European either" (*Sea,* p. 67). If Antoinette becomes the victim in their conflict, he should become the victimizing victor. However, Rochester feels himself the victim; his aggression and tyranny result from treatment he has received from his own family as the youngest and penniless son and from his fear of the unknown and the foreign. Though he managed to acquire all of Antoinette's wealth with no protest from Mason, he suspects he has been trapped by Mason into marrying a woman who has inherited her mother's madness and rumored promiscuity. The development of Rochester's point of view and his growing suspicions concerning Antoinette make clear the Victorian ideology that conflates moral idiocy, madness, and female sexual expression. The dichotomous oppositions of madness/reason, sexuality/control, black/white, and—perhaps generating them all— nature/culture, through which Rochester thinks and attempts to maintain his own place in the system, are, nevertheless, continually threatened.

Throughout the second section, we follow the development of Rochester and Antoinette as antitheses of one another, each clinging to the validity of a perspective of reality in direct opposition to the other's. Antoinette's beauty and that of the island threaten the colonizer husband who conflates them, desiring simultaneously to possess both her and what he calls the secret of the place. In Rochester's imagination, Antoinette, who occupies no place, becomes a place that he both fears and desires to inhabit. He struggles for mastery of what Jean-Paul Sartre has called the "strange hell of beauty" in which appearance, the imagination, dream, illusion, and the feminine are evil.

Rochester's fears stem in part from ignorance of the culture that threatens him. At first, for instance, he does not recognize Christophine's powers: "I looked at her sharply but she seemed insignificant. She was blacker than most and her clothes, even the handkerchief round her head, were subdued in colour. She looked at me steadily, not with approval, I thought. We stared at each other for quite a minute. I looked away first and she smiled to herself . . ." (*Sea*, pp. 72–73). The struggle between the two of them, not only for Antoinette but for moral authority, becomes a major conflict in the novel. Christophine wages her part through all the means at her disposal—her understanding of English "reason" and her West Indian "magic." Though she fails to convince Rochester to change his plans for Antoinette, she does manage to "possess" him, to make him "possessed." In this way she turns his irrational obsession with possessing Antoinette against him.

Following Antoinette's visit to Christophine's house, she keeps her promise to Christophine that she will approach her husband with reasonable questions about his neglect of her. Here Christophine shows a naive hope that recourse to the reason the white legal system claims as its basis will help Antoinette whose property and livelihood it has taken from her. But Rochester has just heard another story from Daniel Cosway, an embittered colored man who slanders Antoinette and her mother and also tries to blackmail Rochester. Cosway's letter appears in full in the narrative, constituting another rupture in voice and point of view in this section. Cosway, a disinherited illegitimate half-brother of Antoinette's, accuses Antoinette and her entire family of inherited madness, accuses Antoinette and her mother of bewitching men, and charges Richard Mason with tricking Rochester into marriage with "a lot of nancy stories, which is what we call lies here." The allusion to "nancy stories" discloses Cosway's own cultural displacement and the conflicts of interest he is attempting to manipulate.

"Nancy" or Anancy tales were originally brought by the Akan, the main group of slaves who first arrived on Jamaica from West Africa.[22] Very popular among the slaves, they characterized a little man with an inferior manner who outwits those opposed to him—a trickster or magician who can turn into a spider if endangered. The Anancy figure may also fly and thus takes part in the oral traditions expressing the longing for wings with which to fly home. In West Africa, storytelling grants carnivalesque license for the impersonation and ridicule of people and objects that are ordinarily powerful

and superior, and this function of the tales survived in the Caribbean, where they might satirize and ridicule white masters. Whites,
then, would perceive Anancy stories as lies and superstitions; to the
blacks they provided an outlet for truths and desires otherwise forcefully suppressed.

Daniel Cosway, in a sense, takes on the deceptive qualities of the
Anancy man at the same time he demonstrates his identification
with the whites of the island by calling these stories lies. Either way,
he betrays his origins. Antoinette declares that Daniel hates white
people, while the maid Amélie insists he reads the Bible and lives
just like white people. Especially in the period following emancipation, the colored class walked this difficult line, preventing the solidarity of blacks and coloreds that might have spurred the native majority to rebel more successfully against the colonial powers. The
other possibility for social change and development, democratic
nationalism, was inhibited, on the other hand, by distrust between
coloreds and whites.[23] Rochester's vulnerable position as foreigner,
however, pushes him, despite any distrust of this strange man, to
seize upon the letter as validation of all his fears and a legitimation
of his own culture's methods of social control. Madness and feminine sexuality must be suppressed in the interests of civilized morality. Only on this wild island could they flourish so abandonedly,
and so Rochester evolves his plan for Antoinette, a plan about which
he need no longer feel any obligations to consult her.

The "trick" that Daniel Cosway plays, however, also turns against
Rochester, first when Cosway threatens to reveal publicly all he
knows about Antoinette's "past" and then when it appears that Cosway's voice has begun to inhabit Rochester's mind. When his words
appear again, they participate in a play of voices, predominated by
Christophine's, and soon emptying Rochester of his own concept of
sanity.

> "And then," she went on in her judge's voice, "you make love to
> her till she drunk with it, no rum could make her drunk like that,
> till she can't do without it. It's *she* can't see the sun any more. Only
> you she see. But all you want is to break her up."
> (*Not the way you mean, I thought*)
> "But she hold out eh? She hold out."
> (*Yes, she held out. A pity*)
> "So you pretend to believe all the lies that damn bastard tell you."
> (*That damn bastard tell you*)
> Now every word she said was echoed, echoed loudly in my head.

"So that you can leave her alone."
(*Leave her alone*)
"Not telling her why."
(*Why?*)
"No more love, eh?"
(*No more love*) (*Sea*, p. 153)

As Rochester narrates his dialogue with Christophine, we see how at first his inner voice challenges her words, then it begins to agree and finally to simply echo them. His thoughts have begun to follow a rhythmic pattern resembling the call-and-response songs of black laborers, as if the culture he has invaded now invades him.

Christophine has come to their house to care for Antoinette, and Rochester has heard her murmuring in patois and singing a song that Rochester recognizes as "dangerous," remarking, "I must protect myself." His efforts at protection do not work against Christophine's words or against Antoinette's. This is the scene in which Antoinette's disembodied voice interrupts the dialogue between Rochester and Christophine.

"She tell me in the middle of all this you start calling her names. Marionette. Some word so."
"Yes, I remember, I did."
(*Marionette, Antoinette, Marionetta, Antoinetta*)
"That word mean doll, eh? Because she don't speak. You want to force her to cry and to speak."
(*Force her to cry and to speak*)
"But she won't. So you think up something else. You bring that worthless girl to play with next door and you talk and laugh and love so that she hear everything. You meant her to hear."
Yes, that didn't just happen. I meant it.
(*I lay awake all night long after they were asleep, and as soon as it was light I got up and dressed and saddled Preston. And I came to you. Oh Christophine. O Pheena, Pheena, help me.*)
"You haven't yet told me exactly what you did with my—with Antoinette."
"Yes I tell you. I make her sleep." (*Sea*, p. 154)

As Christophine intervenes in the section given to Rochester's first-person narration, she revises what he has told us, forcing him to internalize her interpretation. And in this passage he must also listen to Antoinette speak, hear her plead with Christophine, and know that her visit to Christophine was motivated by a desperation to which he had driven her. The sleep Christophine has imposed on Antoinette is dangerous to Rochester, for it places Antoinette somewhere else where she can speak on her own behalf even when she is absent from the scene. Her voice, too, has begun to possess Rochester's mind, and we see that the battle taking place previously in Antoinette's imagination now plays itself out in full force in Rochester's.

While Christophine pleads with Rochester to change his attitude toward Antoinette, to protect her and try to love her again, he calls upon Daniel Cosway's voice to bolster his internal armory of weapons.

> "I will not forsake her," I said wearily. "I will do all I can for her."
> "You will love her like you did before?"
> (*Give my sister your wife a kiss from me. Love her as I did—oh yes I did. How can I promise that?*) I said nothing. (*Sea*, p. 158)

The battle continues as later Rochester reviews the dialogue, inventing new and vicious responses to Christophine's phrases as they chorus in his mind. Rochester's jealousy and rage at the deception he believes his wife has deployed push him over the line and into the irrationality he has projected onto his wife and tried so hard to disown: "She said she loved this place. This is the last she'll see of it. . . . She's mad but *mine, mine* . . ." (*Sea*, pp. 165–166). Here the categories of dichotomous thought that distinguish reason and madness dissolve along with the dissolution of personality or "character." As Rochester marshals his legal forces by threatening Christophine with the police, he also utters the words that allow Christophine to curse him:

> "I would give my eyes never to have seen this abominable place."
> She laughed. "And that's the first damn word of truth you speak. You choose what you give, eh? Then you choose. You meddle in something and perhaps you don't know what it is." She began to mutter to herself. Not in patois . . . (*Sea*, p. 161)

Rochester has also quite literally lost his mind and point of view in the section devoted to it, and the multiple-voiced narrative blasts out of the perceptions of one person to establish formally a social cacophony of intersubjectivity. The now multiply meaningful concept of "possession" makes madness a function of this play of voices rather than an attribute of a single character. Dissolved, character can no longer consolidate, in Wilson Harris's terms, but awaits metamorphosis.

As Christophine's obeah makes its power felt in the formal alterations of realism in the novel's narrative pattern, so too do Antoinette's dreams help her to rescript the fate ordained for her by the nineteenth-century European authority vested in Rochester and in the "realistic" novel *Jane Eyre*. As we have seen, the first dream warns Antoinette of Rochester's approach and threat to her life; it prophesies an ineffectual struggle on her part against him. And, in a way, this scenario does take place in her enslaving marriage and ineffectual attempts to gain Rochester's love. However, the dream also introduces Antoinette to the "secret place" that later frightens Rochester. It initiates their struggle on the ground of imagination and in the realm of obeah magic.

Antoinette dreams her second vision while attending the convent school to which she is sent after the destruction of Coulibri. In the interior world of the convent, things are already carefully split, dualities clear, and knowledge certain: "That was how it was, light and dark, sun and shadow, Heaven and Hell, for one of the nuns knew all about Hell and who does not. But another one knew all about Heaven . . ." (*Sea*, p. 57). Here Antoinette is sure of her own identity and embroiders her name in "fire red, Antoinette Mason, née Cosway, Mount Calvary Convent, Spanish Town, Jamaica" (*Sea*, p. 53). The fire red of the flames at Coulibri thus remains in Antoinette's imagination.

The second dream occurs just before Mr. Mason brings Antoinette out of the protected world of the convent. The opening of the convent gate represents the dissolution of Antoinette's feelings of security and clarity behind the convent walls.

> As we were going out of the convent gate he said in a careless voice, "I have asked some English friends to spend next winter here. You won't be dull . . ."
>
> It may have been the way he smiled but again a feeling of dismay, sadness, and loss almost choked me. This time I did not let him see it.
>
> It was like that morning when I found the dead horse. Say nothing and it may not be true. (*Sea*, p. 59)

Antoinette tries to repress the new and uncertain knowledge of her fate, a fate she has dreamed about.

The effort to silence certain kinds of knowledge corresponds to the effort to maintain a clear demarcation between inner and outer worlds, an effort that fails as Antoinette passes through the convent gate and as she prepares to be married.

> But they all knew at the convent. The girls were very curious but
> I would not answer their questions and for the first time I resented
> the nuns' cheerful faces.
> They are safe. How can they know what it can be like *outside*?
> (*Sea*, p. 59)

The inner world of the convent secures the distinction between private and public worlds of experience. As in the Victorian ideological removal of the home and "natural" feelings from the market and "social" ideas and events, repression and silence must operate— though in ultimately ineffective ways. Antoinette's dream tells a story with her censored knowledge:

> Again I have left the house at Coulibri. It is still night and I am
> walking towards the forest. I am wearing a long dress and thin slip-
> pers, so I walk with difficulty, following the man who is with me and
> holding up the skirt of my dress. It is white and beautiful and I don't
> wish to get it soiled. I follow him, sick with fear but I make no effort
> to save myself; if anyone were to try to save me, I would refuse. This
> must happen. Now we have reached the forest. We are under the tall
> dark trees and there is no wind. "Here?" He turns and looks at me,
> his face black with hatred and when I see this I begin to cry. He
> smiles slyly. "Not here, not yet," he says, and I follow him, weeping.
> Now I do not try to hold up my beautiful dress. We are no longer in
> the forest but in an enclosed garden surrounded by a stone wall and
> the trees are different trees. I do not know them. There are steps
> leading upwards. It is too dark to see the wall or the steps, but I
> know they are there and I think, "It will be when I go up these steps.
> At the top." I stumble over my dress and cannot get up. I touch a tree
> and my arms hold on to it. "Here, here." But I think I will not go any
> further. The tree sways and jerks as if it is trying to throw me off.
> Still I cling and the seconds pass and each one is a thousand years.
> "Here, in here," a strange voice said, and the tree stopped swaying
> and jerking. (*Sea*, pp. 59–60)

In this sequel to her first dream, Antoinette is no longer pursued by the mysterious and malevolent figure, but follows him. What is going to happen "here"? Having read *Jane Eyre*, the reader can guess some of what the dream foretells, recognizing the male voice in the dream as belonging to Edward Rochester and the steps she must climb as leading to Antoinette's attic prison. But why does she not wish to save herself? And what is the significance of the garden, the tree to which she clings desperately? The dirtying of her white dress and her fall suggest a loss of innocence; the garden suggests the archetypal setting for this loss and the accompanying acquisition of moral choice and knowledge. However, Antoinette rejects the possibility of choice and insists that "this must happen." The man controls her completely.

The question of place recurs in the dream. It seems to be the only important question for Antoinette's dreaming consciousness. Furthermore, the setting changes from forest trees, with which she is familiar and which she and Rochester have each visited in her earlier dream, to the enclosed and probably English garden of what we might guess to be Thornfield Hall. The passively obedient Antoinette resists her instructions only once toward the end of the dream when, rather than continuing in response to the direction "Here, here," she stops and holds on to the tree. The tree seems almost alive, and she clings to it while a "strange voice," apparently not Rochester's, advises "Here, in here." The meaning of the tree, the identity of the strange voice, and the location of "here" remain, I think, unknown to us until Antoinette dreams her final vision. And to understand the entire sequence of her dreams, we must read them in the context of Caribbean cultural motifs and also in light of the formal properties of dreams.

As Freud describes the dynamics of dream work, a specific dream logic creates images, symbols, and stories that condense or displace other images and events, those from our unconscious minds and those from our everyday experience. Dream symbols thus become "overdetermined," resistant to exhaustive explanation or any exclusive meaning because of their multiple associations.[24] In this dream logic, spatial relations may indicate relations ordinarily temporal or causal, so that our usual sense of history and event no longer explains the meaning of a dream. Thus, though dreams may appear to us stories, with sequences of actions and characters, their meaning accrues through a logic dissimilar from the logic of narratives. Linguists have noted that the dynamics of condensation and displacement imitate those of metaphor and metonymy.[25] Just as a dream symbol condenses various images, words, or actions into a new, more intensely meaningful image, so does a metaphor bring together the language and objects of one kind of experience with those of another, carrying us from the world of what we know and can articulate to a new world we do not yet comprehend. As a literary device then, the dreams in *Wide Sargasso Sea* point to the code of language making.

We no longer read the themes of identity and conflict of opposites that charge the romantic drama; rather we participate in the formal dynamics of such mythmaking. Antoinette's dreams give her the chance to rewrite her own myth as she learns how to displace the static conflict of identity from which she suffers to create new epistemological ground for its resolution. The novel does not simply oppose one fictional truth to another or one cultural point of view to another, it shifts the ground of interpretation and validity to another world altogether, between fictions and world views. In this in-between space the dream compresses private and public histories, personal and cultural events.

Opposed to already existing "reality," dreams work within the narrative of *Wide Sargasso Sea*, as does obeah, to disrupt its conventions and assert the possibility of another kind of knowledge. The powers of both dreams and obeah depend upon the magic of appearance and illusion, the condensation of historically derived feelings and associations into the utterance of a word, the presentation of a fetish, image, or sign. Words like "marooned" or "possession" become deeply layered and multiple in meaning so that apparently minor moments of the narrative take on a weightier and nearly magical significance.

Through the third and final dream, the novel exceeds and overturns the limitations of its predetermined ending. The ending to *Jane Eyre* depends upon our accepting Bertha Mason's madness as a fact and sign of her subhuman condition. She becomes the monstrous Other, the obstacle in the way of happiness for the self-sufficient heroine of the novel. While Jane feels compassion for "Bertha," Rochester guides the reader to view the two women as antitheses of one another: " 'That is *my wife,*' said he. 'Such is the sole conjugal embrace I am ever to know—such are the endearments which are to solace my leisure hours! And *this* is what I wished to have. . . . Compare these clear eyes with the red balls yonder—this face with that mask—this form with that bulk . . .' "[26]

The concluding pages of *Wide Sargasso Sea*, however, demonstrate a sisterhood between these two female characters that dissolves Rochester's oppositions of the good woman/bad woman.[27] In her third dream, Antoinette wanders through the passageway and discovers a large room with red carpets and curtains that reminds her of a church. She has returned to the inner world represented by the convent, but she has also discovered a room very much like the

"Red Room" in which Jane Eyre was cruelly locked as an orphan child. The tie between these two female characters lies not so much in their relations to Rochester as in their shared experiences of abandonment, confinement, and the need to call upon inner images and voices and make them a part of their outer and shared worlds. Jane hears Rochester calling her name though she is miles from him; Antoinette learns to project her voice into Rochester's consciousness. Jane trusts the voice she hears as real even though she imagines it, just as Antoinette finally trusts the reality of her dream.

Antoinette for a moment, in fact, becomes someone else in her dream, someone who might be Jane Eyre—"I never looked behind me for I did not want to see that ghost of a woman who they say haunts this place" (*Sea*, p. 187). She has previously spied the girl Jane Eyre, also wandering the passageway, looking as if she has seen a ghost. Jane and Antoinette become doubles rather than antagonists in *Wide Sargasso Sea* at the same time that Antoinette recovers her lost ties to the Caribbean women she loved as a child.

In the dream the ghost finally recognizes herself: "It was then that I saw her—the ghost. The woman with the streaming hair. She was surrounded by a gilt frame but I knew her" (*Sea*, pp. 188–189). Self-recognition sets her flying and reunites her with Christophine: "As I ran or perhaps floated or flew I called help me Christophine help me and looking behind me I saw that I had been helped. There was a wall of fire protecting me . . ." (*Sea*, p. 189). This time Christophine's magic has helped Antoinette, and this time she is able to "[look] behind" her, then to "[turn] round," remembering the firing of Coulibri by former black slaves and seeing her own life in the fire.

If Antoinette has walked like the living dead, she has now awakened to fly, fulfilling the traditional slave wish for wings with which to fly "home" or becoming like the Anancy flying trickster, the figure Harris calls "Icarus Anancy."[28] The magic of obeah has helped her in the form of a fetish, her red dress, which she had worn on her voyage to England and which she believes can protect her.

As soon as I turned the key I saw it hanging, the colour of fire and sunset. The colour of flamboyant flowers. "If you are buried under a flamboyant tree," I said, "your soul is lifted up when it flowers. Everyone wants that." . . .

The scent that came from the dress was very faint at first, then it grew stronger. The smell of vetivert and frangipanni, of cinnamon and dust and lime trees when they are flowering. The smell of the sun and the smell of the rain. (*Sea*, p. 185)

The dress falls to the floor "and it was as if the fire had spread across the room." The fetish brings back her memory, teaches her what she must do, reminds her of the name "embroidered in fire red" at the convent school.

As Christophine's obeah and the dream awaken Antoinette's powers, she is able to read her own life, reinterpreting and finally rewriting the elements of its myth.

> Then I turned round and saw the sky. It was red and all my life was in it. I saw the grandfather clock and Aunt Cora's patchwork, all colours, I saw the orchids and stephanotis and the jasmine and the tree of life in flames. I saw the chandelier and the red carpet downstairs and the bamboos and the tree ferns, the gold ferns and the silver, and soft green velvet of the moss on the garden wall. I saw my doll's house and the books and the picture of the Miller's Daughter. I heard the parrot call as he did when he saw a stranger, *Qui est là? Qui est là? (Sea*, p. 189)

In her vision she recrosses the sea, returning to Coulibri and seeing again its furnishings and paintings transported from England and the quilt made by a slave owner's wife. A Caribbean symbol of the soul, the parrot that died in the Coulibri fire comes to life again and responds to Antoinette as to a stranger. The parrot's call demands not that she name who she is, but who is *there*. She must place herself in order to know her soul. The threatening garden wall of her earlier dream metamorphoses into the garden wall at Coulibri where the tree of life had bloomed and decayed. That it now flames signals a return in Antoinette's imagination to an even further forgotten history in the ancient Arawak legend of the flaming tree. The red dress triggers the reenactment of this legend, reminding Antoinette of the flamboyant tree that lifts the soul when it flowers. As Wilson Harris has described it, the ancient Amerindian story tells of the fight between the native Arawaks and Caribs: "The tree is fired by the Caribs at a time of war when the Arawaks seek refuge in its branches. The fire rages and drives the Arawaks up into space until they are themselves burnt and converted into sparks which continue to rise into the sky to become the Pleiades."[29]

We can now identify one powerful element in the image of the tree, swaying with life, to which Antoinette clung in her earlier dream and speculate that the strange voice guiding her into its branches came from ancient sources and a race she could only know through a dream.[30] Her return to the Caribbean in her final vision unites her with all of its peoples—the transported English and white Creoles of her family, but also the older native races, and finally the blacks from whom her "real" life had inevitably estranged her.

Not only does Christophine appear to help Antoinette, but Tia, too, appears and calls to her: "The wind caught my hair and it streamed out like wings. It might bear me up, I thought, if I jumped to those hard stones. But when I looked over the edge I saw the pool at Coulibri. Tia was there. She beckoned to me and when I hesitated, she laughed. I heard her say, You frightened? And I heard the man's voice, Bertha! Bertha! All this I saw and heard in a fraction of a second. And the sky so red. Someone screamed and I thought, *Why did I scream?* I called 'Tia!' and jumped and woke" (*Sea*, p. 190). Tia repeats Christophine's earlier words questioning Antoinette's fear of the obeah feathers in the central scene of the novel, recalling Antoinette to the place where "I belong and . . . where I wish to stay." This is the place from which she spoke in Part II, interrupting Rochester's dialogue with Christophine, making her voice heard in spite of his efforts to silence it. The reminder of obeah recalls too the "secret place," "the hidden place" that had frightened Rochester and that he swore to take away from Antoinette by taking her to England.

Transformed into the flying trickster, Antoinette spins her web, lifting her soul above the flames, burning like the Pleiades in a constellation of all the peoples of the Caribbean. She commits a crime, not that of suicide but of flight, *marronage*. She rejects "the man's voice" and his name for her and chooses instead her black friend, rekindling their childhood ties through the wall of fire. She can make this choice, not because she has consolidated her character, but because she has lost and multiplied it, become enslaved, and thus joined the history of the blacks on the islands, learning from them traditional means of resistance.[31] The heterosexual romance and "failed marriage" give way to a community of women in which Antoinette overcomes her inheritance of betrayal and learns from the ancient Arawaks the visions of metamorphosis that fulfill her multiplicitous and heterogeneous Caribbean identity. The dream condenses into "a fraction of a second" all the private images, cultural symbols, and conflicts of her social world. When she awakens and sets out through the door into the same passageway, Antoinette again crosses the gates separating outer and inner realities, but this time by her own choice and with the knowledge of her own power. She finds this power in her ability to act where she actually is—in the midst of two worlds and in a new fictional reality, the wide Sargasso Sea that dissolved nineteenth-century European distinctions between public and private experience, legitimate and illegitimate sexuality, madness and reason, primitive and civilized behavior, dream and reality, even death and life.

In the colonial setting of the novel, we see how the European mind conflated the feminine and the dark Other of the colonies. When Freud referred to women as the "dark continent," he expressed a pattern of thought characteristic of his period. While Antoinette's enslavement to Rochester parallels the history of the black Africans in the colonies, hers is sexual slavery, different yet the same. Thus she joins a community of black women in her final leap, while borrowing from all of black and native cultures in her quest for place.

My interpretation differs from readings of *Wide Sargasso Sea* that analyze the relationship between Antoinette and her mother as a failure in bonding that cannot be redeemed. Several recent critics of Rhys focus on the mother-daughter tie, drawing on North American and European psychologists such as Nancy Chodorow, D. W. Winnicott, and Jean Piaget.[32] This particular female relationship is, of course, important to understanding the protagonists' psychological dispositions; however, to focus on it centrally from the perspective of European psychology seems to me to restrict the notion of character to something that can be judgmentally diagnosed as either intact or disturbed due to a determining dynamic within the nuclear family. Sometimes the notion of the subject supplants that of character, but again, the "subjects" of Rhys's texts are perceived as silenced (and therefore disturbed, disallowed) due to an absent mother.[33]

Interpreting Antoinette's quest as one for place, resolved by a spiritual and historically located collectivity, suggests a notion of female identity very different from that argued by much of contemporary feminist literary criticism. Toril Moi has divided contemporary feminist thought into two camps, the "Anglo-American" and the "French."[34] These categories seem reductive in light of the writing of some feminist critics, such as Margaret Homans, who attempt to bridge the two theoretical approaches. However, one element that all three perspectives assume, whether emphasizing identity through social experience or the splitting and exclusion of the female self through language, is the dynamics of the European family.

The mother/father/female child triangle patterns, for example, Nancy Chodorow's theory of female identity through mother-daughter bonding that has influenced critics such as Elizabeth Abel and Judith Kegan Gardiner.[35] The dynamics of this pattern, introjected onto the unconscious and writ large in the realms of the Symbolic and the Imaginary, guide the writings of "French" feminists such as Julia Kristeva, Hélène Cixous, Luce Irigaray, and Jane Gallop.[36] Combining the analysis of experience with that of discourse in shaping women's identities, Margaret Homans has questioned "whether or not anything differentiates women's relation to discourse . . . from the discourse of other marginalized groups, such as colonial writers, or racial and ethnic minorities." She revises Rachel Blau DuPlessis's phrase "(ambiguously) non-hegemonic" to describe "not only white women's relation to hegemonic male culture but also the relation between women from marginalized groups and any male authority. This seems to be the case whether the authority is held by white men or by men of subordinate races and nationalities who, oppressed themselves, are nevertheless hegemonic relative to women in their own groups."[37] Homans cites passages from novels by Toni Morrison, Alice Walker, and Margaret Atwood as evidence for her point that the representability of female identity in dominant discourse becomes problematic for these writers when they distinguish it from race or cultural conflicts. Racial oppression, she argues, figures in the texts as explicit victimization. She states that at the point of female identification, the authors and their characters have more in common with women of the ruling race and class; rather than make this connection, however, the texts represent their oppression as women through silence. She views the choices made by the characters (Eva Peace's "'choice' of one leg over two") as masking their oppression as women.

If we were to follow Homans's theory in reading the ending to *Wide Sargasso Sea*, Antoinette's calling of Tia's name and leaping to her death would register as a moment of victimization, when she identifies with those who are racially and culturally oppressed. She speaks, but she dies. However, the moment is dramatized as a choice, and while Antoinette makes it by speaking, she speaks through a dream, her voice heard only by Grace Poole, who decides that she, too, was dreaming. Does the silenced choice then defer to an overriding theme of racial conflict by masking Antoinette's specifically female oppression?

In light of these questions, it appears odd that those readers who perceive Antoinette as victimized in the end perceive her as a victim by virtue of her sexual status, her weak or failed bond with her mother, and/or her quintessentially "feminine" qualities. I think that *Wide Sargasso Sea* reveals even further complexities in the "(ambiguously) non-hegemonic" woman's position. A female character who is neither white nor black demonstrates the cultural and historical determinants of racial Otherness and the ways that sexual oppression can tie even the granddaughter of a slave owner to the descendants of his slaves more strongly than to her actual blood relations. In this case, the protagonist finds, at the moment of her oppression as a woman, a suggested, if not explicit, connection to women of the ruling race and class since she does see herself in Jane Eyre, but, significantly, she discovers that she has more in common with the women of the oppressed race and class. From this point or these points of identification, it becomes possible for such doubly marginal women to retrieve from their histories, as does Antoinette, ways to discredit the dominant discourse, entering yet countering it from "elsewhere." Elsewhere may become possible through maternal or sisterly identification, but even successful bonding does not occur without conflict, and it is Antoinette's conflicted relationships with her mother, Tia, Christophine, and Jane Eyre that contribute to her discoveries. In addition, this concept of elsewhere need not be confined to the realm of suppressed "semiotic" pulsations that Julia Kristeva describes as characterizing the mother-child dyad and revolutionary modernist writing, but extends to a cultural network of spiritual kinship, layered in historical conflicts and the unconscious.

The predominantly Caribbean setting of *Wide Sargasso Sea* allows Rhys to articulate the complex interrelationship between the condition of oppressed races and cultures under European imperialism and the masculine oppression and silencing of women within European society. In her earlier novels, the settings are European, but similar patterns of enslavement and resistance shape her protagonists. In the first novel she wrote (the third published), Rhys writes of a colonial woman, exiled in England on the eve of the First World War. In *Voyage in the Dark* sexual and cultural conflict become coextensive, this time in the "modern" early decades of the twentieth century.

Four

Voyage in the Dark

Carnival/Consciousness

*T*oward the middle of *Voyage in the Dark*, the protagonist Anna Morgan thinks to herself, "Everybody says, 'Get on.' Of course, some people do get on. Yes, but how many? What about what's-her-name? She got on, didn't she? 'Chorus-Girl Marries Peer's Son.' Well, *what* about her? Get on or get out, they say. Get on or get out."[1] That Anna and "they" perceive getting on as getting married reflects the conventions of the nineteenth-century realist novel in which, as Rachel Blau DuPlessis has pointed out, the female protagonist must either marry or die: "Why are these endings in marriage and death both part of a cultural practice of romance? Marriage celebrates the ability to negotiate with sexuality and kinship; death is caused by inabilities or improprieties in this negotiation, a way of deflecting attention from manmade social norms to cosmic sanctions."[2] Jane Eyre provides the perfect example of a friendless orphan who manages her sexual and kinship negotiations successfully; Maggie Tulliver in Eliot's *The Mill on the Floss* gives an example of a heroine who fails, who commits an "impropriety" and so must die.

The "they" who say "Get on" might include some readers and critics of Rhys's novels who seem to admire them in spite of their themes and especially in spite of their characters who definitely do not "get on." Not only do Rhys's heroines not get on; they do not die properly, with remorse for their improprieties or with a satisfying integrity of self.

The endings to Jean Rhys's novels, then, often become the sites of critical puzzlement and debate. The ending to *Wide Sargasso Sea*, occurring as a dream, appears to some readers as a passive flight from reality, to others a suicide and yet a triumph. The ambivalence is heightened if the reader approaches Antoinette's "character" from a European psychological point of view, expecting to judge her integrity or her ability to unify her "self" and triumph as an autonomous individual. For feminist readers, the problem becomes especially acute since we wish to draw well-deserved attention to Jean Rhys as a woman writer and perhaps feel that to do so we must somehow redeem her seemingly "failed" female characters. If we are unable to view them as victorious, we become trapped in victimology.

Recent readings of *Voyage in the Dark,* Rhys's first novel but third to be published (1934), show similar assumptions at work concerning the interpretation of character, assumptions that become particularly problematic in the moral judgments made concerning the novel's ending. *Voyage in the Dark* presents another female character exiled between two worlds. Anna Morgan is also marooned—in the sense of wrecked and abandoned—but, in her case, on the island of Britain, where her complex history and identity as a West Indian are suppressed and where she suffers from poverty and sexual exploitation. At the novel's beginning, she works as a member of a traveling chorus troupe, then gives this up to become the mistress of a man much older than she; when he grows tired of the affair, she resorts to prostitution. Discovering that she is pregnant, Anna undergoes an illegal abortion that causes her to hemorrhage badly. The doctor who attends her remarks cynically, "She'll be all right, . . . ready to start all over in no time, I've no doubt." In the final lines of the novel, Anna repeats his words: "I lay . . . and thought about starting all over again. And about being new and fresh. And about mornings, and misty days, when anything might happen. And about starting all over again, all over again . . ." (*Voyage,* p. 160).

Giving the novel its finely crafted shape and saving it from the melodrama suggested by its plot, narrative juxtapositions of several voices, all spoken from Anna's first-person point of view, delineate the powerful cultural conflicts that Anna internalizes. These conflicts map her unconscious, giving voice to several "selves" and to at least two different and conflicting modes of ironic commentary. Recognizing the narrative fragmentation and the various narrating voices, critics look for resolution to the conflicts and unification of the various selves as a sign of Anna's success as a heroine. And most often, they must concede her "failure," commenting on her nostalgic or "childish" return to her past and wishful thinking as substitutes for successful integration and adaptation to the present.[3]

Readings of the ending are complicated by the now well known fact that Rhys's publisher asked her to change the original version in which Anna dies from the abortion.[4] Rhys altered the last lines, heightening their ambiguity, and also cut out large sections of the final part of the novel. Since Rhys apparently preferred her original version, some critics read the published one as censored and uncharacteristic of her writing. Others defend the published version. Both arguments rely on notions of formal or thematic unity to make their cases. The aesthetic value of unity matches the criterion for character "success" that lies behind frequent critical judgments of Anna. The prevailing disunity of her consciousness in the last section of both versions and her inability to make her past and present "fit" remain signs of her failure to progress beyond what may be perceived as her degraded condition or, in more sympathetic readings, her need for an absent mother.[5]

But as the mythmaking strategies in *Wide Sargasso Sea* indicate, the notion of a unified autonomous self conflicts with the protagonist's quest, a quest for place within a collective history and pluralist culture. European and North American psychological theories of identity and ego development impose inappropriate or only partially appropriate values on texts that emerge from a Caribbean context. Even Lacanian psychoanalysis, with its acknowledgment of the decentered subject, remains focused on the individual's internalized oppositions and differences within European patriarchal society, ignoring broader cultural differences and collective histories.

Perhaps the most important signal of the importance of Caribbean history and culture to our understanding of *Voyage in the Dark* appears in its ending and in the choices Rhys made in rewriting it. In the brief final section of both versions of the novel, when Anna is suffering fever and delirium from loss of blood, long passages in italics portray her return, in fantasy, to her Caribbean homeland and, specifically, to its celebration of Carnival. The images recalled in these passages are frightening in their grotesqueness. From a white European point of view, they appear especially threatening, and in both versions Anna recalls the voices of her father and aunt: "*A pretty useful mask that white one watch it and the slobbering tongue of an idiot will stick out—a mask Father said with an idiot behind it I believe the whole damned business is like that—Hester said Gerald the child's listening—oh no she isn't Father said she's looking out of the window and quite right too—it ought to be stopped somebody said it's not a decent and respectable way to go on it ought to be stopped . . .*" (*Voyage*, p. 158). At first in this section, Anna watches with the rest of her family, separated from Carnival by "the slats of the jalousies" and by her white Euro-Creole heritage. Later, however, she becomes part of Carnival's festivities—"dancing forwards and backwards backwards and forwards whirling round and round" (*Voyage*, p. 159).

Like Antoinette, Anna has always identified with the native and black people of her island, a home she deliberately recalls in as much concrete and sensual detail as possible throughout the novel, beginning with its first paragraph: "It was funny but that was what I thought about more than anything else—the smell of the streets and the smells of frangipanni and lime juice and cinnamon and cloves, and sweets made of ginger and syrup, and incense after funerals or Corpus Christi processions . . ." (*Voyage*, p. 7). While memories of island celebrations thus frame the novel, they cannot provide an easy or nostalgic return to an idyllic past. Anna has always known that even her best friend and nurse, Francine, must have disliked her "because I was white . . . I would never be able to explain to her that I hated being white" (*Voyage*, p. 60). Like Antoinette, she is estranged even from her "home" and most painfully from the people she admires but from whom the history of colonial conquest has separated her. Her participation, in the end, in the celebrations of Carnival represents a significant cultural choice—but one that brings with it a dizzying surrender to something considered "not decent" by her family.

The chaos of carnival voices and the cultural conflicts of the concluding passages markedly intensify what appears throughout the narrative as several fields of consciousness in which various voices speak. Some are spoken by Anna or different versions of Anna, some by those who give shape to and interpret her conflicting identities, internalized voices of "they" who say "Get on or get out." The get-on-or-get-out passage provides an excellent example of what Mikhail Bakhtin has called the "internal dialogization" of novelistic "heteroglossia." The style of *Voyage in the Dark*, with its multiple voices focused within first-person narration, seems to deliberately exhibit this quality of the novel, an exhibition made possible by the "social heteroglossia" enriching the differences and contradictions within the character.[6] The first line of the passage, "Everybody says, 'Get on,'" is spoken by the first-person narrator, addressing herself. It sets up a dialogue, anticipating a response. But even before the response appears, the line itself is divided dialogically by its quotation of what "Everybody" says so that already two voices speak. The second line, "Of course, some people do get on," replies, but in the same narrative voice as the first line, a commentary or extension of the first thought. The third line, "Yes, but how many?" introduces a second voice within the speaker that questions and criticizes the official commentary quoted by the first voice. The next two lines, "What about what's-her-name? She got on, didn't she?" argues back, presumably in the now merged voice of the first narrator and "Everybody," whose position she has taken for the moment. The merged voice then quotes another, from a newspaper headline, in support of her position, "Chorus-Girl Marries Peer's Son." Then the questioning, critical voice responds, "Well, *what* about her?" indicating the inadequacy of the evidence and expressing frustration at the ideology that prevails in spite of the logic of numbers and probability. The last two lines appear to circle back to the first, repeating what "they" say: "Get on or get out, they say. Get on or get out."

The repetition contains an important difference, however, acquired by the phrase's movement among the various voices of the internal dialogue. Like the passage discussed in Part I, in which Anna's repetition of the phrase "Oceans away from despair" takes on a new meaning, so has the phrase "get on," especially with the addition of "or get out." The lack of social logic behind the ideology has already been exposed; the addition of "or get out" exposes a simplistic either-or thinking in popular opinion. The repetition, however, indicates a futile irony—no matter how simplistic, how illogical, "they" will still say it, and anyone who questions or criticizes will find no alternative. The passage has become an ironic commentary on the power of popular opinion, fed by the official, quoted words of newspapers, and masking the social reality of young women in Anna's position.

Similar dialogization occurs in *Wide Sargasso Sea*. The first line, for instance, quotes another "they": "They say when trouble comes close ranks, and so the white people did." We could read the mad play of voices in Rochester's mind in which he argues with Christophine, himself, and Antoinette as a similar display of novelistic heteroglossia, and, indeed, conflicts of voices, both external and internal, seem to shape the style of all of Rhys's novels. In *Voyage in the Dark*, however, we see the tie between this deliberate polyglot and the events of Carnival.

According to Bakhtin, the novel's unofficial, seemingly disorganized language developed in "the lower levels, on the stages of local fairs and at buffoon spectacles, [where] the heteroglossia of the clown sounded forth . . . where all 'languages' were masks and where no language could claim to be an authentic, incontestable face."[7] While Bakhtin discusses the European festivals of the Middle Ages, his descriptions parallel those of Caribbean carnivals, similarities due in great part to the cultural interdynamics of conquest that brought European peasant influences to the Caribbean.[8] West Indian writers, like Jean Rhys, have direct access in their own lives to the languages of Carnival and, in adopting the form of the novel, bring it close to its historical sources.

Of course, Jean Rhys's writing was also influenced by European modernism, and its peculiar form of irony as well as its emphasis on spareness, fragmentation, and interiority complicate the effects of carnival languages in her writing. It may be helpful to describe the ways various voices appear in *Voyage in the Dark* and the dialogic positions they take.

Some of the voices appear in memories, marked by ellipses, quotation marks, or italics or inserted in the narrative through the conventional "I would pretend . . ." or "I thought of . . ." Others appear, not as memories but as commentaries, often parenthetical or, again, distinguished by italics. Through her own various voices Anna sometimes coaches herself (*"It's soppy always to look sad. Funny stories—remember some, for God's sake"*), or makes naive wishes (*"This is a beginning. Out of this warm room that smells of fur, I'll go to all the lovely places I've ever dreamt of. This is the beginning"*), or comments ironically, with an unaccountable sophistication, on her own situation (*"This is England, and I'm in a nice, clean English room with all the dirt swept under the bed"*). The formal play of voices and the clash of cultures that sparks them parallels the carnival theme of the final section. Considering them together, we can discern at least two different kinds of irony in the novel, one influenced by European modernism, the other by carnival traditions of satire and the grotesque. Both kinds of irony are at work throughout the novel, sometimes merging, sometimes playing against one another, but always moving the narrative away from a purely interior or subjective consciousness to the formal system of language and public discourse or into a collective cultural history.

Returning, for a moment, to the get-on-or-get-out passage, we see in it the same kind of irony expressed through internal dialogization that we find in the italicized passage concerning the "nice clean English room with all the dirt swept under the bed." Both passages challenge an official and prevailing rule, but the concluding voice expresses futility or defeat in the face of the rule's power. In this sense, we see a modernist irony at work, one that concentrates on the negative, acknowledging loss of power and hope. Paul Fussell has described the irony of the First World War and its laughter as ". . . the laughter of mortals at the trick which had been played on them by an ironical fate." Such irony, he states, resulted from the war being so much worse than expected and from the reversal of the "Idea of Progress" it brought about.[9] While Fussell describes a completely masculine world and alteration in masculine consciousness, he nevertheless describes very well the kind of irony expressed in Rhys's novel with its feminine characters and setting. The great trick played on Anna and most young women of her class is precisely in the promise of "getting on" (another way of assuming progress), finding love, marrying a duke, and the reality is indeed much worse than expected. In a sense, Anna has joined a war that waged for control of women's labor and sexuality, and it too takes place in 1914, the year in which *Voyage in the Dark* is set. In the next chapter, I will go into more detail concerning the nature of this war and its battle over and on women's bodies. Here I want to concentrate on the specifically female modernist irony developed in the novel.

Making a rough distinction, we can read three narrative voices in *Voyage:* the first narrates present events in England, the second recalls past associations in Dominica, and the third comments ironically on the gap between the first two. Juxtapositions of the first two voices portray a double consciousness like the dual personality social scientists note as characteristic of marginal individuals caught between two conflicting cultures.[10] The third voice first appears in the second chapter, following Anna's meeting with Walter Jeffries and the beginning of her affair with him. He has taken her to dine at a hotel restaurant, in a private room with adjoining bedroom. Anna resists his attempts to seduce her but then accepts the money he sends the next morning. In spite of feeling ill, she goes out shopping and buys a new outfit of clothing. The passages narrating her interaction with the saleswomen include the paragraph in italics, previously quoted, in which Anna almost chants her hopes: *"This is a beginning. Out of this warm room that smells of fur I'll go to all the lovely places I've ever dreamt of. This is the beginning"* (*Voyage*, p. 24). Here she believes the promise made to her, naively accepting the possibility of love and getting on.

When she returns to her room, however, her landlady evicts her, saying, "I don't want no tarts in my house, so now you know" (*Voyage*, p. 25). Faced with illness and homelessness, Anna writes Walter, asking him to visit. Here all three narrative voices come into play:

> I went out and posted the letter and got some ammoniated quinine. It was nearly three o'clock. But when I had taken the quinine and had lain down again I felt too ill to care whether he came or not.
>
> *This is England, and I'm in a nice, clean English room with all the dirt swept under the bed.*
>
> It got so dark but I couldn't get up to light the gas. I felt as if there were weights on my legs so that I couldn't move. Like that time at home when I had fever and it was afternoon and the jalousies were down and yellow light came in through the slats and lay on the floor

in bars. . . . Then Francine came in and . . . changed the bandage
round my head and it was ice-cold and she started fanning me with a
palm-leaf fan. (*Voyage*, p. 26)

Francine's attentions bring her relief and happiness. In the gap between that childhood contentment and her present condition, in
which she is already marked a "tart" and becomes "too ill to care,"
appears the newly ironic third voice. The italics link it to the earlier
passage concerning new beginnings, but the connection is one of
contrast. Naiveté has changed to cynicism. The landlady's reinterpretation of her status and her dependency on Walter effect the
change.

This narrative technique of contrasting and disjunctive voices
achieves, nevertheless, a shifting formal unity that depends on the
dialogic intervention of the ironic third voice. Irony emerges from a
perceived gap between some ideal and a reality that falls short of or
obliterates the ideal. For Fussell, in discussing the effects of World
War I on masculine literary consciousness, the gap between the ideal
of progress and the actual experience of the war's horrors generated
an ironic laughter. Georg Lukàcs has described novelistic irony
more broadly as bridging the chasm separating the "problematic
hero's" ideals and the social reality he encounters. According to
Lukàcs, irony indicates a subjective self-recognition aimed at both
the author and the author's heroes.[11] As a formal device, it becomes
objective, abolishing the subjectivity it recognizes and giving the
novel, which would otherwise be shapeless, its formal cohesion.
Rhys has retained the naive character and the ironic narrator of the
classical novel described by Lukàcs. The irony in this example belongs, however, to the modernist period, indicating the sense of loss
and betrayal noted by Fussell. The phrase *"dirt swept under the
bed"* recalls Fredric Jameson's discussion of modernist irony as expressing a perceived gap between authentic existence and actual experience, a gap that stands in for knowledge of colonialism as a determining condition of subjectivity. That knowledge remains under
the bed, so to speak, in early twentieth-century England, intent on
defending the privatized middle-class values that enjoin Anna to
"get on." In recognizing such hypocrisy and speaking for that which
has been silenced or swept from sight, the ironic voice in this passage
and others like it becomes an objective, formal means of exposing and
naming the gap from which it emerges. In this sense it participates
in the negativity that Bakhtin associates with the twentieth century
but also opens up the narrow vision both he and Jameson see in European modernist irony.

Bakhtin traces the changes that the grotesque realism of medieval carnival imagery underwent through the Renaissance, romantic, and modern periods. He criticizes twentieth-century theories of the grotesque for allowing modernist forms to determine their concepts. Discussing Wolfgang Kayser's work, Bakhtin states, "Kayser's definitions first of all strike us by the gloomy, terrifying tone of the grotesque world that alone the author sees. In reality gloom is completely alien to the entire development of this world up to the romantic period."[12] A full definition of grotesque realism must acknowledge the liberating transformations of "all that was frightening in ordinary life . . . into amusing or ludicrous monstrosities" that characterized carnivals in the Middle Ages. The modernist period is responsible for narrowing our vision of the grotesque to the hostile, the alienated, and to what Bakhtin perceives as an existential dread of life.

The irony expressed in Anna's third voice when it remarks upon the dirt swept under the bed expresses that negativity and modernist despair. In addition, the "weights on my legs" and fever that Anna suffers in this scene portray an existential anxiety and paralysis rather than the comic physical degradation Bakhtin describes as essential to carnivalesque imagery. Anna's social isolation and disillusionment preclude any shared comic laughter that might have transformed the alienation portrayed by her physical symptoms. Her disillusionment results from a rise and fall of expectations for social mobility and personal happiness that would only be experienced by marginalized, working-class women. The deflation of Anna's innocent beliefs in love, beauty, and happiness continues throughout the novel in this specifically female modernist irony, aimed at her own sexual naiveté and the sexual hypocrisy that destroys it. Yet consistently she names that hypocrisy and thus helps to reveal the sources of her disillusionment.

For example, after Walter leaves Anna and she begins entertaining other men, she is able to reflect on women's faith in clothes, a faith she had previously shared: "The clothes of most of the women who passed were like caricatures of the clothes in the shop-windows, but when they stopped to look you saw that their eyes were fixed on the future. 'If I could buy this, then of course I'd be quite different.' Keep hope alive and you can do anything, and that's the way the world goes round, the way they keep the world rolling" (*Voyage*, p. 112). The anonymous but powerful "they" appears in her consciousness now as recognition of social forces opposed to and defeating her earlier dreams. As the irony registers Anna's growing awareness of these official voices and the forces of society, so does it formally move from subjectivity to objectivity, relocating Anna's conflicts in the formal system of language and literary conventions. In this way it provides a way out of interiority, a mediating voice between conflicting private and public experiences.

Dialogic in nature, the ironic narrative voice depends upon an increasingly multiple perspective. For example, Anna's use of the word "lady" transforms its meaning several times, according to her experiences and growing awareness. When she and her friend Maudie go out walking in the first chapter, Maudie comments, "There's one thing about you . . . you always look ladylike." Anna replies, in the spirit of a working girl, "Oh God . . . who wants to look ladylike?" But we suspect that she does because the introductory passages have already clued us to Anna's outsider status among the chorus members and her rather fine sensibility. Compared with Maudie, she is very young and shy, and it matters to her that Walter Jeffries "didn't look at my breasts or my legs as they usually do." On the other hand, her stepmother, Hester Morgan, who Anna later discovers has cheated her out of an inheritance, speaks "an English lady's voice with a sharp, cutting edge to it." In her reply to Maudie at least three voices dialogue with one another concerning the meaning of "lady"—one that attempts a flippant working-girl attitude and covers a second voice that secretly longs to be considered a lady, and a third that despises the cruel snobbery in her stepmother's ladylike voice.

After Anna begins her liaison with Walter, following his visit during her illness, she comments again on the qualities of a lady. Stepping out of her room, she is followed by her landlady, who reminds her that she's been evicted: "But she stayed there staring at me, so I went outside and finished putting on my gloves standing on the doorstep. (A lady always puts on her gloves before going into the street.)" (*Voyage*, p. 29). The parenthetical comment might well appear in quotation marks or prefaced by "they say," for it clearly expresses an internalized rule for middle-class feminine behavior. The parentheses highlight its ironic tone, which is directed both at the "they" who implicitly say this and the Anna who has internalized it. It also points to the gap, now repeatedly exposed by the landlady's remarks, between Anna's image of what she wished to become and the way others perceive her. Her earlier ambivalence has become more directly cynical, critical of herself and the social forms that distinguish "ladies" from "tarts."

In a third perspective on the word "lady," Anna treats it explicitly as a word, giving it an embodied, objectlike status. Abandoned by Walter, she has moved in with a woman named Ethel who brings men to their flat presumably for manicures, insisting repeatedly that she is "really a lady." Anna thinks, "A lady—some words have a long, thin neck that you'd like to strangle" (*Voyage,* p. 120). Here the ironic narrative voice openly and violently rebels, at the same time moving Anna's perceptions into the realm of language and its words. It is as if she has acknowledged the power of the words said by "Everybody," given them actual bodies, and thus made them also vulnerable to her now angry desire for revenge. It is not surprising after her discoveries about Hester's deceit that she should want revenge, but the rebellion also follows the end of all her hopes for the relationship with Walter. The double betrayal of her only female relative and her male lover forces her to recognize the grand "trick" played upon her. She harbors no further illusions. And while such complete disillusionment should indicate the modernist irony we have already found in *Voyage,* here I think it verges on another, historically embedded language—that of carnival satire.

Carnival laughter results from the direct confrontation with terror, the grotesque, and a rebellious "turnabout." The ritualistic chant that Jean Rhys quotes in her autobiography, spoken by her real-life friend Francine, practices this turnabout: "Francine would say, 'Tim-tim.' I had to answer 'Bois sèche,' then she'd say, 'Tablier Madame est derrière dos' (Madam's apron is back to front)."[13] The fictional Francine speaks only a part of this ritualistic exchange, ending with the response "Bois sèche," which Rhys states referred to an obeah god. The allusion to reversal, what Bakhtin calls the "logic of inside out" or "from front to rear," remains in Anna's memory of her black friend. And the logic shapes her increasingly rebellious attack on both the idea and the word "lady."

In the spirit of Carnival, too, Anna parodies Hester, imitating and exaggerating her ladylike voice: "Now that I've spoken you can hear that I'm a lady. I have spoken and I suppose you now realize that I'm an English gentlewoman. I have my doubts about you. Speak up and I will place you at once. Speak up, for I fear the worst. That sort of voice" (*Voyage,* p. 49). At times, her parodies eliminate punctuation, running Hester's phrases and sentences together to emphasize their monotonous, oppressive attempts to exclude all other voices: "Because don't imagine that I don't guess how you're going on. Only some things must be ignored some things I refuse to be mixed up with I refuse to think about even" (*Voyage,* p. 54). Such imitation and parody through excess characterized Carnival festivities in which blacks and coloreds imitated their masters' European dress, dance styles, and class distinctions, but with an exaggeration that ridiculed. Hester's fraud has declassed Anna, who, in Hester's eyes, was always reduced to the station of a black, as evidenced by her un-ladylike voice.

As Bakhtin states, Carnival allowed the play of many voices, languages from all strata of society, liberating them from the prevailing order.[14] It's not surprising, then, that Hester's attempts to maintain the prevailing order concentrate on the voice: "I tried to teach you to talk like a lady and behave like a lady and not like a nigger and of course I couldn't do it. Impossible to get you away from the servants. That awful sing-song voice you had! Exactly like a nigger you talked—and still do. Exactly like that dreadful Francine. When you were jabbering away together in the pantry I never could tell which one of you was speaking" (*Voyage*, p. 55). Hester battles with Francine over Anna's voice, while Anna, through her memories of Francine's stories, songs, and laughter, struggles to maintain the multiplicitous language of Carnival, using its principles to resist the reduction of her self to a one-dimensional identity.

Throughout the novel, Anna's acquaintances refuse to listen to her descriptions of the West Indies, confuse it with other "hot places," and call her names like "the Hottentot." When she explains her background to Walter, he merely humors her:

> "I'm the fifth generation born out there, on my mother's side."
> "Are you really?" he said, still a bit as if he were laughing at me.
> (*Voyage*, p. 44)

But Anna persists, describing a slave list she once saw on her mother's family's estate, a Venezuelan girl she knew at school, and the boatman Black Pappy. When Walter says he prefers "cold places," Anna stops speaking. Her memories surface, however, when she and Walter make love, an act that somehow identifies her with the mulatto girl whose name she had seen on the slave list: "*Mailotte Boyd, aged 18. Mailotte Boyd, aged 18 . . . . But I like it like this. I don't want it any other way but this*" (*Voyage*, p. 47).

Walter's upper-class masculine and very English preferences silence Anna's voice, which contains the voices of multiple cultures and races, a multiplicity that gives her comfort and a sense of identity. Silenced, she accepts identification with the slave girl, entering, in her relationship with Walter, a slavelike dependency and submission. Though Walter is portrayed as a decent enough man by the standards of his own class, he nevertheless treats Anna as a master would a slave, commenting on her lovely teeth, for instance, and insisting that her virginity is "the only thing that matters." Walter expresses his attitudes in a language more sophisticated than that of Anna's landlady or friends, but nevertheless, in all of their eyes, Anna can be one of two or at most three things—a "Virgin," the name given her by the chorus members at the beginning of the novel, or a "tart," the name her landlady bestows upon her, or somewhere in between, a kept mistress, but this becomes only a step on the way to prostitution. In this scenario, the official dichotomy of lady/whore (lady/"nigger" in Hester's version) works forcefully to obliterate all the voices within Anna, all the selves she once was or might have become.

Wilson Harris has described one of the Caribbean slave's methods of survival and resistance in the following way: "[the slave] found himself spiritually alone since he worked side by side with others who spoke different dialects. The creative human consolation . . . lies in the search for a kind of inward dialogue and space when one is deprived of a ready conversational tongue and hackneyed comfortable speech."[15]

The voyage from Dominica to England places Anna in a slavelike position. Deprived of the mixed language of patois that she shared with Francine, deprived of even the opportunity to describe her Caribbean experiences to people who would believe or value them, Anna finds "creative consolation" in "inward dialogue and space." That space opens even further in the final passages when Anna's inward dialogue takes her back to the Constance estate of her mother's family and to the time of Carnival.

When Anna first becomes aware of her pregnancy, her memories of Dominica intensify; she tries hard to remember, as if her memories can shield her from what is happening in the present. Like Antoinette, she has been in danger of losing her memory, of becoming a zombie, dead while living only as others, alien to her, see her. Through her memory, she attempts to return to her mother's home, recalling the road, mounting her horse, riding by the sea and through the coconut palms along the road. Francine's voice appears in parentheses here: "(Francine says that if you wash your face in fresh coconut-water every day you are always young and unwrinkled, however long you live)," emphasizing the female culture and bonding central to her memories. That Anna quotes Francine so frequently also indicates the degree to which Francine's voice has become a part of Anna's, constituting the internal dialogue necessary to her spiritual survival.

The journey to Constance Estate contains, like Carnival, which she soon recalls, beauty, pleasure, and terror. It becomes a metaphor for Anna's life voyage: "It took three hours to get to Constance Estate. It was as long as a life sometimes." The more certain of her pregnancy she becomes, however, the more her memories focus on the kind of argument portrayed most intensely in the concluding Carnival passages—arguments over Caribbean cultural practices and beliefs: "and Anne Chewett used to say that it's haunted and obeah— she had been in gaol for obeah (obeah women who dig up dead people and cut their fingers off and go to gaol for it—it's hands that are obeah)—but can't they do damned funny things—Oh if you lived here you wouldn't take them so seriously as all that—" (*Voyage*, p. 139). The voice that prevails, however, convinces her that she has undergone metamorphosis and become something other than human: "—they look like people but their eyes are red and staring and they're soucriants at night—looking in the glass and thinking sometimes my eyes look like a soucriant's eyes . . ." (*Voyage*, p. 139). Later, prefiguring her abortion, she dreams of returning to an island, on board ship with a dead child. The island "was home except that the trees were all wrong."

Fear and alienation predominate in these memories, the inevitable feelings of an exile returning to a home in which she was always an outsider so that the home was never quite right. Knowledgeable of its culture, she remains nevertheless afraid of it. Anna's visit to the abortionist, her return to the flat she shares with Laurie, the pain she experiences and the bleeding are all punctuated and made meaningful by memories of these earlier fears. Soon the multiplicitous internal voices and faces become composites, so that the white face of a man with whom she has had sex, the white face of the doctor, and the white Carnival mask condense into the same image. Similarly the voice saying "Stop, please stop," at first Anna's voice speaking to the man with the white face, then speaking to the doctor, metamorphoses into both her aunt's attitude toward Carnival and the landlady's voice observing about Anna's bleeding that "it ought to be stopped."

These two condensed elements of Anna's delirium are central to understanding the role of Carnival in this passage. The white mask becomes the image that brings together all of Anna's most immediate and fearful visions. It represents the trick played upon her by Walter, by England and its white culture, and by her own naiveté, "Like that time at home with Meta, when it was Masquerade and she came to see me and put out her tongue at me through the slit in her mask" (*Voyage*, p. 153).

However, carnival masks symbolize transformation and metamorphosis, the visual image of turnabout. Anna recalls in detail the masks worn by the players as she watched from behind the jalousie shades:

> —the masks the men wore were a crude pink with the eyes squint-
> ing near together squinting but the masks the women wore were
> made of close-meshed wire covering the whole face and tied at the
> back of the head—the handkerchief that went over the back of the
> head hid the strings and over the slits for the eyes mild blue eyes
> were painted then there was a small straight nose and a little red
> heart-shaped mouth and another slit so that they could put their
> tongues out at you— (*Voyage*, p. 158)

These masks clearly imitate to excess, to the point of ridicule, the faces of pink, mildly blue-eyed, straight-nosed, and painted-mouthed white men and women. Commenting on the differences between the masks worn by the men and those worn by the women, Deborah Kelly Kloepfer has argued that the wire covering of the women's masks portrays the silencing of all women.[16] This interpretation ignores the fact that the black women wearing them are imitating white women, "their dark necks and arms covered with white powder." It also ignores the irony of Anna's uncle's statement, "—you can't expect niggers to behave like white people all the time." The blacks do not behave like white people (they dance and sing), but they "act" like white people, parodying the whites' behavior, including the censorship imposed upon white women within their own culture.

The wire mesh, covering the whole face and worn by the black women, suggests another turnabout in white-black relations enacted by the Carnival players. A common punishment administered to slaves for intoxication consisted of a wooden mask fitted tightly onto the head with slits for eyes, a triangular space for the nose, but no mouth opening.[17] It is interesting to compare this instrument with that used in seventeenth-century England as a punishment for "scolds." To punish the woman accused of what we might call too much voice, a mask constructed like an open frame was fitted over the whole face. A metal lever with sharp points on it was forced into her mouth, and the "brancks," as it was called, tied in the back with a long string by which the woman was led about.[18] By simply parodying what they observed in white sexual relationships and gender behavior, the black women confront the white "ladies" with their own subordinate and silenced condition, one paralleled to that of the black slaves in the visual representation of muzzling.

Anna's memory of this particular mask effects a turnabout in her consciousness concerning the alliances she wishes to make and point of view that she takes. The argument over Carnival, whether it ought to be allowed or "ought to be stopped," that her white relatives carry on prompts her to reverse her position and to take up again her journey home. As she listens to "their voices . . . going up and down," Anna's fears are altered by sudden understanding: "I was looking out of the window and I knew why the masks were laughing" (*Voyage*, p. 159). In the original version, an additional line explains, "But I knew why they were laughing   they were laughing at the idea that anybody black would want to be white."[19] In both versions, Anna's moment of understanding the blacks' point of view transforms her from a distant and frightened observer to a giddy participant. In both versions the carnivalesque heteroglossia intensifies; past and present, Caribbean and English voices enter the delirious dialogue. Now, in her vision, she joins the dancing, and when Walter's voice interrupts, saying "You ought to be going," rather than returning to her room as she would have done during their affair, she balances herself on a saddle and begins her horseback journey again, taking the same road, but with a different perspective and arriving at a different place.

The earlier memory of this journey concluded with the frightening figure of another silenced woman, a "woman with yaws . . . her nose and mouth were eaten away" (*Voyage*, p. 130). This time Anna's ride takes her to the same "turning where the shadow is always the same shape—shadows are ghosts you look at them and you don't see it only sometimes you see it like now I see—." What she sees now is not the diseased beggar woman, but "a cold moon looking down on a place where nobody is a place full of stones where nobody is" (*Voyage*, p. 160). The description suggests that her home no longer exists, but has become a ruin, reminiscent of the ruined Coulibri in *Wide Sargasso Sea*, creator of ghosts and nobodies. Discovery of this more accurate image of her home where both parents no longer live and where she can in reality no longer return signals the deciding point in Anna's consciousness of her multiplicitous selves. She may succumb to others' views of her and become nobody, or she may persist: "*I thought I'm going to fall nothing can save me now but still I clung desperately with my knees feeling very sick*" (*Voyage*, p. 160). The passage indicates her persistence and also that her journey is not yet complete.

Death completes her journey in the earlier version and may have seemed to Jean Rhys a more logical closure for the novel. It is certainly more logical by the literary criteria Rachel Blau DuPlessis has identified that demand either marriage or death for a novel's heroine. Adding ambiguity rather than closure, the published ending completes Anna's journey in a different way. Though Rhys cut large sections of the final chapter for the published version, she cut only a few brief lines from the scenes describing Carnival. Her decision to concentrate on those scenes indicates the importance of carnival images and logic in the formal dynamics of the novel and suggests that they will figure in its conclusion.

When Anna repeats the doctor's words, "ready to start all over again," with her more hopeful vision of "being new and fresh," it seems at first that she has learned nothing but simply returned to her previous naiveté and wishful thinking. Taken in the context of the Carnival passages, however, this inner dialogue with herself recalls one of the most important aspects of carnival logic and laughter.

Anna has undergone what we might call a series of bodily degradations, beginning with the sexual bartering that initiates her affair with Walter, continuing in her relations with other men in which she exchanges sex for money, and resulting in her nearly fatal abortion. This is probably the only work of fiction in the early twentieth-century that describes abortion from the woman's point of view, and in doing so it borders on the "grotesque realism" that Bakhtin describes as essential to carnival language. Grotesque realism depends upon the body and bodily life, but as collectively, not individually, experienced. It represents the cycles of fertility, pregnancy, deterioration, dismemberment, and decay, and involves the "essential principle of degradation." This collectively experienced cycle of life is opposed to the European realistic convention of "character." In the realist convention, Bakhtin argues,

> the process of degeneration and disintegration . . . (the second link of
> becoming) drops out and is replaced by moral sententiousness and
> abstract concepts. What remains is nothing but a corpse, old age de-
> prived of pregnancy, equal to itself alone; it is alienated and torn
> away from the whole in which it had been linked to that other,
> younger link in the chain of growth and development. . . . Hence all
> these sterile images representing "character," all these professional
> lawyers, merchants, matchmakers, old men and women, all these
> masks offered by degenerate, petty realism.[20]

We might add to his list all these virgins, tarts, and fallen women, women who must die to compensate for their errors in negotiating sexual and kinship relations.

We should modify, however, his concept of the whole and of the community in which the cycles are realized. Resisting all along not so much her status as prostitute per se as the reduction of her identity to a single dimension, Anna has sought aid from Francine. She also seeks identification with the slave Mailotte Boyd and recalls the collective voices of black Caribbean women, a quest that culminates in her sudden understanding of the women's Carnival masks and laughter. She can only fully join their community, however, if she can share the spirit of the laughter which, as Bakhtin indicates, "has not only a destructive, negative aspect, but also a regenerating one."[21] To do so, Anna must make a choice concerning the voices she hears.

When the doctor remarks, "You girls are too naive to live, aren't you?" Laurie laughs, and Anna listens "to them both laughing and their voices going up and down." Their cynical laughter expresses the modernist irony of loss and betrayal; it also stands in for and obscures knowledge of an entire sex/gender and colonial system. It pays tribute to the modernist fear of life that Bakhtin claims opposes life and death in a gesture contrary to the true carnival spirit of grotesque realism. This is the gesture and the despairing vision that Anna refuses when she repeats the doctor's next words, "Ready to start all over again in no time, I've no doubt": "I lay and . . . thought about starting all over again. And about being new and fresh. And about mornings, and misty days, when anything might happen" (*Voyage*, p. 160).

While traditional Carnival renewal depended upon fertility and pregnancy—what Bakhtin describes as the adult woman's bodily "degradation" for the sake of new life—we might see Anna's vision of "starting all over again" as enacting a specifically female turnabout on this logic. In Anna's earlier dream, the dead child becomes a "boy bishop" who wears a priest's robes and a ring. From his coffin, he rises and bows: "His large, light eyes in a narrow, cruel face rolled like a doll's as you lean it from one side to the other" (*Voyage*, p. 140). The vision of cruelty supplants the "new life" promised by pregnancy, making it clear that for Anna, in her isolation and poverty, the birth of a child can only oppress her. In the dream, she thinks, "I ought to kiss the ring," indicating the further submission to social and patriarchal authority required by her pregnancy. When she awakens from this dream, however, she continues "dreaming about the sea" and envisions her journey home where she understands *"why the masks were laughing."*

The moment of understanding and alliance with the masked black women in her Carnival vision follows the phrase "their voices . . . going up and down." In her vision, the voices belong to her aunt, uncle, stepmother, and father. The same phrase appears after Anna hears Laurie's and the doctor's cynical laughter, "their voices going up and down." Thus Anna joins together two discussions of moral decency—that of the doctor and Laurie, who are laughing at Anna's (and Laurie's) moral condition, and that of her relatives, who are debating the decency of Carnival. Conversely, she associates herself with Carnival and chooses to join it, as object of disapproval *and* as member of a community of satirical revelers. Her understanding of the masks and their laughter, rather than the laughter of modern European cynicism, allows her to transform the meanings and values attributed to the masking of her own identities.[22] Unable to give birth, she refuses the doctor's interpretation of her body as following a socially illicit cyclical pattern and, instead, returns to her island home as a participant in its carnival culture. Through her imagined return, she enacts another kind of cycle, beginning again and perhaps changing the meaning of the abortion into an event that regenerates her own life.

Though the original version of the ending is the only one to include the reason for Anna's understanding of carnival laughter, the revised version suggests the possibilities for renewal implicated in that understanding. In giving the revised ending this suggestion of possible renewal, Rhys has completed Anna's voyage and simultaneously written beyond the apparent narrative requirement that the protagonist die.

Further, Anna's repetition of the doctor's words in this final scene gives the dialogical answer to the doctor's earlier repetition of her words ("Oh, so you had a fall, did you?"). In this way, the text's despairing modernist irony and its accompanying European point of view speak alongside, but do not suppress, the renewal of life that gives the laughter of Carnival its satirical joy.

The lingering tone of wishful naiveté reflects Anna's isolation in reality from her chosen community and gives the ending its ambiguity. Conjuring "elsewhere," she remains, after all, in the social context of modern Europe.[23] Nevertheless, following a pattern made more explicit in *Wide Sargasso Sea*, Anna has "awakened," gone "wild," and, in spirit, flown to join the black and native women of her island home. Rejecting the names—"Virgin," "tart," "Hottentot," "foreigner"—given her by English dichotomizing, she sustains her multiplicitous identities. She has not triumphed as an individual, up against society, but rather found the place and the people from which she can envision new life.

Part Three

Other Women

Five

Voyage in the Dark

The Other Great War

"Oh, so you had a fall, did you?" the doctor said. His hands looked enormous in rubber gloves. He began to ask questions.

"Quinine, quinine," he said; "what utter nonsense!"

He moved about the room briskly, like a machine that was working smoothly.

He said, "You girls are too naive to live, aren't you?"

Laurie laughed. I listened to them both laughing and their voices going up and down.

"She'll be all right," he said. "Ready to start all over again in no time, I've no doubt."[1]

Unlike Anna, who lies either silent or powerless to be understood, the doctor speaks with all the authority vested in the medical profession. He speaks too with the power of a physician who has discovered, by treating Anna's hemorrhage, her illegal action, and the cynicism of one who believes he has already seen and understood everything about her. In the previous chapter, I discussed the ambiguity, exacerbated by the existence of two different versions, of the ending to *Voyage in the Dark*, focusing there on Anna's inner voices and visions. Here I would like to shift attention to the doctor's words. His dialogue opens onto a historical context, European rather than Caribbean, in which Anna's experiences in England are given meaning and which her voices and visions oppose.

I present two approaches to understanding this European historical context: one derives from a structuralist view of traditional kinship patterns and their observable breakdown in the modern period, and the other consists of a historical narrative, though not a unified or consistent one, describing a European war other than the Great

War, yet just as profound in its social and psychological implications—a war waged over and on women's bodies. The dual approach
seems to me appropriate because in presenting and responding to social violence against marginalized women in modern European society, Rhys's texts appear to draw on mythical elements of ritual,
violence, and sacrifice that become most explicit in *Good Morning,
Midnight;* nevertheless, the narratives remain grounded in specific
social and historical dynamics. Scenes of sexual exchange in the
novels suggest the common ground for both kinds of analysis.

Before examining more closely then the implications of the doctor's remarks, we will move from the ending of the novel to its beginning pages where we find a scene of sexual barter between Anna
and Walter Jeffries defined through a shopping trip in which Anna
acquires a pair of stockings. Anna's meeting with Walter takes place
not in the home of relatives or friends, not at a social event to which
both have been invited, not even in a cafe or shop, but on the street.
They immediately negotiate the chance encounter through money
and commodities:

> Everybody laughed. We paired off. Maudie went on ahead with the
> tall man. The other looked at me sideways once or twice—very
> quickly up and down, in that way they have—and then asked where
> we were going.
> "I was going to this shop to buy a pair of stockings," I said.
> They all came into the shop with me. I said I wanted two pair—
> lisle thread with clocks up the side—and took a long time choosing
> them. The man I had been walking with offered to pay for them and I
> let him. (*Voyage,* p. 10)

Before they know one another's names, a certain transaction takes
place. Walter's payment for Anna's stockings, after he looks her over
"in that way they have," enacts a ritual of barter that signifies the
sort of relationship they will develop. It is more important than any
introduction in determining the nature of this accidental meeting—
a meeting which, because of its lack of formal social organization,
demands the definitive moment and narrowing of possibilities that
the purchase creates.

Walter continues negotiations by asking Anna to dinner. In a private restaurant room, the significance of their earlier transaction becomes clear. As a preface to his attempted seduction, Walter refers
to the stocking incident: "He said, 'You've got the loveliest teeth.
You're sweet. You looked awfully pathetic when you were choosing

those horrible stockings so anxiously.' And then he started kissing me . . ." (*Voyage*, p. 19). His words remind Anna of more than their earlier meeting. Rather than complimenting Anna's face, eyes, or hair, something associated with feminine expressiveness and beauty, Walter comments on her teeth, a strange choice that brings to mind the examination of horses or slaves for sale. His paternalistic descriptions of Anna as pathetic and the stockings she chose as horrible imply her lack of confidence and taste, attributes reflecting the wider opportunities and choices of Walter's social class. Indeed, he reiterates these distinctions the next morning by sending twenty-five pounds with a request that she buy some stockings and "don't look so anxious when you are buying them." In these preliminaries to his caresses, Walter names their relationship in terms that convey an expected sexual exchange, the nature of the goods exchanged, his power to choose and to assess their quality, and his own class superiority. Anna thinks her friends would "shriek with laughter" over the initial failure of his seduction because she knows that that exchange of sexuality is precisely what characterizes socially their relations.

Anna's father's death and her aunt's fraud have declassed her, and homelessness in an alien culture has placed her in a social position similar to that of the spiritually isolated slave described by Wilson Harris. As discussed in Chapter 4, the play of voices that characterizes this novel's narrative style portrays Anna's methods of resistance and survival, and while working for her spiritually, they respond to a condition, similar to the slave's, of economic exploitation and alienation. Retrieving memories of cultural pluralism and carnival rebellion from her past in the Caribbean, she nevertheless enacts in her present life in England in 1914 the reductive exchange of her body for her living.

The bartering between Anna and Walter continues when he visits during her illness (she has written asking him to come) and brings food, wine, and a comforter. The diction of the passage deepens the contrast between Anna's hopes of finding love and the social reality of their relationship:

> He was standing in the doorway. I could see him against the light in the passage. . . .
> He came to the bed and put his hand on mine. . . .
> He took a book of matches out of his pocket and lit the gas. . . .
> He came in again with a lot of parcels . . .
> He kissed me and his face felt cool and smooth against mine.
> (*Voyage*, p. 27)

The exclusive use of the pronoun *he* from the very beginning of this scene is noticeable because of the contrast it presents to the degree of expected intimacy in their relations. Anna's refusal to use Walter's name implies a displacement from the immediacy and uniqueness of his presence. The pronoun shifts his identity for her to a simply masculine one; his name is arbitrary and irrelevant to their relationship, just as it was in their first meeting when the purchase of stockings "named" them before any introductions were made. By putting Walter's personal identity to the side, the pronoun connotes Anna's continued desire for something he both is and is not.[2] She expresses this wish during his previous attempt to seduce her: "Soon he'll come in again and kiss me, but differently. He'll be different and so I'll be different. It'll be different. I thought, 'It'll be different, different. It must be different'" (*Voyage*, p. 20).

Anna can offer her company and sex in these negotiations, and eventually she must sleep with Walter to finalize their arrangement. In the meantime, they prepare and sign a contractual agreement, beginning with Walter's proposal of sexual relations, continuing with his gift of money, and agreed upon by Anna in writing when she sends the note requesting his visit. Anna recognizes the significance of these gestures and learns as she goes how to enter such agreements. She also attempts, through her memories of Francine, who cared for her during a childhood illness, to make "different" the meaning of the new arrangement with Walter by associating it with the caring friendship of Francine.

The relationship with her black female nurse and this one with Walter cannot, however, compare except as a reversal of caste positions. Walter "keeps" Anna, and she believes she loves him. This love requires that Anna see herself in ways defined by the class and power dimensions of the exchange agreement. She describes his house: "There was the light on over the sofa and the tray with the drinks, and the rest of the house dark and quiet, and not friendly to me. Sneering faintly, sneering discreetly, as a servant would. Who's this? Where on earth did he pick her up?" (*Voyage*, p. 42).

Walter's friends ask the same questions, though not so discreetly. On an outing, Walter's cousin Vincent and another woman discuss Anna as if she were not present:

> Germaine was staring at me. "She looks awfully young, this kid,"
> she said. "She looks about sixteen."
> "Yes," Vincent said. "Dear old Walter, whom we all know and
> love, has been doing a bit of baby-snatching, I'm afraid." . . .
> "She's on the stage, is she?" Germaine said. . . .

"It was at Southsea," I said.

"Oh, it was at Southsea, was it?" Vincent said.

They began to laugh. They were still laughing when Walter came in.

"She's been giving you away," Vincent said. "She's been telling us how it all started. You dirty dog, Walter. What in God's name were you doing on the pier at Southsea?" (*Voyage*, pp. 71–72)

Anna cannot participate in the scene's language; they have appropriated it and used it to ridicule her. So she finds recourse in inarticulate and violent action: "I was smoking, and I put the end of my cigarette down on Walter's hand. I jammed it down hard and held it there, and he snatched his hand away and said, 'Christ!' But they had stopped laughing" (*Voyage*, p. 72). Anna's inability to defend herself with words and her exclusion from the class values expressed in the conversation among the other three indicate that, though the exchange relationship between her and Walter may appear to be mutually agreed upon, he controls it. He and his friends name Anna by refusing to name her; by denying her participation in shared dialogue, they exclude her from the language with which they constitute their identities and values. Her exclusion does not happen incidentally but necessarily. She must be present and her presence denied in order for Walter and Vincent to voice their conceptions of who they are.

Anna's wishes, from the beginning, that this relationship both continue and be different reflect the in-between status of her role as mistress. Since she is not and cannot become Walter's wife, the house that a wife might have entered as home gains its right to sneer at her, and Walter and his friends patronize and demean her. Their socially justified contempt is what she would like to be different, and she remembers, whether accurately or not, Francine's sincere concern for her in contrast to the false pretence at monogamous love scripted in the role of "kept woman" or mistress. In the arrangement, she forfeits even a prostitute's right to buy and sell her body to those whom she chooses and at a price she sets. What little emotional and financial independence from any one man that a prostitute might enjoy is denied Anna, and she becomes instead a passive, dependent, and vulnerable commodity. As a mistress, or a prostitute pretending through love and exclusivity to be a wife, she loses her voice; her silence guarantees the good woman (wife) and bad woman (prostitute) opposition in a stable dichotomy that her voice as kept woman might undo, threatening to reveal the close ties, economically and politically, between wife and prostitute.[3]

If women enter language only as negation or Other, as much recent feminist criticism has argued,[4] here we see inscribed specific
class and cultural dimensions of that silencing. We also see the
choices made by women who may position themselves differently
from one another within the social system of language. Germaine
shares Vincent's laughter in this passage; however, she fares little
better than Anna in the sexual exchange upon which the gathering
depends. When later Anna comments on Germaine's attractiveness,
Walter replies that she's old and will be "blowsy in another year."
Furthermore, it seems that Germaine has stretched too far the terms
of her agreement with Vincent, asking for more money than he's
willing to give. Walter remarks, foretelling his own departure, "She
thought she had her claws well into him. It's a very good thing he's
going away" (*Voyage*, p. 73).

The text also silences Anna's first sexual experience with Walter
through a cryptic passage in italics followed by a blank space:

> When I got into bed there was warmth coming from him, and I
> got close to him. *Of course you've always remembered, and then
> you forget so utterly, except that you've always known it. Always—
> how long is always?* (*Voyage*, p. 31)

"It" has no textual referent here and remains mysterious, open to
interpretation. Perhaps "it" refers to the warmth she feels, perhaps
to the sexual act or the gesture of submission involved in her identification with the mulatto slave Mailotte Boyd (*"Mailotte Boyd, aged
18 . . . . . . But I like it like this. I don't want it any other way but
this"*). In the original version of *Voyage in the Dark*, a passage appears in the last Carnival scenes alluding to an earlier sexual encounter.[5] Perhaps that is what Anna has forgotten "so utterly." The
reader might also speculate about the meaning of "it" in light of Jean
Rhys's diary descriptions of being sexually molested as a child.[6] In
the published text of the novel, however, the passage seemingly refers to something that cannot be said, that must be deferred by the
pronoun. The blank space following the lines confirms the imposi-
tion of silence.

Only later does Anna reflect that "it had been just like the girls
said, except that I hadn't known it would hurt so much" (*Voyage*,
p. 32). The blank space reveals Anna's metamorphosis from "Virgin"
to "tart," through an experience "said" by others, that denies further
her right and ability to speak beyond the recognition of pain.

When Walter leaves Anna, he hands her over to Vincent, who

gives her money and attempts to explain Walter's point of view. Though Anna and Walter had originally negotiated their own agreements, Anna now has no voice at all in her affairs; the two men arrange it all. Her only alternative to a degrading dependency on a man who will no longer recognize her is to attempt all over again the kind of barter and negotiation that tied her to Walter. The details differ only slightly. This time she gives a manicure, he takes her to dinner, she sleeps with him, and in the morning she finds five pounds in her handbag. Before leaving Anna for good, "he" gives her fifteen pounds.

Why must Anna exchange her sexuality for her livelihood? Why doesn't she find a job or take advantage of the singing lessons Vincent arranges? Why doesn't she at least try to "get on"? Her passivity irritates critics such as Peter Wolfe, who contends that if Anna had "more fiber," she might have kept her "honor."[7] Such critical judgments assume again the values of nineteenth-century realist fiction, particularly in regarding female chastity as honor. In this sense, Wolfe merely repeats Walter's view of Anna's virginity as "the only thing that matters" and misses the critique of character itself, as moral and literary value, developed in Rhys's writing. Not surprisingly, Wolfe considers Rhys's multivocal characters to be "dull," "dispossessed urban spinsters."[8]

By tracing the dissolution of "character" and its reconstitution in fragmented and multiplicitous forms, *Voyage in the Dark* also reveals the changing social structures of sex and gender in the modern period. It does so from the perspective of a woman most severely affected by the changes and in a way that makes evident a double crisis in European history: the decline of colonial power marked by the First World War and a simultaneous breakdown in traditional patterns of kinship based on the exchange of women.

The kinship studies of Claude Lévi-Strauss suggest a framework for understanding this breakdown. Lévi-Strauss has analyzed kinship as a system of exchange; he argues that the exchange of women between family groups in exogamous marriage ensures the establishment and growth of civilization.[9] His studies distinguish two types of systems: "elementary structures" that prescribe certain marriages, forbidding all others, and "open" systems that preclude, through the incest taboo, some marriages, leaving open all other possibilities. Though open systems do not prescribe specific marriage alliances, a class-structured society nevertheless requires more general constraints and prescriptions. The exchange of women in exogamous marriage in open systems exercises such control by confining women to the family and sustaining a domestic/public division in social organization.[10] However, in modern urban society, not all women are "frozen" in the family and controlled by its norms.

Rhys's novels portray single women, without family ties, acting as individuals in the public world. Free agents, albeit reluctantly, they find their own jobs and create their own social relations outside of family constraints or protection. Though socially independent, they find few opportunities for economic independence. In 1911 women constituted less than 28 percent of the labor force. Sixty-six percent of these women worked either in textile manufacturing or in "personal service."[11] Only the war opened new opportunities for women to earn their living, but most of these emerged in industry and heavy production work. Even typing and office work did not become available to more than a few women until the 1920s, and these women, like the chorus girls of the time, were vulnerable to sexual advances and exploitation.[12] Women earned less than half, often closer to one-third, of wages paid to men in the same jobs, and many full-time women workers failed to earn subsistence wages.[13]

In these conditions, prostitution becomes a possibility, though not a clearly defined one, since the operating distinctions blur between terms such as "kept woman" or mistress, "tart," and prostitute. Moreover, pinning these labels on women who are simply single and alone indicates a subversive sexuality in their very existence. Because kinship networks do not claim and classify them, their presence signals illicit sexuality as they become susceptible to the prostitution of which they are suspected. Anna's father has died, her stepmother has betrayed her, and her uncle has given up responsibility for her. There is no one to give her away in marriage; no exchange between families can take place, and she is thrust into the world on her own.

Anna and other single working women violate the domestic/ public distinction that the traditional exchange of women requires and maintains as ideology if not actuality. This structural change creates social scenes of erotic ambiguity. As René Girard remarks in his discussion of Lévi-Strauss's analysis of marriage laws: "the language of kinship . . . is no longer spoken in certain societies, most particularly our own. . . . And there is no code of conduct telling people how to behave toward others and what behavior to expect in return."[14] Women like Anna embody such uncertainty.

During the time that Rhys was writing, other events indicate that the transgression of domestic and public boundaries became a socially perceived phenomenon. We find a sign of the rupture of this system of exchange in the statistics regarding marriage and divorce, which show both a decreased rate of marriage and a greatly increased number of divorces. In addition to the statistical data itself, there appear significant changes in the census categories used to organize the data. Most notable is the formulation of new statistical categories for the years 1935–1946. Rather than listing the number of divorces as before, new headings distinguish numbers of "Divorced Men" and "Divorced Women." The heading for divorce changes from "Civil Conditions" to "Justice and Criminal Proceedings."[15] The changes indicate that by the mid-thirties when Rhys published *Voyage in the Dark*, officials considered the status of individuals rather than the marriage unit and, at the same time, they perceived the phenomenon of divorce as a social problem requiring the same procedures that adhere to deviance and crime.

According to Samuel Hynes, men in authority during the Edwardian period perceived sex itself as a social problem. "Sexologists" such as Havelock Ellis and Edward Carpenter who wished to liberate individual sexual feelings from social constraints came into conflict with conservatives who battled to preserve the institution of marriage from divorce reform. Conservatives associated divorce with the falling birth rate; "a high birth rate meant men for the armed forces, men for the Empire, and men to swell the industrial labor force at home." Hynes continues: "it was possible to conclude that the Marriage Question and the problem of Imperial Defence were related, and to blame the impending decline of England on women."[16] The blame fell most heavily on feminists who challenged the exclusively masculine political system in which laws governing women's lives were made solely by men. The "war between the sexes" escalated to such an extent that men went to another war in 1914 with relief, "as a husband might leave a nagging wife."[17]

The blame for the Empire's decline fell also on "foreigners" like Anna who remind the English of their troublesome colonized "other." When Anna and her flatmate Ethel see a movie called *Three-Fingered Kate*, Ethel complains about the actress: "'Well,' she said, 'that girl who did Three-Fingered Kate was a foreigner . . . Couldn't they have got an English girl to do it? . . . It was just because she had this soft, dirty way that foreign girls have. And she stuck red curls on her black hair and she didn't care a scrap. Her own hair was short and black, don't you see? and she simply went and stuck red curls on. An English girl wouldn't have done that'" (*Voyage*, pp. 93–94).

The *real nature* of a woman's body, at stake in Ethel's xenophobia, was also the central issue in battles that took place from the late Victorian through the early modern period between men, and between men and women, over "sex." The specific issues involved in

popular and legislative debates included the regulation of prostitution through forced medical exams, the questions of birth control,
custody of children following divorce, abortion, the physical and
psychological meaning of maternity, and the nature of female desire—including lesbian sexuality. Women's bodies became fields for
battles over what Hynes calls "other social issues."

We might, however, construct a historical account of another European war, in which "other social issues" mobilize invasions of
"the Other," escalating up to and through the outbreak of World
War I. My description of these invasions hardly constitutes a unified
narrative history. Their overall theme, however, constructed through
convergences of various kinds of texts, including that of Rhys's
novel as well as primary and secondary historical sources, suggests
both the dynamics of male/female power struggles of the period and
the tendency of dominant history—with its focus on the Great War
and its divisions into Victorian, Edwardian, and modern—to obscure the significance and connections among these battles. Even
social historians like Hynes who refer to "the war between the
sexes" see the issues as debates and legislative reforms participating
in a progression of liberal social changes. The "war" is trivialized by
patronizing humor (references to "nagging wives," for example) and
suffragist strategies condemned simplistically as violence. Feminist
historians such as Judith Walkowitz and Mary Poovey are retelling
the story of this war, exposing the dominant ideology that has ob-
scured it, but also making the oppositions and spaces within dominant ideology more visible.

In the doctor's words at the end of *Voyage in the Dark* are embedded, I will argue, a history of violent changes and shifting oppositions in the representation and regulation of women's bodies from
the 1840s through the early 1900s. Two invasions that frame the
time period of this war are the medical exams required by the Contagious Diseases Acts of the 1860s through the 1880s and the forced
feeding of feminists in prison on the eve of the First World War. But
we might note also the earlier debate of the mid–nineteenth century over chloroforming women in childbirth and the intense attrac-
tion and repulsion the drug's physical effects on the silenced female
body exerted on operating physicians. As Mary Poovey has brilliantly analyzed, doctors argued the issue as determinant of their
own professional status as well as the sexual "nature" of women.[18]

Poovey marks the eighteenth-century introduction of forceps de-
liveries as the beginning of medical supervision of women's bodies, especially in childbirth, that was increasingly institutionalized

through the 1850s. She describes a set of assumptions that legitimated such supervision:

> This set of assumptions—that woman's reproductive function defines her character, position, and value, that this function is only one sign of an innate periodicity, and that this biological periodicity influences and is influenced by an array of nervous disorders—mandates the medical profession's supervision of women. . . . This set of assumptions is also the physiological basis offered for what was generally held to be woman's greater emotional volatility, for the development of her artfulness or cunning, and for the notion that woman is, by definition, disease or disorder.[19]

Considering again the doctor's claim that Anna will soon be ready to "start all over again," we can see a cynical inversion of the assumption concerning women's innate periodicity that Poovey describes. Anna's sexual activities, whatever they may be and whatever their reproductive results, are viewed by the doctor as cyclical. He views the sexual exchanges of prostitution that contemporary feminist historians have understood as a female occupation, social and economic in its nature, as an inversion of woman's innate biological periodicity. In this sense, he follows the eighteenth- and nineteenth-centuries' dominant medical views, though he expresses them with a modernist twentieth-century irony.

Poovey points out, however, that the increased supervision and control she describes was not gained through joined efforts on the part of a united patriarchal medical profession; rather she locates oppositions within the profession and its ideologies that erupted in the chloroform debates of 1847–1857. She argues that the chloroform debates politicized the silenced female body, a silence that "produces an excess of meanings" as the body becomes a token of dispute over the nature and authority of the medical profession. In spite of their divergent professional interests, both sides of the argument nevertheless agreed on the undesirability of "scenes of an indelicate character"—the involuntary sexual excitation induced by both ether and chloroform. Reading the sedated woman's moans and gestures as inappropriately sexual, groups of medical men intensified the competition among themselves while simultaneously legitimating continued and diligent control of the excessive female body. Poovey concludes that by constructing, within their own opposing constituencies, the need for such control, the medical profession acknowledges that the silenced female body "can also create an ambiguity that defies the entire medical community's attempts to maintain control."[20]

When Anna hallucinates the long horseback journey to her mother's family estate, she thinks, *"I'm going to fall,"* and then says, "I fell . . . I fell for a hell of a long time then." The doctor repeats her words, "Oh, so you had a fall, did you?" Rhys's text makes explicit his misreading of Anna's silenced, bleeding, and delirious body as a sign of her sexual nature. His efforts to control it consist in an act of definition, the words implying that he knows all about her, what she does, and why. Yet he clearly does not and cannot know her, neither the inner voices and visions that constitute her problematic subjectivity, nor the social conditions through which she has come to lie beneath his smoothly functioning, machinelike hands. The words "ready to start all over again in no time" reveal his assumptions of a biological periodicity in Anna's nature, but they also express, by what remains absent from them, an institutional undecidability that shadows his authority to define Anna. Precisely *what* will she be ready to start all over again? Sleeping with men, with one man, walking the streets, receiving men in her room? In his claim to know Anna, he admits an inability to define her, socially and erotically, that historically plagued the theories and policies of medical science. In his statement, "I've no doubt," he raises the question of his own authority even as he asserts it, a question dependent upon his perceived ability to read the meaning of Anna's body.

While the status of the medical profession was at stake in the chloroform debates, questions concerning its moral authority and political power fueled the late-Victorian battles over the Contagious Diseases Acts. From the point of view of feminists who fought for their repeal, these laws, passed in 1864, 1866, and 1869, constituted invasions of the female body they described as "instrumental rape."[21] The acts required arbitrary examination by medical and police authorities of women suspected of prostitution. Any unaccompanied woman on the street, especially any poor woman, might be submitted to forced examination.

Judith Walkowitz has described the problem facing advocates of the Contagious Diseases Acts who were asked to define "prostitute." William Harris, the assistant commissioner of the metropolitan police, responded: "Speaking of London, I should propose that any woman who goes to places of public resort, and is known to go with different men, although not a common streetwalker, should be served with a notice to register."[22] A pamphlet written in 1882 by an "Ex-Constable of the Devonport Division" argued that female promiscuity was inherent: "In every large town without exception, where a woman has a chance of this course and runs no danger of serious loss or inconvenience, and possesses the means of deluding her friends, she will embrace it."[23]

Even the influential physician and author of the acts, William Acton, found these police definitions a bit too severe. In his early studies, Acton argued that women engaged in prostitution only on a temporary basis and could be reintegrated into respectable society. At this point in his efforts to institute the acts, Acton faced arguments from religious opponents who perceived the absolute ruin of women through male lust, which would, in their view, be legalized in the regulation of prostitution. According to Walkowitz, his early position justified "controlled heterosexual outlets for men" by arguing that under regulation a woman could "pass through this stage of her existence with as little permanent injury to herself and as little mischief to society as possible."[24]

Later, when he faced the arguments of the Repeal Campaign, Acton changed his definition of prostitution, asserting in 1869: "The public should be made fully aware of the fact we are not legislating for 'soiled doves' but for a class of women that we may almost call unsexed."[25] With this new definition of prostitutes as an irredeemably corrupt class, Acton fought Repeal arguments on behalf of prostitutes' civil rights. Walkowitz concludes: "The failure to provide a statutory definition of the common prostitute is consistent with the traditional legal treatment in Britain of women and outcast groups—as the "Other,"—an entirely negative and collective presence before the law."[26]

Reading Anna's body as that of the irredeemable prostitute, the doctor who attends her repeats the early evangelical view of prostitutes as forever ruined *and* the later Acton view of prostitutes as undeserving of civil rights and respect. His remark "You girls are too naive to live, aren't you?" comments ironically on the early humanitarian/religious and later feminist view of prostitutes as victims— naive girls, seduced and abandoned. It includes too the cynical medical man's recognition of the life-and-death danger they face. The doctor has perhaps saved Anna's life, yet from the very dangers that his profession, by assuming legal and political powers, has perpetuated. When Laurie responds by giggling, she acquiesces to his authority, cynicism, and power to define her, as well as Anna, in these historically conditioned yet still undecidable terms. She giggles, but does not speak, and thus takes a position similar to the one Germaine occupied in earlier scenes that silenced Anna—one complicit in the symbolic system that denies her a voice by denying her and Anna a "respectable living" and possibly even a life.

The Contagious Diseases Acts both protected and controlled prostitution until the late 1880s, when influential feminists succeeded in repealing them. While in force, the laws helped maintain the demarcation between public and private lives by marking the sexual status of women according to their appearance in public, enforcing the confinement of "respectable" women in their homes. One point that repealers of the acts continually made was that the laws did not distinguish between a woman who lived in a monogamous relationship with one sailor, for instance, and one who bartered her sexuality with several or numerous men. Josephine Butler argued that by reducing all unmarried sexually active women to the status of prostitutes, the laws demoralized them to the point of accepting prostitution as a way of life. The argument highlights the effect of the acts in maintaining the dichotomous opposition between prostitute and wife, excluding the mistress as a third and threatening term. Anna occupies a necessary and necessarily silent position in a system that, among other things, divided women and made them ignorant of and hostile toward one another. The laws protected too the sexual double standard and class divisions that allowed men to participate in affairs with prostitutes and thereby refrain from threatening the chastity of women of their own class and the stability of the bourgeois family. But with the repeal of these laws and the increasing appearance of single women attempting to earn their own living, women on the street and in public began to embody a greater and uncontrolled erotic ambiguity.

Another army joined the fray at this time, that of the Purity Crusades and their offshoot, the Social Hygiene Movement. Anna alludes to the social power and commercial influence of their rhetoric when she notes an advertisement in the newspaper: "What is Purity? For Thirty-five Years the Answer has been Bourne's Cocoa" (*Voyage*, p. 49). Worried that her stepmother will ask her what she is living on, Anna recalls the ad, with a difference in meaning: "'What is Purity? For Thirty-five Years the Answer has been Bourne's Cocoa.' Thirty-five years . . . Fancy being thirty-five years old. What is Purity? For Thirty-five Thousand Years the Answer has been . . .'" (*Voyage*, p. 50). The ideology of purity joins millennia of patriarchal silencing of women's sexual experience in Anna's repetition of and inability to complete the ad slogan. The tone of the passage, though ironic, indicates the female modernist despair characteristic of much of Anna's internal dialogue. The pervasive threat she faces perhaps warrants her despair.

The Purity Crusades, launched in the late 1800s, adopted militaristic language and coercive police measures. When in the early twentieth century former repealers of the Contagious Diseases Acts and prominent feminists joined forces with doctors whom they had previously opposed, the Social Hygiene Movement succeeded the Purity Crusades with even greater moral force and social authority.[27]

In connection with the previous chapter's discussion of the role of carnivals, it is interesting to note that the Purity Crusades targeted immediately the working-class "Fancy Fairs" or English street festivals. Judith Walkowitz has described the fairs as a "traditional form of working-class entertainment [that] represented easy social intercourse between the sexes and defiance of work and time discipline."[28] She argues that abolishing the fairs constituted "a general assault on traditional lower-class sexual mores" and reflected fear of active female sexuality.

The movement's ostensible enemy was venereal disease, and it adopted repression and force as methods of attack. Anna and her acquaintances suffer, not only from the hostility of landladies, but the stares of policemen and harassment from detectives, who enter their rooms demanding references and certificates. Ethel complains that the police treat her "as if I was a dirty foreigner," a remark that indicates the combined fear of foreigners and of female sexual activity fueling the movement's assaults on working women.

The physical, psychological, and spiritual effects of this war, if not as spectacular as those of the Great War on men, were nevertheless profound. In perceived connection with the decline of imperial confidence, this battle also challenged Western notions of the individual. As the change in census categories indicates, the concept of the individual officially replaced that of the marriage or family unit, questioning the traditionally masculine meaning of "individual" and making it problematic for male and female social identity. Women had won the right to own property during the Victorian period, becoming economic individuals, though still lacking the political status of voting citizens. Now the government counted all women as individuals in marriage and divorce for the first time. Such official status, symbolically at least, grants women social agency and an autonomous, coherent self, long definitive of the male citizen. In literature, women writers such as Dorothy Richardson and Virginia Woolf make definitive contributions to the modernist movement and its challenge to realist fictions, including that of the bourgeois ego, while a heightened ambivalence toward women and sex becomes apparent in works by male writers like James Joyce and D. H. Lawrence. The tendency to think of the single woman as fascinating yet sexually deviant marks an ambivalent attempt to place her in categories that will once again explain her nature, define her status, and control her associations with other women: "Why do you go around with Laurie? Don't you know she's a tart?" (*Voyage*, p. 109).

As the system of kinship exchange that maintains sexual/social relations breaks down, more "primitive" bartering occurs in attempts to reconstitute acts of exchange in other ways. Class and sex relations continue, but not in the same system—or, rather, within that system as it breaks down, as power and its manifestations reorganize.[29]

The urban context significantly determines the nature of these transformations. Organized around industry and mass production, the city throws thousands of otherwise unassociated individuals together. Whatever their backgrounds, in public in the city, they move about alone, unknown, and unrecognized by the majority of people they encounter. Individuals must establish the social meaning of such encounters through symbols and codes—of dress, speech, gesture.[30] Discussing the breakdown of kinship systems, René Girard has even hypothesized that "if sufficient information were available, we could evaluate the mediative role of such cultural manifestations as clothing styles, entertainment, and so forth in determining marriage alliances."[31] Thus Anna's obsession with clothes signifies both feminine belief in artifice, which she recognizes as false hope, and the social necessity for costume, which she recognizes as life-determining:

> About clothes, it's awful. Everything makes you want pretty
> clothes like hell. People laugh at girls who are badly dressed. Jaw,
> jaw, jaw. . . . "Beautifully dressed woman. . . ." As if it isn't enough
> that you want to be beautiful, that you want it like hell. As if that
> isn't enough. But no, it's jaw, jaw and sneer, sneer all the time. And
> the shop-windows sneering and smiling in your face. And then you
> look at the skirt of your costume, all crumpled at the back. And your
> hideous underclothes and you think, "All right, I'll do anything for
> good clothes. Anything—anything for clothes." (*Voyage*, pp. 21–22)

Gestures and speech play a role, too, in establishing meaning in chance encounters between anonymous people. When Maudie and Anna pick up the two men in the beginning pages of the novel, Maudie's gestures signal the possibilities for the meeting and lead immediately to a new organization of the four people. She giggles and jokes:

> "Yes, we're taking the air," Maudie said. "Not all of it, of course."
> Everybody laughed. We paired off. Maudie went on ahead with the
> tall man. (*Voyage*, p. 10)

When Maudie and Anna find jobs with the chorus, they act as free agents, like men, who sell their labor power in exchange for wages. In this exchange, their labor power takes on the character of a commodity.[32] But unlike men, their labor power consists in their being women and sexually attractive enough to work on the stage or as models. Hence they become sexually suspect and susceptible to encounters that socialize them for the open exchange of sexuality in prostitution. Working for wages requires some talent and ability rather than exclusively sexual qualities. When Anna exchanges her sexuality for money, clothes, or rent, however, she makes of her labor power a purely sexual commodity. Marx wrote that labor power becomes a commodity in the act of exchange, even through direct barter, and so it is with Anna's sexuality.[33] Commodity exchange reduces the value of the object to its exchange value:[34] "'My dear, I had to laugh,' she said. 'D'you know what a man said to me the other day? It's funny, he said, have you ever thought that a girl's clothes cost more than the girl inside them?'" (*Voyage*, pp. 38–39). Sexual bartering reduces Anna's self to her sexuality and to a price. It is this flattening of her identity, rather than the career of prostitute per se, that Anna's multiplicitous voices resist.

Like any other commodity, Anna's sexual attractiveness must be reproduced. Immediately after meeting Walter, Anna spends the money he sends on expensive clothes; she has henna shampoos to make her hair lighter; and at dinner, "the nails shone bright as brass." Anna wonders why and how she is living her own life, which seems, in the Marxist sense,[35] estranged from her:

> Only sometimes, when I had got back home and was undressing to go to bed, I would think, "My God, this is a funny way to live. My God, how did this happen?" (*Voyage*, p. 35)

> When he touched me I knew that he was quite sure I would. I thought, "All right then, I will." I was surprised at myself in a way and in another way I wasn't surprised. I think anything could have happened that day and I wouldn't have been really surprised. "It's always on foggy days," I thought. (*Voyage*, pp. 131–132)

What happens to Anna seems unrelated to her, and she is alienated from her "self": ". . . it was like looking at an old photograph of myself and thinking, 'What on earth's that got to do with me?'" (*Voyage*, p. 37).

Somewhat paradoxically, Anna's past helps her recognize what happens to her socially in the present. In the color and caste hierarchy of the West Indies, women who could not marry wealthy white men might become their mistresses. When her stepmother Hester complains of Anna's father and the "illegitimate children wandering all over the place called by his name" (*Voyage*, p. 54), we become aware of a similar sexual system, but with different values, that has been a part of Anna's life. As Hester says, "My idea of a gentleman an English gentleman doesn't have illegitimate children and if he does he doesn't flaunt them" (*Voyage*, p. 54). West Indian colonials, however corrupt and decadent, often recognized the exchange as a social relationship and acknowledged kinship.[36] The mistress or kept woman in this system might retain, through acknowledgment of kin, her voice and some influence over her life. Nevertheless, the respectable wives from England were bound to voice shock and disapproval as a means of distinguishing themselves from "other" women by sexual and racial caste: "And you being told they were your cousins and giving them presents every Christmas and your father had got so slack that he said he didn't see any harm in it" (*Voyage*, p. 54).

The gifts Walter gives Anna affirm in a similar way their illicit social relation. The significant factor is not the gift itself, but the symbolic nature and repetition of the act that maintains a relation of exchange and asymmetrical power.[37] These arrangements between Anna and men more wealthy and powerful than she, and on whom she must entirely depend, maintain the caste relations of sex and class. When Walter gives responsibility for Anna to his cousin, when Anna refuses help from Vincent and ends up sleeping with Carl, when Anna becomes pregnant and must return to Walter for money for her abortion, it becomes clear that the exchange takes place among men in a general suprafamilial system, a system more compatible with the anomic urban environment and the increasingly corporate nature of power in the early part of the century. However, the system does not form well enough at this point to sustain itself beyond improvisation. With no means of independence, yet in the situation of an independent person, Anna is abandoned by Walter, Vincent, and Carl. She must endure the abortion and others' naming her a prostitute "ready to start over again in no time."

The "dirty foreigners" to whom Anna is linked, the germs of venereal disease, and the pathology attributed to the prostitute converge as shadows to this period's notions of health and morality. Sanitation, health, and morality become one in their contributions to the nation's strength while female sexuality and disease threaten it. For instance, one critic writing in 1935 describes *Voyage in the Dark* as a neurological study of a pathological woman. Warning young girls that it may demoralize them, she advises the reader to be secure in character, position, and virtue.[38] Her reformist brand of criticism clearly associates the moral qualities of character, position, and virtue with health. Michel Foucault has argued that these associations began in nineteenth-century medical discourse and eventually became common to more popular discourse: "In the ordering of human existence [medicine] assumes a normative posture, which authorized it not only to distribute advice as to a healthy life, but also to dictate standards for physical and moral relations of the individual and of the society in which he lives."[39] He states that discourse links medicine with the "destinies of states" and "it takes its place in that borderline, but for modern man paramount, area where a certain organic, unruffled, sensory happiness communicates by right with the order of a nation, the vigour of its armies, the fertility of its people, and the patient advance of its labors."[40]

Though Foucault does not focus on women in his discussion, his words bear particular significance in light of the legislative and moral authority over women's bodies given to doctors through the Contagious Diseases Acts and later the Social Hygiene Movement. The blame for the Empire's decline that fell on women coded them as the carriers of disease in a cycle considered both natural to women (their innate periodicity) and socially evil. The cycle appeared to be contained within the prostitute; yet it actually involved her circulation as commodity in an exchange among men that linked her directly to the respectable wife.[41] Venereal disease infected respectable women through their husbands, who carried and circulated the disease, not through other women. Yet as repealers of the acts repeatedly pointed out, only prostitutes and never their more culpable clients were punished. Occluding men's participation in the circulation of disease, the acts again upheld the dichotomy of private and "public women," silencing the voices of the latter while acquiring for the masculine medical and legal institutions further control over all women's bodies.

By the time that doctors and nurses were collaborating in the torture of suffragists in prison, their complicity with institutions of social control, especially control of women, was publicly acknowledged and accepted by many. Already outsiders, Anna and other Rhys heroines often succumb to illness, madness, and their accompanying hallucinations, presenting to other characters and some readers a larger and threatening disease. But rather than signifying moral sickness, madness and illness in these novels suggest instead turmoil and upheaval in the constitution of self and identity, a challenge to the illusions of a unified masculine ego and an honorable feminine "character."

The social crises of a threatened Empire seem to have demanded and found a victim, a sacrificial image that Anna, bleeding from the abortionist's blunders, easily fulfills.[42] In the battle over and on her body, she sustains the wounds and receives the blame. The doctor's cynical remarks imply her guilt, justifying the sacrifice. But they also open onto a historical undecidability concerning the nature of women's sexuality, an undecidability made possible and exacerbated by women's silences. Into this space enter Anna's private voices and carnival visions, presenting an alternative meaning to the doctor's words and heightening the ambiguity of the novel's ending.

The other European war that I have indicated in this chapter extended ideologically through the period between the two World Wars. In the spread of psychoanalytic doctrine and in the increasing popularity of progressive "sexologists" such as Havelock Ellis, who opposed William Acton, the Contagious Diseases Acts, and the purity campaigns, medical science and psychology nevertheless continued to define women's sexuality and place them "naturally" in the service of the family and state. But again, dominant ideologies competed with one another; oppositions opened spaces for exploring and questioning traditional institutions. In Rhys's *Quartet*, Paris of the 1920s provides a social context for such an exploration that questions in particular the institution of marriage.

Six

Quartet

"Postures," Possession, and Point of View

Among all of Jean Rhys's novels, only *Quartet*, her first novel to be published, presents a character whose identity is clearly European. Marya Zelli is English, married to a Pole and living in Paris during the 1920s. Nevertheless, Caribbean themes and images structure the novel's plot and narrative style and become central to the dispossession of "character" developed as narrative technique. Instigated by an act of exile and exchange, in which Marya is transferred from her imprisoned husband to a wealthy lover, conflicts of possession and obsession transform a happy female vagabond into a "captive attached to somebody's chariot wheels." The "possession" of Marya becomes meaningful, however, in the context of bohemian Paris; lacking a West Indian past through which to interpret her present life, her sole defense consists of a female modernist irony that criticizes but does not effectively transform the "chariot" to which she is bound or even the meaning of her bondage. Critics who become annoyed at the passivity of Rhys's protagonists, and even those sympathetic to their weaknesses, tend to attribute to her first "heroine" a condition of pathological masochism.[1]

It is important to examine this concept of female masochism, to place it in its context of psychoanalytic thought, and to ask what interests it serves as an evaluation of character. By tracing the Caribbean allusions in *Quartet* and interrogating the concept of masochism, we can see how colonial conflicts of power model the sexual conflicts of even this most European of all Rhys's novels. In its concern with point of view, as both theme and narrative problem, the novel explores relations of sadomasochism in a modernist experiment that questions our North American and European assumptions about personality and character.

But as soon as she put the light out, the fear was with her again—
and now it was like a long street where she walked endlessly. A redly
lit street, the houses on either side tall, grey and closely shuttered,
the only sound the clip-clop of horse's hoofs behind her, out of sight.[2]

Marya Zelli's fear stems from the abrupt change brought about in
her life following the imprisonment of her husband Stephan for
theft. The images convey the blind, imposing authority of married
and family life from which Marya is now excluded. The street's red
light suggests the status of a woman shuttered out of houses and left
to walk alone in the public streets. It foreshadows Stephan's final
condemnation of her as *une grue*—"loose woman." With Stephan,
she had felt vaguely content: "For she was reckless, lazy, a vagabond
by nature, and for the first time in her life, she was very near to being
happy" (*Quartet*, p. 14). But now, "loosened" from her marriage,
Marya returns to the same situation she faced when she and Stephan
met: "No money. Nothing at all. . . . My father and mother are both
dead. . . . I owe for the dress I have on" (*Quartet*, p. 19). The long,
winding Parisian streets that had previously promised adventure
now reveal to Marya her sexual vulnerability and represent the social preconditions to her dispossession of character.

Her perceptions of everyday life alter quickly, along with the style
of narration and the images that convey these perceptions. Previously the narrator has addressed the reader: "Marya, you must understand, had not been suddenly and ruthlessly transplanted from solid
comfort to the hazards of Montmartre. Nothing like that. Truth to
say, she was used to a lack of solidity and fixed backgrounds" (*Quartet*, p. 15). The distance maintained here between the narrative stance
and the character described implies that, although Marya's past has
not been solidly fixed, her identity as a character, distinct from the
voice of the narrator, rests secure. This security dissolves with Stephan's confinement. A new and more direct style now confuses the
narrator's voice and Marya's, posing a question of identity.

When Marya receives a letter from Stephan confirming his imprisonment, the narrative voice describes the breakdown of Marya's
sense of security and contentment in a style that exhibits a similar
and related breakdown:

It was a vague and shadowy fear of something cruel and stupid that
had caught her and would never let her go. She had always known
that it was there—hidden under the more or less pleasant surface of
things. Always. Ever since she was a child.

> You could argue about hunger or cold or loneliness, but with that
> fear you couldn't argue. It went too deep. You were too mysteriously
> sure of its terror. You could only walk very fast and try to leave it
> behind you. (*Quartet*, p. 33)

Here the vacillation from one identity to another, less sure and terrifying one, takes place. First the narrator's voice speaks Marya's
thoughts indirectly. Then a general meditative "you," spoken to no
particular person, refers self-reflexively back to the speaker; yet
readers cannot be sure if this speaker is Marya or the narrator or all
of us in this more direct expression of Marya's fear. The ambiguous
"you" contrasts especially with the previous direct address, "Marya,
you must understand . . ."

Critics have noted the vacillation in narrative stance exemplified
in this passage and attributed it to an autobiographical confusion of
author with character less controlled in this novel since it was Rhys's
first.[3] Most critics read the novel as a recounting of Rhys's affair
with Ford Madox Ford (Heuffer) and her experience living with him
and his common-law wife Stella Bowen.[4] Certainly the affair with
Ford gave Rhys material for her fiction; however, it is a mistake to
reduce narrative experiment to an autobiographical fallacy. The passage quoted above does not so much identify author with character
as invite the reader to take Marya's point of view. Or rather, accounting for the various possible references for "you," it diffuses the
point or place from which she perceives, speaks, acts; readers may
position themselves in one or more of those places.

The dissolution of distinctions between character, narrator,
reader, and—possibly—author poses the question of identity formally while the various voices state its theme: "In the morning she
went back to the Quai des Orfèvres and was given a permit to visit
the Santé Prison. Marya Zelli, aged twenty-eight years, British by
birth, Polish by marriage. . . . And so on, and so on" (*Quartet*, p. 35).
As Marya's social dislocation increases, fewer transitional passages
appear; scene, episode, and image are sharply juxtaposed. The text
shifts from traditional third-person narrative to narrated interior
monologue and back again. Increasingly, the style develops into the
deliberate fragmentation that characterizes Rhys's later novels. In
Quartet we see the coincidence of this style's emergence with creation of an outcast, displaced figure.

As I have argued in previous chapters, the detachment of voice
and identity from speaker, the question of place or position, shapes
Rhys's writing in her later novels, and I would argue that it does so

here as well. The positioning (or posturing) of voices and bodies, taking up or inhabited by various points of view, is precisely what concerns Rhys's narrative technique in *Quartet*. Rhys first published the novel in 1928 under the title *Postures*. She also considered the title *Masquerade*, suggesting, along with deception, the metamorphoses of power enacted through masks and alluding to colonial hierarchies of sex, race, and power.[5] In *Quartet* point of view may disguise, deceive, possess, or dispossess the speaker.

Other allusions to Caribbean culture mark the posturing of *Quartet*'s characters. When Marya first realizes the implications for her of Stephan's imprisonment, she thinks of the Parisian streets with fear; however, when the Heidlers, wealthy patrons of the arts, offer her a place to stay, the streets become the sites of more ambiguous carnival scenes. Sitting in a cafe, "she thought of [the streets] without fear, rather with a strange excitement" (*Quartet*, p. 47), and outside the cafe, she stands on the street, "looking at the Lion de Belfort fair—the booths, swings, the crowds of people jostling each other in a white glare of light to the gay, metallic music of the merry-go-rounds" (*Quartet*, p. 47). Here the fair suggests excitement, possibly sexual excitement associated with its working-class origins and traditional license, but the images of "people jostling," the "white glare," and "metallic music" render the fair a harsh and possibly false scene of joy. Marya has met H. J. and Lois Heidler only a few times and noted a solid, almost brutish sturdiness about him, a deadened and suspicious look to her. She receives their offer with feelings of dismay; on the other hand, Heidler's solidity suggests warmth and security to her in spite of her sense that he wants something more of her than what might be expected from a houseguest.

Later, when Stephan encourages Marya to stay with the Heidlers, she walks back to her tram wondering "why she had ever thought the matter important at all." A merry-go-round set up at the Porte d'Orléans helps her to suppress her earlier misgivings more completely. She watches a little girl, "holding tightly on to the neck of her steed, her face tense and strained with delight." The sight of such manic pleasure relieves Marya: "The merry-go-round made her feel more normal, less like a grey ghost walking in a vague, shadowy world" (*Quartet*, p. 57). Both of these early passages draw upon carnival scenes to express the ambiguity of the streets for Marya, who is now confronted with their "endless labyrinth," and the self-deception that accompanies her social displacement.

The weekly experiences of waiting in the long lines of women to visit Stephan in the prison Santé, then walking the streets alone, "possessed by pity as by a devil," make her realize the waste of her life. "And her longing for joy, for any joy, for any pleasure was a mad thing in her heart. It was sharp like pain and she clenched her teeth" (*Quartet*, p. 74).

In these lines the language of possession, pleasure, and pain mixes in telling ways. Marya does not indulge masochistically in her dependency and suffering but, longing for joy, chooses reluctantly the situation that Stephan, Heidler, and Lois all seem to approve for her—that of dependence on a man who will become her lover. Bohemian Paris offers little else for an untrained, attractive young woman, especially one "vagabond by nature." She might model for an artist, which she does for Lois, or try for a job on the stage, which Lois assesses realistically: "Well, I hope you're not thinking of trying for a job as a *femme nue* in a music-hall. They don't get paid anything at all, poor dears" (*Quartet*, p. 52).

Eventually Marya experiences herself painfully as Other and in the most concrete way—the "other woman." In spite of their bohemian ways, the Heidlers live by a game composed of strict categories and codes for social behavior. In this code, the other woman becomes the object of their desires, and they assume their prerogative to inflict pain upon her. From their very first meeting they speak of Marya in her presence in the third person, as if she were not there. In an argument among the three of them, Heidler shouts at Lois, "No, let me talk to her . . . you don't understand how to deal with this sort of woman; I do" (*Quartet*, p. 103). The category "this sort of woman" conflates in Heidler's mind with another candidate for the position of Other, the tribal "savage":

> Her head had dropped backwards over the edge of the bed and from that angle her face seemed strange to him: the cheek-bones looked higher and more prominent, the nostrils wider, the lips thicker. A strange little Kalmuch face.
>
> He whispered: "Open your eyes, savage. Open your eyes, savage."
> (*Quartet*, p. 131)

Heidler thus identifies Marya as Other sexually and even racially, though no information appears in *Quartet* to give her any background other than English. Positioning her as doubly Other, he forces her into "playing the game" according to his rules; he gives Marya another name, like Rochester's renaming of Antoinette, to appropriate her for his use: "he was forcing her to be nothing but the little woman who lived in the Hotel du Bosphore for the express purpose of being made love to. A petite femme. It was, of course, part of his mania for classification. But he did it with such conviction that she, miserable weakling that she was, found herself trying to live up to his idea of her" (*Quartet*, p. 118).

Rhys's narrative style revolts against this mania for classification and, at the same time, formalizes the pain and confusion it causes. It seems to one critic that "the abrupt shifts into the thoughts of another character—often the one against whom the heroine is reacting—destroy the continuity of the narrative and weaken its psychological verisimilitude."[6] But Rhys is not interested in narrative continuity and verisimilitude, rather in the forces that disrupt such unities. That the voices of Heidler and Lois inhabit Marya's mind indicates the degree to which she has been possessed, deprived of an authentic point of view, if such a thing exists, and eventually metamorphosed into a zombie, ". . . a thing. Quite dead" (*Quartet*, p. 123), or a soucriant, "as if all the blood in my body is being drained, very slowly, all the time, all the blood in my heart" (*Quartet*, p. 156). As she is possessed, Marya becomes obsessed: "Then her obsession gripped her, arid, torturing, gigantic, possessing her as utterly as the longing for water possesses someone who is dying of thirst" (*Quartet*, p. 117).

It is the "game" that makes such evil obeah possible, and the game depends upon marriage—Marya's interrupted marriage and the Heidlers' threatened one. Lois allows, even encourages, Heidler's affairs but "doesn't want to be given away; she doesn't want anybody to know" (*Quartet*, p. 89). The "well-trained domestic animal," "definitely of the species wife," must submit to H. J., even become procuress for him, to deter him from leaving her permanently. In an early scene she appeals to Marya:

> Her voice trembled. Marya was amazed to see tears in her eyes. . . .
> "You know," Lois added, "H. J., I love him so terribly . . . and he isn't awfully nice to me."
>   They sat side by side on the divan and wept together. (*Quartet*, p. 53)

Such sisterly sympathy disappears, however, as the posturing trio repeat among themselves actions of sadomasochistic torment. Marya bows to Lois, who, like Sade's Juliette, joins in torturing the Justine figure rather than become the victim herself: " 'Let's go to Luna-park after dinner,' she said. 'We'll put Mado on the joy wheel, and watch her being banged about a bit. Well, she ought to amuse us sometimes; she ought to sing for her supper; that's what she's here for, isn't it?'" (*Quartet*, p. 85). In this dialogue we see how completely the carnival image has lost its ambiguity and solidified into cruelty. Here the inversion of joy and pain does not signify a liberating turnabout, but the successful appropriation and possession of another human being.

Marya's methods of resistance resemble those of Antoinette and of Anna; they range from mockery and sarcasm, to running away, to the physical violence she inflicts on both Heidler and herself. Her mockery inverts the values of the world that oppresses her. The Heidlers' well-fed good health and energetic intelligence, for instance, become synonyms for evil in Marya's and the narrator's satiric character descriptions. Marya imagines a conversation with Heidler:

> She'd talk and all the time her eyes would be saying, "I loved you. I loved you. D'you remember?"
> But he wouldn't look at her eyes, or if he did he'd look away again very quickly. He'd be feeling healthy-minded, outrageously so. He'd long for cold baths and fresh air. Can't she explain and get it over?
> "Didn't I tell her that she made me feel sick? The extraordinary persistence of this type of woman." (*Quartet*, p. 177)

To Heidler, Marya now represents a diseased Other, one whose illness is contagious and threatens him. She *does* suffer recurring spells of real illness; he *has* in actuality informed her that she makes him sick. Marya and the narrator do not, however, acquiesce to the association of disease with evil and immorality in Heidler's confused projections. When a woman in a cafe makes a nasty remark, the narrative describes her as " . . . very healthy looking . . . with long, very sharp teeth" (*Quartet*, p. 70). It is helpful to again consider the context of social reform movements of the early twentieth century, discussed in the previous chapter, that made health and purity their slogans, while harassing working-class women and depriving them of their civil liberties. In this light, we can see in Rhys's first novel the gestures of turnabout that make illness oppose the established order of the healthy, unified ego, complacent in its cruelty.

Both the narrator and Marya mock Lois's reasonable and well-informed discussions, her "healthy" frankness of mind:

> Lois also discussed Love, Childbirth (especially childbirth, for the subject fascinated her), Complexes, Paris, Men, Prostitution, and Sensitiveness, which she thought an unmitigated nuisance.
> "Clergymen's daughters without money. Long slim fingers and all

the rest. What's the use of it? Those sort of people don't do any good
in the world."

"Well, don't worry," answered Marya. "They're getting killed off
slowly." (*Quartet*, p. 61)

Unhealthily "obsessed" with Heidler, Marya's unconscious mind
nevertheless sees through his posturing, classifying, and rationaliz-
ing. While she is ill and confined in Cannes, her dreams deride his
pretenses at religious feeling:

> "God's a pal of mine," he said. "He probably looks rather like me,
> with cold eyes and fattish hands. I'm in His image or He's in mine.
> It's all one. I prayed to Him to get you and I got you. Shall I give you
> a letter of introduction? Yes, I might do that if you remind me. No
> trouble at all. Now then, don't be hysterical. Besides Lois was there
> first. Lois is a good woman and you are a bad one; it's quite simple.
> These things are. That's what is meant by having principles. Nobody
> owes a fair deal to a prostitute. It isn't done. My dear girl, what
> would become of things if it were? Come, come to think it over.
> Intact or not intact, that's the first question. An income or not an
> income, that's the second." (*Quartet*, p. 22)

Mocking Heidler, Marya also reflects critically on the class and sexual hypocrisy that divides women, the myth of the good woman/bad
woman and its collusion in the morality of money and property.

Her inversions of bourgeois values, like the allusions to carnival
scenes and masquerade, do not, however, help her transform the
meaning of her possession by the Heidlers. Though resembling the
methods of a slave, these gestures do not give her escape. She begs
him to "say something nice to me" and lies "quivering and abject in
his arms, like some unfortunate dog abasing itself before its master"
(*Quartet*, p. 131). In the novel's climactic scene, after Heidler has
abandoned Marya, she screams at her husband: "You think I'd let
you touch him? I love him." A delicious relief flooded her as she said
the words and she screamed again louder: "I love him! I love him!"
(*Quartet*, p. 184). The scene contrasts sharply with the final pages in
Wide Sargasso Sea when Antoinette dreams and then enacts her rejection of Rochester's enslavement and chooses instead kinship with
her black friend Tia.

Why don't the Caribbean motifs work for the protagonist in *Quartet* as they do for Antoinette in *Wide Sargasso Sea* and, to a certain
extent, for Anna in *Voyage in the Dark*? Why is it that these same
motifs actually measure the degree to which she has been subjected

to the wills of others? I think the answer lies in the novel's social setting, in the Montmartre scene of upper-middle-class Paris where, in Bakhtinian terms, Carnival is co-opted into an "official feast." The official feasts of the Middle Ages, according to Bakhtin, "did not lead the people out of the existing world order and created no second life. On the contrary, they sanctioned the existing pattern of things and reinforced it."[7] The feasts in *Quartet* occasionally resemble those of true carnivals; for instance, at the Bal du Printemps and at other numerous cafes and bars of Montmartre, couples "shake themselves and turn with abandon" and a cacophony of voices assaults Marya's ears along with "the nasal music of the concertina of the *bal musette*" (*Quartet*, p. 73). Their official nature shows, however, at LeFranc's, where the Heidlers take Marya to dine and Monsieur Le Franc thinks of Marya, "Ah, the *grue!*" It is true that, afterward, they watch two naked women dancing, while a woman resembling Gertrude Stein with "the head of a Roman emperor" paces and watches. Lois exclaims: "I'm bored, bored, bored! Look here. Let's go to a music-hall, the *promenoir* of a music-hall, that's what I feel like. Something *canaille*, what?" (*Quartet*, p. 85). Lois's associations with the rabble are limited to the trendy, however, to just what is allowed at these official feasts in which class snobbery, cliqueishness, and fashionable appearances preside. Lois keeps up appearances by insisting that Marya be present at her parties. She then humiliates the necessarily silent Marya in front of the guests, claiming all the while to be "terribly fond" of her.

On her own behalf, Marya makes vague attempts at imaginary alliances with other women. Confined to the Hotel du Bosphore in a way that closely parallels Stephan's imprisonment, she imagines "all the women who had lain where she was lying" (*Quartet*, p. 119). Thinking with tender nostalgia of her husband, she empathizes with other trapped and degraded human beings, especially women: "Soon, for her sentimental mechanism was very simple, she extended this passion to all the inmates of the prison, to the women who waited with her under the eye of the fat warder, to all unsuccessful and humbled prostitutes, to everybody who wasn't plump, sleek, satisfied, smiling and hard-eyed" (*Quartet*, p. 125). But unlike the spiritual kinships of women with whom Antoinette and Anna choose to ally themselves, these women can provide no alternative cultural myth through which Marya might revise the meaning of her captivity. The renewal promised by carnival mockery eludes her, and she is left with the despair of modernist irony and satire.

Hence, she appears a masochist, a weak and self-destructive woman, even to herself ("weakling that she was"). Having thought of herself already in terms of a soucriant, a victimized vampire from whom all the blood has been drained, she awakens from a drugged dream one morning to discover that she has bitten her own arm. Even so, Marya is able, through the narrator's voice, which comes close to and sometimes merges with her own, to comment satirically on discussions of "sensitiveness" and "weakness":

> Heidler said: "Lois doesn't believe in fate, and she doesn't approve of weakness."
> "Oh, it's a damn convenient excuse sometimes," answered Lois.
> The two women stared coldly at each other.
> "After all," remarked Marya suddenly, "weak, weak, how does anybody really know who's weak and who isn't? You don't need to be a fine bouncing girl to stab anybody, either. The will to stab would be the chief thing, I should think."
> Heidler coughed. (*Quartet*, p. 87)

The dialogic perspective within the narrative does not find fulfillment in an alternative cultural language or myth, as we have seen; however, I think we might place it within the European context in which it appears, especially the context of psychological debate concerning the concept of "masochism" that took place during the 1920s. This debate participated in a larger one concerning the "nature" of female sexuality and involved such important figures in the history of psychoanalytical and social-psychological thought as Sigmund Freud, Karen Horney, and Havelock Ellis. Its ideas were current in Paris in the 1920s, furnishing topics for the "well-informed" and "intelligent" discussions that Lois loves and that Marya mocks.

Karen Horney began challenging Freud's assumptions regarding the "primacy of the phallus" and "penis-envy" in the early 1920s. Throughout the 1920s and 1930s she continued to criticize accepted psychoanalytic thought regarding women and to propose that the "dread of women" on the part of men and a male-oriented society contributed to the inhibitions and conflicts felt by modern Western women. Between 1922 and 1926 she debated with Freud in an exchange of papers on the psychoanalytic theory of femininity.[8] Horney's 1922 paper, which initiated the exchange, questioned the assumption that women felt their bodies to be inferior and argued that such a perception of female bodies resulted from a male-oriented culture. She also suggested that women might experience a pleasurable sexuality of their own. Freud put forward his theory two years later, insisting upon the inferiority of the female body and the development of femininity through penis-envy. Then in 1926 Horney published two papers, one arguing that Freud's view of women was a male fantasy, resulting from unconscious fears of women, that women enjoyed sexual desire and physical/psychological pleasure in motherhood that was undermined by their social subordination.[9] In the second paper, discussing frigidity in women, Horney states, "Our culture, as is well known, is a male culture, and therefore by and large not favorable to the unfolding of woman and her individuality."[10] Always beginning with clinical data, she opposed prevailing psychoanalytic theories with empirical evidence that led her to cultural critiques of marriage. She viewed marriage, with its accompanying social ideals of romantic love and monogamy, as responsible for what had previously been diagnosed as inherent physiological/psychological disorders in women.[11]

The ideas Horney developed in these early debates led to a full critique of the concept of female masochism, which she felt related directly to the institution of marriage. From 1929 to 1933 she confronted not only Freud but also Helene Deutsch in her battle against antifemale psychoanalytic theories. Deutsch argued that women must renounce clitoral pleasure in favor of desire for a child and, to be normal, must accept their instinctual masochistic tendencies.[12] Horney presented in response her 1933 paper, "The Problem of Feminine Masochism." The basic ideas were not new to her theory of femininity, but she extended it to challenge this specific concept. Horney argued that the social conditions of modern Western societies induced the kind of masochism psychoanalysts found in their patients and that, in particular, the institution of marriage in our culture contributed to this phenomenon.

Among the conditions of women's lives and of marriage, Horney cites many that describe Lois's life with Heidler and Marya's connections to both Stephan and Heidler. These include the estimation of women as inferior to men, the economic dependence of women on men or on family, the restrictions of women to spheres of life concerned primarily with emotional ties, sexual repression and lack of outlets for expansiveness, and a surplus of marriageable women, "particularly when marriage offers the principal opportunity for sexual gratification, children, security, and social recognition."[13] These constraints destroy women's chances to establish secure and confident identities or to develop their own voices and points of view. They become vulnerable to other people's views of them and susceptible, like Marya and Lois, to their manipulation and control.

The conditions described by Horney certainly apply to male-female relations as Rhys's characters experience them and, according to Horney, are likely to produce any or all of the following masochistic symptoms: an inhibited and emotionally dependent personality; a weak and helpless self-image; the use of weakness and helplessness in struggles for power and as reasons for special consideration; and the tendency to behave submissively, to be and feel exploited, to confer responsibility on men. All of these symptoms are aspects of the masochistic tendency "to arrange in fantasies, dreams, or in the real world, situations that imply suffering; or to feel suffering in situations that would not have this concomitant for the average person."[14]

According to Horney, then, the social conditions of women's lives in modern Western culture generate the attributes of clinically diagnosed masochism. Horney's study points out the contradiction between a diagnosis of masochism as pathological and the theory that it results from women's physiological nature. If both theses were correct, all women would be naturally masochistic and, at the same time, neurotic, implying a nonexistent model of unnatural but normal womanhood. Her analysis reveals the logical contradictions and masculine fantasies informing some critical evaluations of Rhys's heroines as masochistic and thereby representatives of an archetypal "Woman."[15] Attempting "to shake off this [masculine] mode of thought,"[16] as did Horney in reading her clinical data, we discover instead in Rhys's novels the specific social conditions that create an insecure and dependent ego in women. The narrative in *Quartet* reveals the social construction of an uncertain and vacillating feminine point of view.

In her attempts to combat what she perceived as psychoanalytic misogyny, Horney failed to take into account something Freud wrestled with: the *construction* of gender and sexual identity through the unconscious. Freud is most radical in his theories of female sexuality when he questions the difficult "very circuitous path" that leads to "the ultimate normal feminine attitude."[17] Horney bases her arguments on biological characteristics (as does Freud at times) and assumes female desire for heterosexual relations and motherhood to be natural as well as normal. In this respect, her theories are seriously flawed, especially from a Lacanian perspective.[18] Yet because Horney moves analytically between cultural institutions and the unconscious and because this analytical orientation leads her to focus on heterosexual marriage as an institution, her theories have descriptive power. Most important, they contribute to the discourses of "Love, Childbirth . . . , Complexes . . ." to which *Quartet* alludes and which are the conditions for the kinds of questions the novel can raise and explore.

Thrown together in ways that enhance the social causes of masochism described by Horney, Lois and Marya dramatically enact its symptoms, giving to Heidler the role of tormentor and borrowing some of his tricks when it suits them.[19] Lois—who enjoys no other sexual relation, has no children, believes women to be inferior to men, and depends on Heidler economically, emotionally, and socially—competes with Marya and every other available woman for Heidler's continued support. She sacrifices her integrity, compromising and complying with her husband's desires; she inhibits expression of her own wishes, limiting them only to the need to keep up appearances. But like Caribbean planters' wives, who so abused their slaves, Lois behaves in sadistic ways as well, admiring and attempting to ally herself with the master by becoming like him in an exaggerated manner.[20]

> [Lois] made an impatient and expressive gesture, as if to say:
> "D'you suppose that I care what you are, or think or feel? I'm talking about the man, the male, the important person, the only person who matters." (Quartet, p. 81)

> Lois . . . sat very straight, dominating the situation and talking steadily in a cool voice.
> "We must get Mado another hat, H. J."
> Heidler looked sideways at Marya cautiously and critically.
> "She must be chic," his wife went on. "She must do us credit."
> She might have been discussing the dressing of a doll. (Quartet, p. 85)

Unable to forge any alliances and finding no one to imitate, Marya vacillates between begging Heidler to "be kind to Lois" (Quartet, p. 106) and threatening fantastically to "strangle your cad of a Lois— kill her, d'you see?" (Quartet, p. 130). She feels "like a marionette," complicit in their possession and control of her: "It seemed to her that, staring at the couple, she had hypnotized herself into thinking, as they did, that her mind was part of their minds . . ." (Quartet, p. 98). And she longs "to assert her point of view."

While the debate over the "nature" of female sexuality and the concept of female masochism opened wide during the 1920s, it began to close in the next decade with the victory of the traditional Freudian view. Female masochism as a natural and simultaneously neurotic aspect of women's development became analytical dogma and also gained much popular support in the early decades of the twentieth century through the widely read work of the British sexologists, in particular Havelock Ellis.

Ellis's multivolumed and much-printed *Studies in the Psychology of Sex* represented a progressive challenge to Victorian taboos by arguing that women experienced a natural sexual passion. However, Ellis defined female sexual desire as heterosexual, maternal, and (here, quite unlike Horney) masochistic. In the interplay of Horney's and Ellis's theories, we see some of the social limitations to arguments possible during this time. Both Ellis and Horney believed in an innate heterosexuality and an innate wish in women for motherhood, while Horney criticized the masculine bias in psychoanalysis and the feminine subordination instituted in marriage. She based her counterarguments most often on what she considered natural or biological conditions unique to female sexuality that the masculine orientation in psychoanalysis simply missed. Her critique lost out, however, to orthodox Freudian views of the "normal feminine attitude" and then to those popularized by Ellis, who stated that only in marriage could a woman's natural sexuality unfold. Female desire expressed itself, Ellis argued, in modesty and reluctance and then took "delight in experiencing physical pain when inflicted by a lover, and [expressed] an eagerness to accept subjection to his will."[21] Such pleasure in pain, he wrote, "is certainly normal" and complemented the masculine desire to exercise force which "may easily pass into a kind of sadism, but . . . is nevertheless in its origin an innocent and instinctive impulse."[22] Influential during the Edwardian period, Ellis's views, unlike Horney's, became widely popular during the 1920s and 1930s especially, and ironically, through the many marriage manuals published during those years.

Readers and critics of Rhys's novels have inherited, I would argue, the official psychoanalytic and popular conclusions of a debate that had earlier, during the time that Rhys began writing, opened to question the nature of female sexuality. We tend to read *Quartet* not in the context of Horney's challenges but with attitudes similar to those expressed in the 1935 review of *Voyage in the Dark* mentioned in the preceding chapter. That reviewer found in the novel a neurological study of a pathological woman. The reviewer's language mimics that of a clinician, assuming that the reading public will accept and understand such terms. Focusing exclusively on an individual woman's "character" or personality, it forgoes any discussion of how those traits develop within certain social conditions and in interaction with others who have the power to categorize "that type of woman." I am not arguing that Rhys read Horney's papers or followed the debate I have described; I think the questions posed by the debate were available to her through the cultural climate in which she wrote, and her Caribbean background provided insight into racial and sexual power relations that opened to dialogic questioning in her writing any official conclusions about feminine masochism.

Though the narrative stays close to Marya's perspective, *Quartet* works with the problem of point of view and in this way inscribes thematically and stylistically the dialogic questioning of official judgments. Each character almost ritualistically states his or her pretensions at understanding the other's point of view:

> She looked at Marya with a dubious but intelligent expression as if to say: "Go on. Explain yourself. I'm listening. I'm making an effort to get at your point of view." (*Quartet*, p. 51)

> "I'm not saying," he told her, with a judicial expression, "that I don't see your point of view." (*Quartet*, p. 106)

Marya's possession dispossesses her of point of view. Through recurring suggestions of another character's interiority within hers and through the fluctuation in narrative voice that tends to merge with Marya's, we perceive the process of psychic displacement. For one must stand on stable and certain ground long enough to develop a perspective that may be described as a particular point of view, and Marya's stance is constantly endangered. Moreover, no cultural myth other than that of female masochism is available to her as a means by which to transform the meaning of her degradation or to renew her life. The critical questioning of that myth in this novel finds expression through a modernist irony that inverts bourgeois values but cannot transcend despair.

In Bakhtin's discussion of the changes in carnival imagery throughout literary history, he identifies Romanticism and its influences in modernism as transforming the meaning of the carnival so that it loses its regenerative qualities to angry satire.[23] The mask becomes a way to deceive, to keep a secret; the marionette becomes "the puppet as victim . . . the tragic doll."[24] Whatever traces of ambiguity and potential joy emerged in Marya's initial loosening from her marriage disappear as she becomes more and more isolated from any community or subculture that might have preserved the original popular nature of the carnival motifs in the novel. Her fear of life represented in the life of the streets becomes the overpowering force, and she is consumed in the official feast of the Heidlers' marriage.

The irony of the novel is fulfilled when we realize that Marya has found a place for herself. No longer allowed to wander the streets ("it wouldn't do to leave the girl trailing round Montparnasse looking as

ill as all that"), nor to see her own friends, nor finally to stay with
Stephan on his release, Marya finds her place within the fold of the
family. A loose woman, she's been tightened up, regulated, controlled. The ambiguous threat she once posed to the Heidlers' marriage as a helpless and available woman no longer subverts the rules
of their game.

Marya loses her place again at the end of the novel when she defies Heidler's injunction against seeing Stephan, who has been re-
leased from prison. Assuming the double standard as the founda-
tional rule to his game, Heidler insists, "I've never shared a woman
in my life, not knowingly anyhow, and I'm not going to start now"
(*Quartet*, p. 147). He no longer visits Marya and sends her only small
amounts of money, not enough for her to help Stephan or to leave
France with him. In the final, rather melodramatic scene, Stephan
plans to kill Heidler, and Marya hysterically threatens him with the
police. Stephan strikes her so that she falls, hitting her forehead on
the edge of the table and losing—literally now—her consciousness.
Stephan hurries outside where a Mademoiselle Chardin waits to
pick him up. She wants to go to a hotel she knows: "'Encore une
grue,' he was thinking" (*Quartet*, p. 186).

Though initially displaced into the Paris of the 1920s and bohemian life, supposedly free of bourgeois prejudices and Victorian attitudes toward marriage and sexuality, Marya finds herself in a situation resembling Antoinette's in the nineteenth-century setting of
Rhys's last novel, *Wide Sargasso Sea*—that of a woman driven to illness and madness or neurosis, confined by a man she loves, and
seemingly acquiescent in her fate. The same power dynamics appear
in this modern setting in different forms, characters, and ideologies—a reorganization of sex and power under the guise of sophistication. We are reminded of Christophine's complaints about neo-
colonialism: "These new ones have Letter of the Law. Same thing.
They got magistrate. They got fine. They got jail house and chain
gang. They got tread machine to mash up people's feet. New ones
worse than old ones—more cunning that's all" (*Sea*, pp. 26–27). And
perhaps Lois's tolerance of her husband's in-house affair differs little
from the plantation wife's acceptance of her master/husband's extramarital sex life on the estate.

Bohemian experimentation of the 1920s promised adventure and
liberation. Reading *Quartet*, however, we discover the shadow side
to the sexual revolution; the institution of marriage still regulates
the sexual lives of women. It constructs socially a feminine identity
that then conveniently, if illogically, fits a psychological diagnosis of
pathological yet normal female masochism. The Heidlers' marriage

imprisons Marya as brutally as the Santé imprisons Stephan. It confines Lois and ultimately H. J., too, but their voices prevail and gain power in the official feast that the erotically ambiguous figure of a marginalized woman threatens. Taken in, her identity spliced and reassembled, Marya becomes the other woman, the mistress who finds her place but loses her point of view within a tormented and oppressive marriage.

Jean Rhys initiated her narrative experiments in an exploration and critique of feminine masochism as engendered through modern European marriage; her second novel to be published, *After Leaving Mr. Mackenzie* (1931), addresses social and literary conventions of romance, countering them through narrative repetition that reveals the illusion of "character" in the context of a social backlash against female independence and adventure.

Seven

After Leaving Mr. Mackenzie

Repetition and Counterromance

"And I felt as if all my life and all myself were floating away from me like smoke and there was nothing to lay hold of—nothing.

"And it was a beastly feeling, a foul feeling like looking over the edge of the world. It was more frightening than I can ever tell you. It made me feel sick in my stomach."[1]

Julia Martin's existential nausea feels as beastly and foul as that of any modern hero; her *angst*, however, results from a dizzying freedom experienced specifically as female. She has longed for adventure and chosen her freedom, but not without having to recognize the strings attached: "I wanted to go away with just the same feeling a boy has when he wants to run away to sea—at least, that I imagine a boy has. Only, in my adventure, men were mixed up, because of course they had to be. You understand, don't you? Do you understand that a girl might have that feeling?" (*Mackenzie*, p. 51). The men mixed up in her adventure have included a husband and a series of lovers, the last named Mr. Mackenzie. It appears that the adventure itself has faded, leaving only the men and Julia's dependence upon them. She seems, at this point, unable to make any choices other than those that repeat a pattern of poverty, loneliness, and sexual exchanges with men who view her, as Heidler views Marya, as a certain "type" of woman.

Romance has already failed the female protagonist in this novel, and quest appears to have died with it. The reader might wonder whether this is another "prequel" like *Wide Sargasso Sea*, a novel that somehow ended before it began, but in this case ended badly, inconclusively. However, possibilities reopen within the narrative for both romance and quest plots, possibilities that conclude with repetition of all that has gone before. This novel does not progress, its heroine does not "get on," but neither does she decline in the ways that Anna or Marya might be described as declining in social and moral status. Rather, readers' expectations for a conventionally ascending or descending narrative are continually thwarted as the novel's structure circles phlegmatically back around itself.

The regressive, circular plot structure formalizes a crisis of representation that the images of nothingness thematize. The impossibility of representing a female "self" or subject is exacerbated by the protagonist's extreme marginality, historically conditioned by the aftermath of World War I, and inscribed in narrative frames that portray the psychological consequences of a social setup. Images of ghosts, zombies, a veiled mother, mirrors, and the framed portrait of a masklike female face all point to "something else," "somewhere else" that continually disappears. Excluded, silenced, it cannot be reached, and, as the novel's counternarrative suggests, it is perhaps an illusion after all of conventional narrative sequencing. As in Rhys's other novels, the heroine attempts to follow conventional romance sequencing by looking for a hero, but the "hero" fails to become one. Her best chances lie in alliances with other women, but opportunities for these dissolve, too, as she simultaneously misses possibilities for self-discovery. In this counternarrative, things neither change nor remain the same; they repeat in reverse and with only slight differences.

*T*he novel ends with a scene that also preconditions its beginning. And it begins with a scene that we realize in retrospect might have given it a hopeful conclusion. In the second chapter, Julia, who has just received notice, through his lawyer, from her ex-lover Mr. Mackenzie that this will be the last check he can send her, approaches him in a restaurant:

> She said, "Oh, yes, look here, this cheque . . . This cheque I got today. I don't want it."
> "Good," said Mr. Mackenzie. "Just as you like, of course. You're the best judge of that." . . .
> She picked up her glove and hit his cheek with it . . .
> "I despise you," she said.
> "Quite," said Mr. Mackenzie. He sat very straight staring at her.
> (*Mackenzie*, p. 33)

At this point she has very little money left and is demoralized by her dependency. Yet this action denies him the right to debase her altogether; it comprises a small but spirited act of resistance to his now indifferent power. As a conclusion, it would have signaled moral triumph and hope for Julia's "character"; as a beginning, it suggests we may have reason to admire Julia, to see her as a plucky heroine and expect an ending in real love or at least self-knowledge. Her meeting with sympathetic Mr. Horsfield, who has witnessed this scene reflected in the cafe mirror, enhances our expectations.

The novel, however, refuses to fulfill the expectations it raises. In the concluding chapter, Julia meets Mr. Mackenzie on the street in Paris. He takes her to a bar for a drink, and she requests that he loan her some money. In this final scene, the reader feels something similar to the eerie displacement and replacement we experience reading the ending to *Wide Sargasso Sea.* We know the character has been here before, someplace outside and before the text, in this case not in a fictional precursor, but in a kind of ghost text that haunts the one we're reading.

Julia describes herself frequently as a ghost and seeks some ineffable knowledge in corpses, dances with skeletons, and sees "the ghost of herself coming out of the fog to meet her" (*Mackenzie,* p. 68). The ghost text floats outside but also through the novel, making the characters appear only to disappear, and the plot, like Julia's life, an insubstantial series of "disconnected episodes." We are reading shadows, reflections, and the traces left afterward—in short, a zombie novel.

While Caribbean motifs do not appear explicitly to help explain the "elsewhere" quality of the narrative, key allusions to "a dark-purple sea, the sea of a chromo or some tropical country that she had never seen" (*Mackenzie,* p. 12) and to Julia's mother's childhood in Brazil suggest places or cultures that provide glimpses of otherness. These allusions color Julia's imagination and guide her renewed quest, but they do not give her an alternative to the novel's regressive structure or a way to "fulfill" her character. The ghost text channels instead a modernist exploration of specifically female postwar disillusionment.

*J*ulia Martin is a woman who has been framed, in almost every meaning of the word. The frame excludes her from the plot progressions of a conventional novel and from the alternative possibilities of spiritual community with other women that we found in *Wide*

Sargasso Sea. Julia's life, for instance, is almost infinitely framed within the narrative. When she describes her life floating away, she is talking to Mr. Horsfield, the man who first encounters her in a mirrored image. She tells the story of her existential anxiety within another story, which Horsfield has identified from its beginning as "the story of [her] life." The frame story begins with Julia's travels in Europe, which she narrates "as if she were trying to recall a book she had read or a story she had heard," and her meeting with a woman painter in Paris for whom she sat as a model. But then within this story, Julia describes a time when "having tea, I started to tell her about myself." The story of her life has become a story about telling about her life—" . . . before I knew where I was I was telling her everything else too. Everything that had happened to me, as far as I could" (*Mackenzie*, pp. 52–53).

As Julia tells the story within the story, she acquires four different audiences: Horsfield, her present audience; the painter, her audience in the past; and also "myself . . . and the woman in the picture." The picture, which hung in the painter's studio, is a reproduction of the familiar portrayal of Modigliani's mistress "lying on a couch, a woman with a lovely, lovely body . . . A sort of proud body, like an utterly lovely proud animal. And a face like a mask, a long, dark face, and very big eyes. The eyes were blank, like a mask . . ." (*Mackenzie*, p. 52). With its blank eyes and masklike face, this reproduction of a portrait represented in a narrative within a narrative might represent to Julia, and to readers of the larger narrative of this novel, a woman "killed [perhaps overkilled] into art."[2] For Julia, however, "it was as if you were looking at a real woman, a live woman." In Julia's eyes, the woman comes to life, as if masking an illusion cancels its illusory quality so that illusion *is* reality or, conversely, "a real woman, a live woman" is an illusion, exactly the feeling Julia has about herself.

When Julia discovers that the painter for whom she sits has not believed a word of her life story, the overrepresented woman in the picture not only comes to life but merges with herself and simultaneously becomes her only audience: "It was a beastly feeling I got— that I didn't quite believe myself, either. I thought: 'After all, is this true? Did I ever do this?' I felt as if the woman in the picture were laughing at me and saying: 'I am more real than you. But at the same time I *am* you. I'm all that matters of you'" (*Mackenzie*, p. 53). The portrait's laughter accompanies the self-recognition Julia feels looking at the picture and the life she sees in it. It is a moment of intensely overdetermined ambiguity, for it is the same moment in which she feels as if all her life and self were floating away. She simultaneously *is* nothing. Or, put another way, she recognizes that she can only be as she is represented.

The moment of existential freedom and terror, which is also a crisis of representation, repeats itself in a later scene in which Julia visits her dying mother. The return "home" to England and to her family takes on qualities of a quest turned around, directed to the past as a possible source of some yet unrecognized knowledge. Though the narrative does not connect them explicitly, it portrays Julia's perceptions of the woman in the portrait and of her mother in similar terms. Both resemble beautiful animals; both have dark skins, high cheekbones, inert bodies. In the company of her mother and in the room's silence, Julia hopes to learn "many deep things that she had only guessed at before" (*Mackenzie*, p. 98). But when she speaks to her mother, begging her to listen, "the sick woman looked steadily at her daughter. Then it was like seeing a spark go out and the eyes were again bloodshot, animal eyes. Nothing was there. She mumbled something in a thick voice, then turned her head away and began to cry, loudly and disconsolately, like a child" (*Mackenzie*, p. 99). Instead of learning "many deep things," Julia discovers "nothing." But she insists to her sister that her mother did "know" her, and that she said something that "sounded like 'orange trees.'" As in her encounter with the portrait, knowledge of herself comprises knowledge of nothingness. Only the allusion to a southern climate mitigates the emptiness she finds.

The connection to the portrait intensifies when, following her mother's death, Julia sits again at the bedside thinking "that her mother's sunken face, bound with white linen, looked frightening—horribly frightening, like a mask. Always masks had frightened and fascinated her" (*Mackenzie*, p. 124). Another allusion, this time a specific reference to Brazil, appears in the narrative when she is on the street and hears the music of a barrel-organ playing a tune to which she gives the words: "*Go rolling down to Rio.*" She seems to insist, yet with heavy irony, on her mother's South American identity and to comment, almost grotesquely, on its "rolling" away.

The dark, masklike qualities of her mother's face and of the portrait of Modigliani's mistress link them in Julia's perceptions of women through whom she might recognize herself. Both are alive *and* dead, both are, or are portrayed as, Third World women, and both represent, through their veiled faces, a profound but always silenced and disappearing truth. Though her mother is "real" and the portrait is not, the real mother can appear only as represented, too, as Julia searches her own memories and her mother's eyes and words

masculine gaze and its reduction of female and colonial identities to
a one-dimensional Other.

Julia might have found in her sister Norah a similar tie of kinship.
Norah, too, has been framed socially and textually in ways that asso-
ciate her with colonial natives. The novel directly compares Norah's
life to that of a slave. Norah has not left home, but stayed to nurse
her mother through years of illness. She has received the praise and
admiration of friends and relatives and basked in "the feeling that
one was doing what one ought to do, the approval of God and man"
(*Mackenzie*, p. 104). But meeting Julia again "aroused some spirit of
rebellion to tear her to bits." Norah rages against the unfair disap-
pearance of her youth and resents those around her who have praised
her but never helped. In a scene resembling the passages narrating
Julia's life story, Norah finds her life framed in a mirror and in another narrative:

> She picked up the book lying on her bed-table—*Almayer's
> Folly*—and had begun to read:
>> The slave had no hope, and knew of no other sky, no other
>> water, no other forest, no other world, no other life. She had no
>> wish, no hope, no love. . . . The absence of pain and hunger was
>> her happiness, and when she felt unhappy she was tired, more
>> than usual, after the day's labour.
> Then she had got up and looked at herself in the glass. She had let
> her nightgown slip down off her shoulders, and had a look at her-
> self. . . . She had laughed at herself in the glass. Like an idiot. (*Mac-
> kenzie*, p. 103)

Or like the reflection of Julia in Modigliani's portrait. The good
daughter of the family has been framed, too, and Julia's presence
forces her to confront her losses.

Norah, however, does not see that she and Julia, however different, share a similar social fate. Instead she finds allies in her friend
Miss Wyatt and in her Uncle Griffeths, both of whom defend and
protect her from Julia and the rebellious feelings Julia engenders in
Norah. In the absence of their dead father, Uncle Griffeths has as-
sumed a somewhat distant but controlling patriarchal authority
while Miss Wyatt, who wears a tie and has "gestures . . . like the
gestures of a man," appears to govern Norah's everyday life. Like the
female painter, Miss Wyatt takes on a masculine presence in the
novel's probably homophobic characterization that gives her power
over both sisters' lives and means of interpreting them. Rather than

renewing her sisterhood with Julia, Norah "[feels] a fierce desire to hurt her or to see her hurt and humiliated." Her wishes are granted on several occasions during Julia's return to London as one by one her relatives place Julia "beyond the pale."

*T*he social recognition of others is crucial to Norah's and Julia's abilities to represent to themselves who they are. The recognition of Norah as a "fine girl" prompts her to fulfill the image in opposition to that of Julia as the wayward daughter. In the narrative framing of Julia's "life story," social recognition makes all the difference in her ability to constitute a "self." The duality of seeing herself as simultaneously nothing and "all that matters" in the Modigliani portrait springs from the narrative frame that places the moment between two layers of social dialogue—that with the painter who coldly discounts Julia's story and that with Horsfield, who listens, sympathizes, and is "filled with a glow of warm humanity." Lack of social recognition from the painter, who perhaps does kill Julia into art by objectifying her in paint and denying her narrative subjectivity, makes possible the abyss; its depths are confirmed when Julia returns home and pulls out old photographs, letters, her marriage certificate, passport, and "the papers about my baby who died and was buried in Hamburg." The documents fail to represent her self: "But it had all gone, as if it had never been. And I was there, like a ghost. And then I was frightened, and yet I knew if I could get to the end of what I was feeling it would be the truth about myself and about the world and about everything that one puzzles and pains about all the time" (*Mackenzie*, p. 54). This passage, because it assesses the value of the experience, hinges the two narratives and their dialogues. The frame dialogue in which Julia receives sympathy and social acceptance from Horsfield makes possible her telling of the story of her life, in which she tells the story of her life, and enables her interpretation of its meaning and promise of truth.

Because Horsfield's acceptance counts for so much, we are tempted to view his character as the potential hero who might rescue Julia from the abyss of nonrepresentation. Through him and through the mirror in which he sees not Julia but Julia and Mr. Mackenzie reflected, the after-narrative of *After Leaving Mr. Mackenzie* returns to past events, reopening their possibilities, reinterpreting their meanings. It almost allows us to ask whether quest and romance will come alive again, as did the Modigliani portrait, whether Julia will have a second chance at truth or love, or possibly even both.

Teasing us with the possibilities for romance and renewed quest, the novel never, however, allows us to read comfortably within those conventions. It subverts them from the beginning through another aspect of its narrative form—the shifting positions taken by the narrative voice that inscribe the problem of Julia's disappearing, ghostlike self. Of all Rhys's novels, the narrative stance in *After Leaving Mr. Mackenzie* remains most distant from its protagonist. We depend on other characters, the third-person narrator, and rather sparse dialogue for our understanding of Julia's dissolving character. We gain much greater access to the thoughts of other characters than to Julia's. With the exception perhaps of the "story of her life" passages, veiled by the narrative and visual frames, her thoughts or feelings are mediated by the narrator or, most often, speculated upon by other characters. This experiment with point of view takes the opposite direction from that in *Quartet;* rather than focusing on the possession of the protagonist's mind by other voices and thus retaining the narrative center in her interiority, this novel moves around the protagonist, viewing her from the exterior, guessing and failing to understand or consolidate her character. Like the Modigliani portrait, she stays masked, even while attempting to come alive. Her perspective remains central in importance yet, at crucial moments in the plot, most unknown.

For instance, the passages preceding Julia's challenge to Mackenzie describe her from his perspective:

> Almost he was forced to believe that she was a female without
> the instinct of self-preservation. And it was against Mr. Mackenzie's
> code to believe that any female existed without a sense of self-
> preservation.
>
> She was irresponsible. She had fits of melancholy when she would
> lose the self-control necessary to keep up appearances. He foresaw
> that the final stage of her descent in the social scale was inevitable,
> and not far off. She began to depress him.
>
> Certainly, she could be very sweet sometimes. But that's part of
> these people's stock-in-trade. You don't take any account of that.
> (*Mackenzie*, p. 27)

In spite of the irony directed at Mackenzie in this passage, we pay attention to his description because it comprises the only information we have received about Julia at this early point in the novel apart from that given in the first chapter by the narrator. The indirect narrated monologue includes this information, for instance: "She had been an artist's model. At one time she had been a mannequin. But it was obvious that she had been principally living on the money given to her by various men. Going from man to man had become a habit. One day she had said to him, 'It's a very easy habit to acquire'" (*Mackenzie*, p. 26). In the first chapter we have learned from the narrator that Julia drinks alone in her room, daydreams, and "would lie on the bed for a long time without moving." On the basis of this previous evidence, we find ourselves affirming, even if hesitantly, Mackenzie's assessment of Julia as "the soft sort." Since the source of our previous evidence mocks Mackenzie, however, we do not wish to be allied with him and hope for counterevidence in Julia's act of resistance.

While our view of Julia is simultaneously veiled and revealed through the narrator's and other characters' perspectives, so are the other characters' views of Julia portrayed as distanced or distorted. In this sense, readers find themselves perceiving Julia much as the other characters do and thus we become potential objects of the kind of ironic criticism that tags Mackenzie. We must see ourselves as readers of "character" with desires similar to the ones that motivate those who deny Julia her subjectivity. The visual and narrative frames that present Julia as enigma invite speculation, promote a desire to interpret and manage her presence, and also stimulate ambivalent feelings of attraction/repulsion. Often, in crucial moments, we see Julia through the eyes of another character who, viewing her framed in a mirror or a doorway, guesses at her mood and her potential actions in the hopes of mastering them. In the instigating scene with Mackenzie, for instance, he is sitting in a restaurant, eating dinner, when "he lifted his eyes from the veal—and there she was, coming in at the door." Terrified by his certainty that Julia will make a scene, Mackenzie seeks the waiter's collusion, then calms down, guessing that "the effort of walking into the restaurant and seating herself at his table would have left her in a state of collapse" (*Mackenzie*, p. 29). But, as he soon discovers, he has guessed incorrectly and the scene becomes "a nightmare" for him. In the meantime, Horsfield has been watching "something fantastic, almost dreamlike," in which both Mackenzie and Julia have appeared to him framed and "reflected in a looking-glass. A bad looking-glass, too. So that the actors had been slightly distorted, as in an unstill pool of water" (*Mackenzie*, p. 37). Julia's "character" has proved other than expected to Mackenzie and to us.

Now Horsfield's gaze replaces Mackenzie's. With his sympathetic eyes, we can feel more comfortable with ourselves as readers of Julia. He guesses that she is lonely, a little older than he had thought, and that when he asks her to his hotel room, she will follow. After hearing "the story of her life," he guesses further:

> He felt that he could imagine what her mother and her sister were like. No money. No bloody money. Bloody money! You might as well say "Bloody money." They would be members of the vast crowd that bears on its back the label, "No money" from the cradle to the grave . . . And this one had rebelled. Not intelligently, but violently and instinctively. He saw the whole thing. (*Mackenzie*, pp. 54–55)

Horsfield's efforts to understand Julia and his impulsive sympathy contrast strongly to the perspectives taken by Mackenzie and also by the painter for whom Julia modeled. Though the painter is a woman, she and Mr. Mackenzie impose a similar masculine gaze upon Julia, refusing to credit her words and wishing only to objectify, consume, or manage her body. The layers of social dialogue which frame Julia's life story are gender-coded according to the quality of the gaze, and their gender characteristics do not match the sexes to which they conventionally belong, but reverse them. Correspondingly, we find that Horsfield and Julia share similar qualities. She has chafed at restrictions and longed like a boy for adventure; he too has sought adventure as a result of dissatisfaction. She acts on impulse to preserve her dignity; he impulsively seeks through her something humane and compassionate in his life.

The narrator presents Horsfield's point of view more complexly and sympathetically than that of Mackenzie. He is first described as

> thinking that he had spent a disproportionately large part of the last six months in getting away from people who bored him. (The last six months had been his kick of the heels.) The habit of wanting to be alone had grown on him rather alarmingly.
> He wondered whether it had been worth while to spend the only legacy he ever had, or was ever likely to have, in travelling about Spain and the south of France, because he had a vague idea that the sight of the sun would cure all his ills and would develop the love of life and humanity in which he felt that he was lamentably deficient. (*Mackenzie*, p. 36)

Perhaps this reflective self-criticism leads him to seek out the unhappy woman he has just observed and, though disappointed by her lack of youth and faded appearance, to continue feeling an interest in and responsibility for her. Through Horsfield, we continue reading Julia, our expectations for plot progression renewed.

The masked face of the Modigliani portrait, the distancing narrative frames, and the shifting but predominantly external narrative perspective all veil Julia's "character" from her own and the reader's views. Such veiling simultaneously conceals the truth she hopes to find and gestures promisingly toward its existence. By simultaneously blocking and provoking the gaze, the veil or mask specifies woman as enigma and therefore guarantor of concealed truth.[5] Discussing cinematic images of veiled women, Mary Ann Doane has argued that the veil's power in these respects depends upon the special significance of the face:

> The face is that bodily part not accessible to the subject's own
> gaze . . . —hence its over-representation [in close-ups] as *the* in-
> stance of subjectivity . . . the most *readable* space of the body.

> The face, more than any other bodily part, is *for* the other.[6]

No wonder that Julia perceives the nude body represented in the painting as proudly revealed but reads the real life of the woman in her blank eyes and masked face. Her powers to simultaneously block and provoke the viewer's gaze, and especially to represent an enigmatic truth, hidden yet guaranteed by the very fact of its being masked, reveals to Julia the symbolic attributes of "woman" in European culture. Denied voice, objectified in art, she is both excluded and elevated by her otherness.

"Getting to the end of what I was feeling" to discover "the truth about myself and about the world" can mean two things for Julia and perhaps both. It can mean that she accepts Western culture's appropriation of "woman" as enigma and, by exploring her own feelings as a man explores the sea or a foreign territory or a woman's face, she will find the promised but concealed truth. It can also mean that by exploring her own internalized otherness, through which she identifies with the masked portrait and her mother's veiled face, she may discover the dynamics of patriarchal culture that pose, through "woman," the question of truth. She may discover that hidden truth is only a promise made possible by the exclusion of women's subjectivity. In a way, these two possibilities appear to cancel one another out, since the first presupposes that Julia's feelings are available for her to explore while the second results in discovery of the means by which her subjectivity is denied. Since, as Mary Ann Doane puts it, "the face is that bodily part not accessible to the subject's own gaze" and the face represents her subjectivity, how can she truly see herself?

If Julia seeks a true vision of herself through the first alternative, that of exploring her own feelings as if they are available and will enable her to solve the enigma of "self" and "woman," her best hope may lie with Horsfield. As we have seen, she and Horsfield share similar feelings, and he is open to exploring them. He also sees her as "woman" and would like to protect her as a "man." Yet his gaze is coded feminine, exempting him from the ranks of those who exclude and debase "woman." If, on the other hand, Julia questions the woman-as-enigma-as-truth equation and its associations with the primitive, the way out of her dilemma lies in exploring the ways she sees other women and herself in them. Her identification with the woman in the portrait and her attempt to know herself through her mother seem promising indications of her ability to ally herself with other women in their otherness. The question remains whether she can join with them, especially whether she can join with them in the carnivalesque laughter that she imagines emanating from the masked face in the painting. Both alternatives and their possibilities for success depend upon the social relations that frame them.

*T*hough Horsfield exhibits feminine-coded qualities of empathy and compassion, he has not had to suffer the same consequences of his wish for freedom and adventure that Julia, because of her sex, has faced. Julia has been framed textually and also socially. Class and sexual differences provide Horsfield with a legacy, an income, and a house of his own to which he can return after his wanderings, which, of course, are far more appropriate to a masculine quest. Horsfield has also fought in the war. This experience, however, becomes dually gender-coded in the gap between its ideology of masculine heroism and the reality of shell shock, the "cracking up" that Horsfield assures Julia he too knows something about.

The different effects on men and women of World War I alluded to in the dialogues in *After Leaving Mr. Mackenzie* help to contextualize the reverse gender coding in the "story of her life" passage in which the female artist asserts a "masculine" and Horsfield a "feminine" gaze. Elaine Showalter has described how the effects of shell shock on thousands of soldiers during World War I threatened to transform their image of courageous and stoic heroism into that of weak, cowardly, and feminine hysteria.[7] The symptoms of shell shock, in fact, matched those diagnosed by Victorian and Edwardian physicians as female hysteria, and they appeared in far too many men to allow authorities to continue accusing each individual soldier of cowardice. At one point during the war, military authorities actually censored medical reports and analyses of the phenomenon in order to prevent their undermining the war effort. Showalter argues that changes in psychiatry and in therapeutic practice resulted from the need to reinterpret these symptoms in men and restore their masculinity. But in the meantime, as Sandra M. Gilbert has argued, women who worked for the war effort on the home front gained independence and a freedom from domestic confinement that exhilarated them. While men found themselves confined to narrow trenches and susceptible to hysterics, women enjoyed mobility in the public world and often earned wages of their own for the first time in their lives.[8] That some women experienced physical and economic independence during the war does not cancel out another effect of the war on women: its erasure of feminist culture. Rather, we can view both results of women's active service to the state as intensifying the misogyny of the period between the wars, a backlash against women's autonomy that thrived in the absence of a strong feminist movement. The battle experiences of some men and women on behalf of the state reversed perceptions of sex/gender attributes in many cases while the absence of a strong feminist culture following the war allowed a silencing of women's conflicts *with* the state.

Julia remembers the war as "a mad, reckless time" and feels suddenly "exultant and youthful" (*Mackenzie*, p. 68). In one conversation with Horsfield, she asserts, "I rather liked the air raids" (*Mackenzie*, p. 152). Though we find it difficult to piece together the fragments of her floating and disconnected life, the reader does realize that whatever adventure Julia enjoyed during the war did not give her the public identity or economic independence ascribed by Gilbert to women during the war years. Rather, she has been far more strenuously engaged in the other war, discussed in Chapter 5, taking place over and on women's bodies. Though she entered it as a youthful rebel, it has defeated her and continues to punish her in the misogynistic aftermath of both wars.

The wounding shots—dislocation, divorce, poverty, the birth and death of her baby—have fractured Julia as severely as trench bombing shocked infantrymen. In a conversation in which an ex-lover named Mr. James describes the changes in his personal philosophy due to the war, Julia maintains a long silence while an inner dialogue takes place: "She was thinking: '. . . When you've just had a baby, and it dies for the simple reason that you haven't enough money to keep it alive, it leaves you with a sort of hunger. . . . And the tart downstairs lends money and buys flowers and comes to see you and cries because you are crying.' "Look here, I don't believe that; you're making it up." All right, don't believe it then'" (*Mackenzie*, p. 112). Though Mr. James feels free to explain the significance of his war experiences, Julia's are silenced. The internalized voice of Mr. James or perhaps a more general "they" refuse her war any public articulation. In spoken dialogue with Horsfield, however, the comparison emerges implicitly:

> She said: "D'you know what I think? I think people do what they have to do, and then the time comes when they can't any more, and they crack up. And that's that."
> "Yes," he said, "and perhaps I know something about cracking up too. I went through the war, you know." (*Mackenzie*, p. 152)

What Julia has "had to do" is leave home, something expected of any man but forbidden, unless in service to the state, to women.

Though the reverse gender coding brought about by the war that history records and that discourse allows brings Julia and Horsfield into sympathetic resemblance to one another, their wars have been separate and hers disallowed. Their sex differences, socially experienced, prevent Julia from being known or rescued while their gender similarities prevent Horsfield from rescuing her as a masculine hero should.

Horsfield does sympathize. He feels an "overwhelming contempt for the organization of society" and imagines telling Julia, "I'm on your side. Can't you see that? I'm for you and for people like you, and I'm against the others. Can't you see that?" (*Mackenzie*, p. 167). However, he simply remains as uncommitted as the narrator's introductory description suggests he has always been. He is never sure of his feelings and often acts in ways that counter his thoughts. The impulses of a hero and those of a "feminized" man cannot be reconciled, yet he retains the masculine privileges that give him choice in the matter. For example, after their first meeting in Paris, Horsfield insists that Julia accompany him to the movies, but immediately his attitude alters: "He decided that when they left the cinema he would find out where she lived, get a taxi, take her home—and there would be the end of it. Once you started letting the instinct of pity degenerate from the general to the particular, life became completely impossible" (*Mackenzie*, p. 45). In spite of his decision, however, he does just the opposite: "'Will you come back to my hotel?' he asked. 'We can talk much better there'" (*Mackenzie*, p. 45).

Following an accidental meeting in London, his thoughts vacillate from one attitude to another:

> He thought: ". . . I can't possibly bring her here."
> Suddenly he saw Julia not as a representative of the insulted and injured, but as a solid human being. She must be taken somewhere . . . She must have a bed to sleep in, food, clothes, companionship—or she would be lonely; understanding of her own peculiar point of view—or she would be aggrieved. . . .
> Undertaking a fresh responsibility was not the way to escape when you came to think of it. . . .
> He suddenly remembered that, after all, he was not in love with Julia; and he thought; "I am not going to be rushed into anything."
> (*Mackenzie*, pp. 168–169)

In this passage, Horsfield's "feminine" sympathies conflict with his unwilling and unfulfilled role as "masculine" hero who must be in love with the woman he rescues. Refusing to rush or even saunter into that role, Horsfield has circled round to a moment existing outside and before the text, the time when he had longed for escape and received a legacy. Once again, he decides to "chuck everything . . . get something out of life before I'm too old to feel. Get a bit of sun anyway" (*Mackenzie*, p. 167). We're reminded again of how similar Julia and Horsfield are, seeking authentic feeling in places elsewhere, southern climates and the sun. And we see again the differences between them: Horsfield's sex and income allow him to make and then repeat such a decision, while Julia makes her own isolated, repetitive, and circular path back to Mr. Mackenzie.

For Horsfield, Julia becomes a means through which he can pursue his own perenially ambivalent feelings and represent a new self to himself. She becomes not a mirrored image of herself, as in their initial meeting, but of his self as he would like to see himself. He cares most for her when he feels more in touch with himself, when he can say, "you've given me back my youth" or "just the touch is wanted—something to set us off. You, and what happened last night, have done that for me" (*Mackenzie*, p. 167). Even when he thinks he knows Julia and sees "the whole thing," the question remains of what she sees. After they have sex in his hotel room, Horsfield acknowledges but does not ask the question: "'. . . the worst of it is,' he thought, 'that one can never know what the woman is really feeling'" (*Mackenzie*, p. 153). The very worst is that the woman herself cannot know.

While Horsfield waffles in his commitment to Julia, she now reads a message from him as "something written by a stranger to someone she had never seen." Her own subjectivity denied her, Julia sees only that she has never seen herself. Invisible, she loses even the consolation of childhood memories and imagined suns. Instead of recalling her mother as the warm center of her life, Julia now remembers the "first time [she] was afraid of nothing . . . afraid in the sun": "The sunlight was still, desolate, and arid. And you knew that something huge was just behind you. You ran" (*Mackenzie*, p. 160).

After receiving some money from Mr. James, she runs again, deciding to return to Paris. Parting from Horsfield, she vents her rage in tears and insults. For his part, "Mr. Horsfield tried to put Julia entirely out of his mind."

While still in England, Julia has come close to pursuing her second alternative: exploring through other women her internalized otherness to discover the dynamics of patriarchal culture that pose woman as enigma-as-truth. At her mother's funeral, she confronts the abyss of nonrepresentation that she continues to discover through the women who seem to "know" her: "her brain was making a huge effort to grapple with nothingness. And the effort hurt; yet it was almost successful. In another minute she would know. And then a dam inside her head burst, and she leant her head on her arms and sobbed" (*Mackenzie*, p. 130). Julia has "abandoned herself." She sees her life now as absurd and painful. Yet "at the same time, in a miraculous manner, some essence of her was shooting upwards like a flame. She was great. She was a defiant flame shooting upwards not to plead but to threaten. Then the flame sank down again, useless, having reached nothing" (*Mackenzie*, p. 131). Efforts at self-representation resurface only to lead her once again to "nothing." If the image of a shooting flame cannot represent her essence, perhaps "nothing" can; or perhaps there is no essence.

The connection between her mother's masked face and that of the Modigliani portrait is crucial to the moment of possible discovery, especially the difference between them. Instead of suggesting life in the truth promised by her veil of white linen, her mother's face represents death. Discovering through her mother's death that the "essence of her [Julia]" is actually "nothing," Julia might have concluded that the promise made in Modigliani's portrait was a false one. She might have recognized her own social condition as a woman in her mother's veiled and now eternally silenced face. Her glimpses of otherness and potential other selves might have led Julia to join, as did Antoinette and Anna, with other exiled or enslaved women.

However, as we have seen, the woman most enslaved and closest to Julia, her sister Norah, has sought her allies in relatives and friends who approve of her only so long as she perceives herself and behaves as Julia's opposite. In turn, when Julia explains to Norah that her sobbing expresses rage, not sorrow, she then turns her rage on Norah and "all good respectable people" whom she wishes "had one face so that I could spit in it." Julia cannot seem to see her own rage in Norah's barely suppressed fury, and she fails to join with her in a gesture of kinship that would upset the family's typecasting of their parts as the good and the bad woman. Instead each woman plays her scripted role, Julia screaming accusations at Norah, who runs to the protection of Miss Wyatt. Miss Wyatt pushes Julia out the door, and Uncle Griffeths, who sees Julia approaching him on the street, crosses to the other side to avoid meeting her.

The woman represented so unsatisfactorily as "mother" has now died, and the promise of her concealed face has disappeared, "rolling away." Shunned by her uncle and, most importantly, turned out of the female household inhabited by Norah and her friend, Julia "was certain that if a stranger were suddenly to appear before her and ask in a sharp voice: 'What's your name?' she would not know what to answer" (*Mackenzie*, p. 142). Nameless, "the dark room was horrible to her" and "the street was a dark tunnel." She has lost her chance to see herself in the lives and deaths of other women and will not be able to join the carnivalesque laughter of the woman in the portrait. All the women in this novel laugh, as does Norah, framed in front of her mirror, alone, and death does not bring renewal. Socially and spiritually buried, Julia can only see others as similarly dead.

Beginning a series of sinister and grotesque incidents, Julia sees a "face . . . all bones and hollows in the light of the lamp striking upwards, like a skeleton's face" (*Mackenzie*, p. 147). Climbing the stairs to her room quietly in hopes of avoiding discovery by her landlady, Julia suddenly screams. Waking everyone in the house, she continues screaming, "Who touched me? . . . Who's that? Who touched my hand? What's that?" (*Mackenzie*, p. 164). Horsfield has accidentally brushed her hand, but Julia "thought it was someone dead."

*P*art III of the novel charts Julia's second return—to Paris, where the novel began, and ultimately to a moment just like the one that must have preceded the text as the condition for all that fails to develop within it. The failure of each of Julia's opportunities and the lack of progression of the narrative leave only "disconnected episodes" announced and enacted by a narrative that parodies both its own "counterform" and the conventional form it ruptures. Returning to Julia's point of view, the narrative nevertheless cannot inform us of her thoughts or feelings. Rather it can only demonstrate the fact that they are not hers. Her perspective has become that of the internalized masculine surveyor that John Berger describes: "She began to imagine herself in a new black dress and a little black hat with a veil that just shadowed her eyes. After all, why give up when so many people had loved her? . . . 'My darling. . . . My lovely girl . . . *Mon amour. . . . Mon petit amour . . .'" (Mackenzie*, p. 182). Now she longs for the veil that will conceal, deceive, and provoke the erotic gaze. Something has changed, however, "something in her was cringing and broken." She cannot meet the glances of the men who pass her.

When one of them follows her, she decides she will tell him "to go off." However, when he turns to look at her, he mutters, "*non alors*," and walks away of his own accord. Julia laughs and thinks repeatedly, "That was really funny. The joke was on me that time" (*Mackenzie*, pp. 187–188). The joke, if it is one, is that she has become invisible and cannot even know herself as the surveyed, not even as a "sight." And, again, she cannot share her laughter with other women. In one episode, Julia longs to explain her life to a strange, beautiful woman who looks "kind and soft." But they do not speak to one another. Instead Julia enters a Pathéphone Salon, where she hears a popular song about impossible returns: "*Pars, sans te retourner, pars.*"

The chapter in which Julia is followed on the street is titled "The Second Unknown"; it parallels a chapter in Part I called "The First Unknown." In "The First Unknown," a man follows her, just as in "The Second Unknown." However, in the earlier chapter, Julia does tell him off, and he responds, "I have some money and I am willing to give it to you. Why do you say that I am *ignoble*?" (*Mackenzie*, p. 59). Though he has subjected her to his gaze, implied that she is for sale and that he ought by rights be allowed to consume her, Julia nevertheless feels cheered by the encounter—"After all, I'm not finished. It's all nonsense that I am. I'm not finished at all" (*Mackenzie*, p. 59). The "unknowns" of the chapters refer, perhaps, to the anonymous men, but also suggest their role in sighting Julia, framing her, and making her unknown to herself.

All of the novel's chapters are titled in ironic ways that emphasize the ghostly status of the text and characters. The chapter "It Might Have Been Anywhere" contains the scene in which Horsfield and Julia have sex in his hotel room. All we know of Julia's thoughts or feelings is that it seems to Horsfield she is willing, "her body was soft and unresisting." We have access only to Horsfield's mind, and through his thoughts are reminded that "one can never know what the woman is really feeling" (*Mackenzie*, p. 153). In sex, Julia truly disappears, losing her place and all subjectivity; yet, if not recognized sexually, she becomes twice or doubly unknown to herself.

Five chapters are named for the characters who appear in them. Seven are named for their settings. Such titles suggest props for a novel that has become a bare skeleton in a way, the remains of an event, its aftereffects. The last chapter is titled "Last," as if making fun of the genre's conventional structure at the same time it reverses the structure by returning in the end to an event outside and before the beginning of this novel's "plot." In this chapter she meets Mr. Mackenzie again, but we know of it only through his eyes, as he sees Julia and, like the "unknowns," follows her on the street. The final pages silence Julia conclusively as Mr. Mackenzie's gaze assesses her—". . . untidy . . . black specks in the corners of her eyes. Women go phut quite suddenly, he thought." The scene repeats an incident that must have happened before, though not in this narrative space, and authoritatively ends the reopening of possibilities for quest and romance. Julia has again, with a repetition that seems unending and yet final, entered the relationship that she had resisted with so much spirit in the novel's beginning pages.

The novel's regressive structure brings Julia's past and the novel's own shadow text within its frame, framing her textually but also, as stated earlier, socially. In some ways the novel's formal structure parallels the experiences of women who found themselves, after the war, loosened from domestic confinement but unable to make their own living or to be recognized as public persons. In her discussion of the period between the wars, Sandra M. Gilbert describes reactions against the independence enjoyed by some women during the First World War: men sought revenge, women felt guilty, and anti-feminism, even outright woman-hating, prevailed.[9] Furthermore, during the late 1920s and early 1930s, increasing unemployment among men was blamed on women workers.[10] Even the popular and "radical" sexologists such as Havelock Ellis urged women to remain at home, fulfilling themselves through marriage and motherhood.[11] Women were punished for their earlier adventures, forced back into a life they thought they had left behind, or abandoned, like Julia, to their fate on the streets. Julia's family has certainly punished her by disowning her, and she has been forced back to a time prefiguring the text, framed by her longings for freedom, denied a voice with which to explain her own "war" adventures, and made a sight—as a spectacle, a ghost, an "untidy" fright. In *After Leaving Mr. Mackenzie*, the zombie's condition of death-in-life becomes a metaphor for the dissolution of female character and also a model for modernist textual experiment with contiguity, memory, and time "after." Haunting the boundaries of public and private experience, Julia's life floats through a novel that takes place, like the war's aftermath, after its main event.

It also takes place in the spaces between one war and another impending one, or between two "unknowns," two framed stories, a text and its ghost—or as the novel's final line describes it, "the hour between dog and wolf, as they say." The hour's in-between status and the text's ghostly qualities suggest possibilities for metamorphosis. However, it is the time and place as "they say" it, not as the protagonist might have transformed it.

Good Morning, Midnight, the last in the series of novels Rhys published between the wars, explores the internal dynamics of the guilt and punishment imposed upon women during this period. Its heroine attempts, like Julia, an impossible return and, like Antoinette, dreams the plot and conclusion of the novel in which she appears.

Eight

Good Morning, Midnight

The Paris Exhibition and the Paradox of Style

Good Morning, Midnight takes place during the same historical period in which *After Leaving Mr. Mackenzie* is set —"the hour between dog and wolf." *Good Morning, Midnight's* text occupies the end of that hour, however, the time nearest the wolf of fascism and the Second World War. Published in 1939, its scenes are set in Paris of 1937, the place and year of the Exhibition Internationale des Arts et des Techniques Appliqués à la Vie Moderne. The novel opens and closes with significant allusions to the exhibition, allusions which set the novel firmly within a Paris of intense social and political conflict, symbolized best perhaps by the two major buildings of the exposition which confronted one another directly on each side of the Champs de Mars—that of the Soviet Union, topped by giant figures of a marching man and woman with hammer and sickle held high, and that of Nazi Germany, crowned by an immense gold eagle grasping a swastika in its claws.[1]

The novel's protagonist, Sasha Jansen, describes the setting in a dream she recounts in the novel's beginning pages. "Everywhere there are placards printed in red letters: This Way to the Exhibition, This Way to the Exhibition. But I don't want the way to the exhibition—I want the way out. There are passages to the right and passages to the left, but no exit sign."[2] In the dream, the placards appear in a London tube station, not in Paris, and the dream's next images present a man who claims he is her father.

Setting the pattern for subsequent readings of Sasha's dream and of the novel, Thomas Staley has written that "unlike nearly every other English prose writer of the period," Rhys's writing "seemed untouched by the devastating political and military events which had occurred and the even more horrendous ones which were on the horizon." He states, "Throughout the thirties Rhys's heroines saw the world from the inside rather than the outside," and concludes that "her work continued to rest on the power of style rather than new subject matter, intuition rather than analysis, the private rather than the public self."[3] Most critics agree with Staley and read Sasha's dream as an indicator of her conflicted psyche rather than a description of a city in conflict. I think we can entertain both possibilities. Throughout this book, I have argued that Rhys's writing undoes such dichotomies of thought as private/public and inside/outside; *Good Morning, Midnight* undoes them to such an extent that style becomes a political question not only touched by but wholly involved with the rise of fascism and the Second World War.

The intense conflicts between right and left that Paris suffered during the thirties and the rise of fascism within France as well as on its border with Germany are important circumstances to consider in our reading of Rhys's most complex and perhaps most disturbing novel. Not political in the conventional sense of discussing governments and ideologies, it nevertheless confronts head-on social violence against women and connects it to the persecution of Jews and other racial minorities. It invokes the temptations of order and peace at any price, problematizing such sacrifices in sexual terms. The social-historical context of the novel also helps us to examine and reconsider some of the critical debates that have arisen, in particular concerning the psychological implications of its very disturbing ending.

"**Y**es—yes—yes . . ." With these final words, Sasha Jansen welcomes into her bed a strange and repellant man, whose white nightgown has haunted her doorway and who has verbally and physically abused her.[4] The shocking choice disturbs us all the more because it is preceded by passages that portray Sasha being sexually assaulted by a man she confuses with this nameless and detested stranger.

Most often, the conclusion suggests to readers and critics some version of two opposing interpretations. The first sees Sasha's welcoming embrace of the nightmarish *commis* (she speculates that he is a traveling salesman) as a welcome to death, a death of self-respect or of the possibility for any unified self at all. Isolation and fragmentation have destroyed Sasha's attempts to reconstruct her life, and in the final scene she submits to the powers of alienation and sexual domination that overwhelm her. Rosalind Miles, for instance, emphasizes the many allusions to death that describe the *commis* and claims, "the man who offers sex, also offers death."[5]

The second interpretation stresses suggestions of rebirth through transcendence of the self in union with another human being. In this meeting with the man she has feared and avoided, parts of Sasha's splintered self seem to combine, implying the potential for a new whole. In support of this view, Peter Wolfe points to the description of Sasha in a fetal position, and Helen Nebeker describes an archetypal theme of passage, through death to rebirth.[6] Most critics, even those sensitive to the sexual submission portrayed in the passage, agree to a certain extent with this view, referring to Sasha's "psychic triumph"[7] or "the need for union beyond its simple erotic dimension."[8] To take either position means to stress some themes and images and to discount others, reducing a compelling ambiguity to a single dimension.[9] I would like to argue that we can best understand the ending's powerful ambiguity through consideration of the specific social conflicts that form the novel's setting and through analysis of the formal strategies that portray the two possibilities that make critics so uneasy. These formal elements and the conflicting social forces of the setting hinge upon one another in an experiment with form that also involves an exploration of power during a particular period in the history of modern Europe.

The man to whom Sasha says yes in this ending first appears in the opening dream, "dressed in a long white night shirt." In the dream he entreats her to "remember that I am your father." Blood streams from a wound in his forehead, and he cries "Murder, murder" until Sasha wakes from her own cries of "murder" (*Midnight*, p. 14). Leaving her room, she encounters on the landing her neighbor, "parading about as usual in his white dressing gown." The costume identifies the two figures; they metonymically replace each other through the white gown that evokes Sasha's dread and fear. The father in her dream implies that Sasha has forgotten his paternal relation; her forgetfulness seems connected to his wound, as if it makes her somehow responsible. Yet she, too, cries "murder" so that the victim's identity blurs in the ambiguity associating guilt and victimization.

The neighboring *commis*, whom she meets after awakening, appears to Sasha as "the ghost of the landing . . . thin as a skeleton" with "sunken dark eyes with a peculiar expression, cringing, ingratiating, knowing . . ." (*Midnight*, p. 14). She says she is always running into him and states, "I don't like this damned man . . ." (*Midnight*, p. 14). In various scenes in the novel she avoids him, physically resists him, and finally welcomes him into her arms. We are tempted to conclude with Miles and other critics in her camp that, by embracing the *commis* in the final scene, Sasha does welcome death. If so, her death is elevated to that of religious sacrifice, for Sasha compares the *commis* (the word also means "appointed one") to "a priest, the priest of some obscene, half-understood religion"; his dressing gown seems to her "like a priest's robes" (*Midnight*, p. 35).

The vision of this "father" completes the longer dream in which Sasha wanders about the passages of a London tube station where placards announce "This Way to the Exhibition." The placards suggest Paris as the dream's latent and more significant setting, and Sasha's inability to find a way out in the dream corresponds to her description of the Parisian street in which she rooms—"What they call an impasse." Her wish to avoid the exhibition brings to the dream image her perpetual anxiety and self-consciousness whenever she inhabits a public place. Though Sasha carefully constructs her days—"I have decided on a place to eat in at midday, a place to eat in at night, a place to have my drink in after dinner. I have arranged my little life" (*Midnight*, p. 9)—she plots them according to rituals of avoidance, hoping to escape the scenes of a previous love affair which still haunt her memories. When she awakens from her dream, she confronts an emotional impasse as she hears a man outside her room singing, "C'est l'amour qui flotte dans l'air à la ronde."

The dream does indicate the threat of death, but also of Sasha's possible complicity and guilt concerning the father-figure's wound. Her guilt is tied to the shame she feels for wanting to "be different from other people," for wishing to disobey the "steel finger [that] points along a long stone passage" (*Midnight*, p. 13). The dream inscribes difference and disobedience, masculine wounds, accusations of murder that blur victim and perpetrator, feminine feelings of shame and guilt, the fear of exhibition or humiliating public exposure, and political oppositions of left and right to which there appear no alternatives. As an introduction it presents both social and psychic conflicts, insisting that they are inseparable, and it suggests in the feminine consciousness that internalizes them an explicitly sexual dimension. As in *Wide Sargasso Sea*, the text of a dream makes possible the scripting of such complexly intertwined conflicts; the overdetermined quality of a dream, its openness and multiplicity, present problems and also various ways of posing, enacting, and resolving them. The dream sets the scene of narrative possibilities.

Good Morning, Midnight develops and brings together many of the elements of Rhys's other novels, the earlier ones as well as *Wide Sargasso Sea*. Like *After Leaving Mr. Mackenzie*, it takes place "after" more significant events, in this case, Sasha's love affair with Enno and, more broadly, Paris of the 1920s. It operates in at least two time frames then, as does *Voyage in the Dark*, the present time of 1937 and the previous decade, and Sasha tries without success to keep them separate. She quotes her friend Sidonie, who has recently given her money to stay for a while in Paris: ". . . one mustn't put everything on the same plane" (*Midnight*, p. 12). Like *After Leaving Mr. Mackenzie*, *Good Morning, Midnight* also brings up the possibilities of romance only to drop them, continuing the narrative through a nameless quest toward something unknown and threatening. The narrative thus counters conventional romance plots and makes interpretation through those conventions irrelevant. The guilt imposed upon and internalized by women between the two world wars, which structures *After Leaving Mr. Mackenzie*, also shapes *Good Morning, Midnight* in its circling around to the past and also, twice, to its own beginnings. Part III of the novel concludes with the same words that open Part I: "The room says: 'Quite like old times. Yes? . . . No? . . . Yes'" (*Midnight*, p. 145). Two more paragraphs appear as if in postscript, and then a final Part IV ensues that returns to the beginning dream, but, as in *Wide Sargasso Sea*, enacting it with important differences.

Good Morning, Midnight also invokes carnival images—masks and fairs—along with allusions to West Indian music and women from Martinique. In this way it posits an "elsewhere" and the logic of turnabout that may cue joyful liberation or madness and modern despair. However, the most important elements of this novel, which it shares with *Wide Sargasso Sea* and *Voyage in the Dark*, are the inscription of social conflict within a dream text and the protagonist's continual efforts to revise, through her visions and through internalized voices, the meaning of a life imbued with that conflict.

Sasha cannot escape, in her dream, the exhibition, nor in her life can she find a way out of her painful self-consciousness. Susan Squier has described her anxiety as "stage fright," linking it to the perpetual pressure Sasha feels to carry off a performance.[10] Always aware that she is acting, Sasha is never convinced of her role or of her interpretation. She recalls a scene in which her employer, whom she calls Mr. Blank, questions her qualifications. As she enters his office, she coaches herself: "Come on, stand straight, keep your head up, smile . . . No, don't smile. If you smile, he'll think you're trying to get off with him . . . Don't smile then, but look eager, alert, attentive. . . . You fool, stand straight . . ." (*Midnight*, p. 24). She has difficulty interpreting his role—"Of course he isn't doing it on purpose. He's just writing a letter . . . He is, he is. He's doing it on purpose . . ." (*Midnight*, p. 24). But Mr. Blank retains the ultimate

authority and finally casts her as a "hopeless, helpless little fool";
on cue, she begins to cry.

Once in a restaurant, Sasha is sure that two of the customers stare
at her, murmuring, "la Vielle." In another restaurant, the waiter and
the customers seem to collude in ridiculing Sasha. "Now everybody
in the room is staring at me; all the eyes in the room are fixed on
me. It has happened" (*Midnight*, p. 50). Later Sasha reconstructs the
scene and is able to piece together what she thinks probably happened: the waiter must have simply remarked to one of the customers that both she and Sasha are English. Nevertheless, Sasha continues to revise both scenes, fusing them in an accusatory question:
"What is she doing here, the stranger, the alien, the old one? . . . I
quite agree too, quite" (*Midnight*, p. 54).

"The stranger, the alien" suffers from social marginality that obliterates identity: "no name, no face, no country" (*Midnight*, p. 44).
Sasha's marginality forces her to play roles without scripts, impro-
vising parts for every situation because no stable social relations define, reinforce, or repeat a particular performance. Knowledge of her
part depends upon her audience and critics—on how others see her.
Her success depends on her ability to interpret their judgments,
which she alternately resists and internalizes. The theatrical images
that recur throughout the novel invoke a playfulness that becomes
simultaneously a matter of life and death. Lacking even the illusion
of a stable self, Sasha's life depends upon her theatrical success.

The audience that ridicules Sasha assaults her in a battle waged
with "voices like uniforms. . . . Those voices that they brandish like
weapons" (*Midnight*, p. 51). They win the war when Sasha surren-
ders and says, "I quite agree too, quite." As instruments of war, these
internalized voices contrast sharply to the voices recalled by Antoinette and Anna from their Caribbean communities of women, and
they differ, too, from the ironically rendered voices enjoining Anna
to act like a "lady." These military voices speak in a social context
of rising fascism and impending war. I don't think it is simply coin-
cidental that Sasha suspects Mr. Blank will interrogate her on her
ability to speak German. Unable or unwilling ("All the little German I know flies out of my head") to speak the language of the
Nazis, who already in 1937 occupy the Rhineland border with France,
Sasha instead recalls the poetry of the Jewish Heine, identifying
with Germans victimized by Germans and with a poet who makes
"little songs" out of his pain.[11] Her association of Mr. Blank with the
language of the Nazis characterizes his authority as fascistic; indeed, he terrorizes and humiliates her. She leaves her job because of

his abuse and only later is able to revise the meaning of her surrender. His power appears to her then as an objective economic force
which she can bitterly analyze:

> So you have the right to pay me four hundred francs a month, to
> lodge me in a small, dark room, to clothe me shabbily, to harass me
> with worry and monotony and unsatisfied longings till you get me to
> the point when I blush at a look, cry at a word. We can't all be happy,
> we can't all be rich, we can't all be lucky—and it would be so much
> less fun if we were. Isn't it so, Mr. Blank? Let's say you have this
> mystical right to cut my legs off. But the right to ridicule me after-
> wards because I'm a cripple—no, that I think you haven't got. And
> that's the right you hold most dearly, isn't it? You must be able to
> despise the people you exploit. (*Midnight*, p. 29)

The nightmare arises when, ashamed, Sasha blames herself for being
different:

> I say: "I want the way out." But he points to the placards and his
> hand is made of steel. I walk along with my head bent, very
> ashamed, thinking: "Just like me—always wanting to be different
> from other people." The steel finger points along a long stone pas-
> sage. This Way—This Way—This Way to the Exhibition. . . .
>   Now a little man, bearded, with a snub nose, dressed in a long
> white night-shirt, is talking earnestly to me. "I am your father," he
> says. "Remember that I am your father." But blood is streaming from
> a wound in his forehead. (*Midnight*, p. 13)

The internalization of the authority of "other people" and her submission to the mechanical power of their steellike commands and
questions prefaces the shift in Sasha's dream to the vision of the
murdered father, or rather, the man who claims he is her father and
thus hopes to assert patriarchal authority at the same time he im-
putes the guilt of patricide. This is the moment in the dream text
when the modern machine, fascistic domination, and patriarchal authority become coextensive with one another. The threat of war ar-
chitecturally represented in the confrontation between the Nazi and
Soviet exposition buildings joins the futurist emphasis on the machine, celebrated in the exhibition's tremendous Italian pavilion devoted to Mussolini's Italy. This threat becomes simultaneously a
sexual threat linked to paternal authority and the subordination of
women in the family, principles held firmly by both the Italian and

German fascists and, it might be argued, democratic and socialist states as well.[12]

In making these connections, Rhys implies a vision and analysis shared by other modernist women writers. In 1936 Gertrude Stein wrote: "There is too much fathering going on just now and there is no doubt about it fathers are depressing. Everybody now-a-days is a father, there is father Mussolini and father Hitler and father Roosevelt and father Stalin and father Trotzky [sic] and father Blum and father Franco is just commencing now and there are ever so many more ready to be one. Fathers are depressing."[13] Virginia Woolf, too, wrote quite explicitly of the tyranny exercised hand in hand by fascism and patriarchy. In *Three Guineas*, published in 1938, just one year before *Good Morning, Midnight* appeared, Woolf describes "the figure of a man, . . . tightly cased in a uniform . . . And behind him lie ruined houses and dead bodies . . ."[14] In Woolf's image, these are the ruined houses and dead bodies she viewed in photographs of the war in Spain, a direct result of fascism and war, but they are also the ruined "private houses" of England and the dead bodies of tyrannical fathers' rebellious daughters. To illustrate her point further, she alludes to the punishment given Antigone, the espoused daughter of Creon, who dared to obey a law higher than his: "And he shut her not in Holloway or in a concentration camp, but in a tomb. And Creon we read brought ruin on his house, and scattered the land with the bodies of the dead."[15] Here Woolf is developing the analysis that made *Three Guineas* at once so radical and so unacceptable to many readers: " . . . that the public and the private worlds are inseparably connected; that the tyrannies and servilities of the one are the tyrannies and servilities of the other."[16]

Woolf's essay addresses and speaks for the "daughters of educated men," middle-class women barred from education and the professions, made to curry the favor of men on whom they were forced to depend for their livelihood. While identifying metaphorically with the plight of prostitutes and marginal women, Woolf nevertheless concerned herself with the sufferings of respectable women, confined domestically, but still placed within the "system of the fathers." Rhys's novels, on the other hand, perceive the same forces at work from the point of view of those women displaced by them, enduring not only the humiliations of dependency but also lacking even the respectability granted by middle-class fathers' incomes.

In this light, we can revise, at least provisionally until we examine the concluding scenes more carefully, the interpretation of the ending of *Good Morning, Midnight* as an embrace, through sex, of

death. If the *commis* in his white nightshirt is metonymically identified with the murdered father in Sasha's dream, the "sex" he offers
is far more than a physical act. It is a nameless and questionable patriarchal authority, demanding submission to tabooed relations and
forcing, through fascistic terror, Sasha's complicity in her own abuse
and death. With this provisional interpretation, we are farther than
ever from the possibility in the final scene of the rebirth that many
critics suggest.

However, the numerous allusions to death and suicide throughout the novel precede scenes that suggest transformation. For instance, when Sasha feels humiliated in a restaurant, her anxiety and
self-consciousness prompt suicidal fantasies—"Now I am going to
cry. This is the worst. . . . If I do that I shall really have to walk
under a bus when I get outside" (*Midnight*, p. 51). Instead of walking
under a bus, Sasha does what some anthropologists claim people do
everywhere when the danger of death looms too menacingly—she
invents a ritual: [17] "I try to decide what colour I shall have my hair
dyed and hang on to that thought as you hang on to something when
you are drowning. Shall I have it red? Shall I have it black? . . . First
it must be bleached, that is to say, its own colour must be taken out
of it—and then it must be dyed, that is to say, another colour must
be imposed on it" (*Midnight*, pp. 51–52). In her fantasy, she even includes the voice of the shaman or priest of the ritual—"But blond
cendré, madame, is the most difficult of colours" (*Midnight*, p. 52).
The ritualistic stripping of the victim's own identity (its own color)
so that a new one may be imposed is precisely enacted in this otherwise ordinary feminine activity.

Sasha repeatedly performs similar rites, all part of what she calls
"the transformation act." She buys a hat, a procedure that takes two
hours and involves an intensely intimate interaction with the shop
girl—"there is no one else in the shop. It is quite dark outside. We
are alone, celebrating this extraordinary ritual" (*Midnight*, p. 70).
The celebration restores calm and order, preventing for a while any
further violence. After she has her hair dyed ("a very good blond
cendré. A success."), Sasha notes, "It's curious how peaceful I feel—
as if I were possessed by something" (*Midnight*, p. 62). With other
people, all very orderly, she watches some fish in a pool in the Lux-
embourg Gardens: "We stand in a row, watching the fish" (*Midnight*,
p. 63). And following the hat purchase: "I feel saner and happier after
this. . . . Nobody stares at me, which I think is a good sign." A man
begins a conversation with her: "I think: 'That's all right . . .'" (*Midnight*, p. 71).

The rituals and their results contain dual possibilities: on the one hand, they create beauty; they allow strangers to meet in orderly ways, enjoying prescribed intimacy; and they restore calm. On the other hand, Sasha must submit to the priestlike administrations of others who manipulate her body, so that she is "possessed by something." The calm achieved seems to require a robotlike order and passivity; it allows safe but empty conversations. While allaying the danger of actual death or suicide, the rituals enact the death of a previous self, restoring peace and order through procedures designed to transform Sasha into someone else.

We might see Sasha as preparing herself for an even larger ritual, the sacrifice foreshadowed by her dream and the priestlike *commis.* We can also see the temptations of order at any price, including the annihilation of unique individual identity. Yet Sasha acts, improvises, defends herself against death. Transforming herself, she connects with others, loses for a moment her fear and paranoia. The dual possibilities of death and rebirth are initiated and recreated throughout the novel in rituals which, while indicating danger, also codify her marginality and temporarily integrate her into a social order.

The rituals allow Sasha to rescript her role; however, as in her dream, she creates a part that then seems to control her, appearing as her fate. Each new role requires a new costume. Again, as for Rhys's other protagonists, clothes become charms or fetishes on which her fate depends. When Mr. Blank humiliates Sasha, she assures herself that if she had only been wearing a particular black dress with embroidered sleeves, the incident could never have happened. She always wears over her other clothes a fur coat that her lover Enno had given to her. She remembers that, at the time of his gift, she had also changed her name from Sophia to Sasha. The coat, she later guesses, is ironically responsible for attracting a hopeful gigolo, the young man who eventually assaults and robs her. "Of course. I've got it. Oh Lord, is that what I look like? Do I really look like a wealthy dame trotting round Montparnasse in the hope of—? After all the trouble I've gone to, is that what I look like?" (*Midnight*, p. 72). Again, she cannot be certain of her role or audience.

Ironically, though, the fur is fake, her hair color is false, and she could not afford the authentic "taste" of the black dress. She consumes and is consumed by a world of artificiality, false objects whose only significance is symbolic, the props of ritual and theater.[18] For Sasha herself is not a "real" person—she is only whatever her appearance, current name, and image make her. When Sasha states, ". . . no name, no face, no country," she adds, "I don't belong anywhere" (*Midnight*, p. 44). Echoing Antoinette's words describing

lack of place, Sasha suggests that selfhood does not result from character but from location. She lacks both the *patria* and the patronym
which would place her in the social order. Though she speculates
that others perceive her as English, she never states for certain her
national identity. We discover, instead, the instability of national
identity for a woman, no longer married, in this period. The "pa-
tron" demands to see her passport twice when she rents a room: the
numbers are missing, she should have put nationality by marriage.
But the marriage has dissolved; it no longer identifies her and really
it never could have—Enno resembled a stranger more than a husband: "He was a chansonnier, it seems, before he became a jour-
nalist. He enlisted during the first week of the war. From 1917 on-
wards a gap. He seemed prosperous when I met him in London, but
no money now—nix. What happened? He doesn't tell me" (*Midnight*, p. 114). Displaced from family, country, and marriage, Sasha
appears to herself and to others as a fake (an illusion, mask, role)
who consumes false objects (fake fur, artificial color) in relation to
others who also lack authentic identity. All is illusion, magic, a
shamanistic trick.

However, she becomes aware of the also illusory but empty and
cruel nature of the apparently stable and consolidated selves enjoyed
by men like Mr. Blank and the "extremely respectable": "They think
in terms of a sentimental ballad. . . . Everything in their whole
bloody world is a cliché. Everything is born out of a cliché, rests on a
cliché, survives by a cliché. And they believe in the clichés—there's
no hope" (*Midnight*, p. 42). With her theatrical gestures Sasha fights
enemies of style and language, the overused metaphors of a stale hypocrisy. Gesture undermines the certainty of what *is*. It mimes and
parodies that which is real and confuses lies with truth.[19] As Rhys's
character realizes, these "respectable tongues" already confuse lies
with truth in their reified formulae for living and dying; but when
one takes into one's own hands the magic of appearances, one grasps
the possibility of turning that magic back against the world. Hence,
in her successful moments, Sasha creates her own rituals, invents
her own transformations; at other times she becomes the victim in
ritualistic sacrifices designed by others.

Though Sasha's anxiety in these situations appears "paranoid, ob-
sessive" to the reader perhaps,[20] she nevertheless represents, in every
way, the perfect victim. In his discussion of ritual sacrifice, René
Girard states,

> If we look at the extremely wide spectrum of human victims sacri-
> ficed by various societies, the list seems heterogeneous, to say the

least. It includes prisoners of war, slaves, small children, unmarried adolescents, and the handicapped. . . . Is it possible to detect a unifying factor in this disparate group? We notice at first glance beings who are either outside or on the fringes of society. . . . What we are dealing with, therefore, are exterior or marginal individuals, incapable of establishing or sharing the social bonds that link the rest of the inhabitants. Their status as foreigners or enemies, their servile condition, or simply their age prevents these future victims from fully integrating themselves into the community.[21]

Girard notes that in most communities women are never fully integrated individuals but retain a secondary status. Nevertheless, he claims that they are not often offered as sacrifices because they belong to families who might interpret the act as murder and counter with an act of vengeance, thereby escalating the violence the sacrifice sought to allay. Girard proposes that the threat of violence among members of a community requires the sacrifice of someone who is both inside and outside the community—someone who will substitute for its members but not provoke retribution. While women in traditional societies may not fulfill the last of these requirements, single women in modern urban societies, especially single foreign women, wanderers and derelicts, may become fully "sacrificeable individuals." Without kin or allies, Sasha can only fantasize her revenge: "One day, quite suddenly, when you're not expecting it, I'll take a hammer from the folds of my dark cloak and crack your little skull like an egg-shell" (*Midnight*, p. 52).

As Girard points out, sacrificeable individuals may be accused of some fundamentally threatening transgression such as parricide, incest, or infanticide. The sacrifice of such a victim, who need not be actually guilty, thus upholds the taboos that make civilization possible and promotes peace and order among a community that came dangerously close to somehow annihilating itself. Living on the verge of a second world war, Sasha recalls the aftermath of the first in the 1920s: "But people are doing crazy things all over the place. The war is over. No more war—never, never, never. Après la guerre, there'll be a good time everywhere . . ." (*Midnight*, p. 114). The Great War, of course, involved more than single opposing communities, as did the Second World War. In their international scope, they created thousands of homeless gypsies like Sasha, her husband, the gigolo, the Russian Jews she meets, even the traveling stranger in the white dressing gown. These marginalized individuals may indeed have committed various crimes. The gigolo, whose national identity, like Sasha's, is entirely uncertain, searches desperately for forged papers. Enno's money, when he could acquire it, came from unknown sources and disappeared just as mysteriously. But only Sasha is associated with the worst crimes since her baby died just after birth. The woman at the nursing home swathed Sasha in bandages to erase all stretch marks from the pregnancy in another ritual act of transformation: "And there he is lying with a ticket round his wrist because he died in a hospital. And there I am looking at him, without one line, without one wrinkle, without one crease . . ." (*Midnight*, p. 61). She had not been able to welcome the birth in the first place because of her poverty. Now, the child dead, all appearances testify to her never having given birth at all; an illusion acquires a life-and-death magic. And then she is haunted by a man, who claims he is her father, claims he has been murdered, and wants her to sleep with him. Circumstances threaten to frame Sasha, making her appear guilty at a time when the precarious communities of Paris and Europe seem about to annihilate themselves once again.

Describing Janet Flanner's letters from Paris to New York during the 1930s, Shari Benstock has highlighted their concern with "French psychology and the stronghold of Fascism within its own borders." Flanner attributed France's indigenous fascism to an inability to accept its status, in relation to Hitler's Germany, as a second-rate European power.[22] By 1932 France was seriously affected by the international economic depression. Unemployment was high and wages low. As one writer describes the economic and political situation of the 1930s: "The French economy entered a period of stagnation that continued to the outbreak of World War II . . . [and] coincided with a declining international position that also lasted throughout the decade."[23] The economic crisis resulted in a shift to "political extremes." In particular, right-wing and fascist groups held forth in the streets of Paris. The largest of these groups, the Croix de Feu, wore uniforms and held mass maneuvers. Another writer, living in Paris at the time, has described a riot that took place in February of 1934. In this confrontation, numerous right-wing groups, including the Crois de Feu and led by the Royalist Action Française party, battled police for days. Shooting broke out, and hospitals filled with the wounded. The mob seemed to this witness clearly intent on a coup, and was prevented from actually succeeding by a wavering leadership.[24]

Other acts of violence erupted in the 1930s, including the murder of the Yugoslavian king and a French official, as they walked through Paris, by Mussolini-supported fascists. Though a socialist was elected prime minister in 1936, he resigned in the midst of chaos and corruption a year later (the year in which *Good Morning, Midnight* takes place), having lost support of even the leftists. Also in 1937 a bomb exploded near the Étoile. At first the Communists received blame for the violence, but it was later discovered that the Cagoulards, a right-wing group, were responsible. At the time of the exhibition's opening, most displays and buildings were not even ready due to the unrest and disorganization caused by severe labor disputes.[25]

The narrative of *Good Morning, Midnight* does not, in any explicit way, allude to these events. It concentrates instead on the intensely rendered perceptions of an isolated and marginalized woman, who wages her own internal battles while inhabiting the violent and chaotic streets of Paris. But as her dream makes clear, these battles are not separate ones. The violence of the public world manipulates Sasha's physical movements, directs her rituals, and threatens her psyche. In the figure of the *commis*, it seeks her out and harasses her with criminal accusations and the threat of death. Her theatrical gestures and ritualistic attempts at transformation seem merely holding operations—with one exception: when Sasha meets an exiled Russian painter, she experiences a moment of carnivalesque community that truly, though temporarily, transforms her. The catalysts of her metamorphosis are the West African masks that line the painter's studio.

In earlier passages, theatrical allusions have signified manipulation, deceit, and desperate artificiality. For instance, Sasha describes the shop in which she worked under Mr. Blank as if it were a stage set: "It was a large white-and-gold room with a dark-polished floor. Imitation Louis Quinze chairs, painted screens, three or four elongated dolls, beautifully dressed, with charming and malicious oval faces" (*Midnight*, p. 17). Sasha says of these dolls, ". . . what a success they would have made of their lives if they had been women. Satin skin, silk hair, velvet eyes, sawdust hearts—all complete" (*Midnight*, p. 18). Indeed the women she works with are called mannequins. Sasha often describes faces as masks and says "you can almost see the strings that are pulling the puppets" (*Midnight*, p. 90). These passages recall Bakhtin's discussion of the mask and the marionette, particularly the change in their meanings that he attributes to romanticism and modernism. In these periods, Bakhtin argues, the mask's earlier carnival significance gives way to a form that "hides something, keeps a secret, deceives . . . ," and the marionette presents "the puppet as victim of alien human forces."[26] Eventually Sasha's own face becomes another prop: "Besides it isn't my face, this tortured and tormented mask. I can take it off whenever I like and hang it up on a nail. Or shall I place on it a tall hat with a green feather, hang a veil over the lot, and walk about the dark streets so merrily?" (*Midnight*, p. 43).

The relationships between Rhys's characters and men remind some readers of more pornographic connotations of wearing a mask. Judith Thurman refers to the woman in *The Story of O* who wears a mask given by her master to excite him. Though he treats her with sadistic brutality, she finds she cannot or does not wish to remove the mask.[27]

The masks that line the painter's studio walls play a different role in the construction of ritual and performance. In this scene, probably the only one of its kind in the entire novel, Sasha becomes neither a victim nor a solitary fanatic, but acts in concert with others. And here we find several clues to her background and the site of other possible identities. At first the masks threaten Sasha; she thinks they must be West African but then says she has seen them before: "That's the way they look when they are saying: 'Why didn't you drown yourself in the Seine?' That's the way they look when they are saying: 'Qu'est-ce qu'elle fout ici, la vieille?' . . . Peering at you. Who are you anyway? Who's your father and have you got any money, and if not, why not? Are you one of us?" (*Midnight*, p. 92). All of these questions target Sasha as the perfect "sacrificeable victim" and give the masks the alienating and cruel intentions that Bakhtin associates with the modernist mask. Serge, however, transforms them by holding a mask over his face while dancing to the Martinique beguine music that is playing on an old gramophone. His dance brings them together, comrades in their exile and in their masquerade. With him, Sasha loses even her compulsive desire for a drink. She begs Serge to continue dancing as a vision of herself appears: "I am lying in a hammock looking up into the branches of a tree. The sound of the sea advances and retreats as if a door were being opened and shut. All day there has been a fierce wind blowing, but at sunset it drops. The hills look like clouds and the clouds like fantastic hills" (*Midnight*, p. 92).

This image describes in part a photograph of Jean Rhys taken during a return visit to her native Caribbean just three years before the publication of *Good Morning, Midnight*.[28] But even if we did not know about the picture, we could identify through the West African allusions and West Indian music the locale of Sasha's vision. The connection with the Caribbean extends throughout the evening as Serge tells her of his encounter in London with a Martinique woman—"She wasn't a white woman. She was half-Negro—a mulatto . . . She was drunk too" (*Midnight*, p. 95). The woman had presented herself at his door, desperately unhappy because of the prejudice and open hostility she encountered. Serge could think of no way to help her. He had the feeling that she "was no longer quite human, no longer quite

still determine this fate and may even script it in accordance with the fulfillment of friendship that now makes her so happy.

Sasha's happiness is short-lived, however. The possibilities for romantic friendship and community promised by her moment with Serge ends when he does not show for their next date. Delmar meets with her instead and bores her with long monologues about the glories of monarchy. Aware that Sasha prefers his friend, Delmar begins to criticize Serge, accusing him of madness and stating, "I've had enough of these people of the extreme Left. They have bad manners. Moi, je suis monarchiste . . ." (*Midnight*, p. 103). Sasha's return to protective cynicism following this disappointment has as much to do with the political implications of the scene as with her psychological state. With the Left, represented through Delmar by Serge, in retreat and the Right, in the figure and voice of Delmar, opposed and on the offensive, Sasha no longer sees a "way out" of the systems of "the fathers"; she is thrust back into the impasse of her dream. The painting she eventually does purchase of the sad-eyed banjo player, "double-headed and with four arms," no longer seems an invitation to happiness; rather it mocks her.

The modernist despair now elicited by the painted banjo player's mockery builds in the ensuing scenes with the gigolo René, as Sasha heads reluctantly, then willingly, toward the exhibition. The impasse Sasha inhabits once again is portrayed in the text through dramatic metaphors that frequently shift to comments on fictional technique. The text's countering of romantic expectations in the failure of Sasha's friendship with Serge seems necessitated by political contingencies, social conflicts that become increasingly related to artistic form and style.

When Sasha meets René, the two "actors" become so aware of their respective performances that he refers to their "comedy": these fictional characters play the parts of theatrical actors who are playing various roles. Sasha's roles include that of a ghost-writer. In this way, René leads Sasha toward a kind of madness associated with theatrical subversions of "reality" and with the question of literary value.[31] They become the producers and directors of their "play," splitting Sasha's role into two parts with two voices, "I" and "she."

In her scenes with René, Sasha attempts to replay the friendly, potentially romantic part that failed with Serge. Even though or perhaps because René announces that he is a "mauvais garçon," Sasha feels sympathy for him; with him she feels "natural and happy, just as if I were young—but really young. I've never been young . . . I've never played . . ." (*Midnight*, p. 155). Of course, she has always "played" in the theatrical sense of the term, and its meaning becomes all the more complex as acting and the theater become metaphors for writing. René persists in discussing his style and the technique of his "métier" while Sasha recalls a time when she landed a job dictating fairy stories for a wealthy woman from Montparnasse. The woman's publisher complained of Sasha's style—too many words of one syllable:

> Sitting at a large desk, a white sheet of paper in front of me and outside the sun and the blue Mediterranean. Monte Carlo, Monte Carlo, but the Med-it-er-rany-an sea-ee, Monte Carlo, Monte Carlo, where the boy of my heart waits for me-ee. . . . Persian garden. Long words. Chiaroscuro? Translucent? . . . I bet he'd like cataclysmal action and centrifugal flux, but the point is how can I get them into a Persian garden? . . . A blank piece of paper . . . (*Midnight*, p. 167)

Thus, Sasha the fictional character becomes Sasha the actress with many masks, one of which is a writer of corrupt fictions. Evidently one of the problems with her ghost-writing is not so much the length of the words but their kind. The opposition between imaginary Persian gardens and words like "cataclysmal action" suggests the modernist artist's problem in the face of twentieth-century technology: how to make it new, how to avoid both clichés of the past and the subordination of art to technical instrumentality. The exhibition's overriding emphasis on "techniques appliqués" promises the triumph of technology; Delmar's political diatribe has effectively silenced the influence of Serge's tears for Van Gogh, and all Sasha can now imagine is a blank piece of paper.

In the meantime, the other "player," René, discusses the importance of technique. And in the passages recounting Sasha's memories of her marriage and its demise, she reminds herself of narrative requirements: "This happened and that happened. . . . Not all at once, of course. First this happened, and then that happened . . ." (*Midnight*, pp. 142–143). With these injunctions on narrative, Sasha attempts to censor what she calls her "film mind," the impulse to reel out memories on the same plane with the present, to juxtapose scenes rather than connect them through the linear logic of chronological time or to distinguish between imagined and actual incidents.

The crimes of parricide, incest, and infanticide with which sacrificial victims are generally charged are those that abolish distinctions essential to the growth of civilized order. The modernist dissolution of distinctions between present and past, public and private, outer and inner experience appears guilty then of degeneration; in its challenge to hierarchy and paternity, modernism is indeed degenerate art. And in modern urban society, women become the perceived focus of this degeneration; their ambiguous presence in the streets and public places and the lack of normative codes of sexual conduct create conflict that requires either their constraint or sacrifice. As in Sasha's scene with Mr. Blank, they may be unable to speak the language in power; their own words may be bound in silence: "Every word I say has chains round its ankles; every thought I think is weighted with heavy weights. Since I was born, hasn't every word I've said, every thought I've thought, everything I've done been tied up, weighted, chained?" (*Midnight*, p. 106).

However, Sasha's ritualistic transformations give her the chance to change, through stylistic innovation, the mechanical directions of the steel fingers in her dream and to possibly rewrite the commands ("This Way to the Exhibition") of their signs. Sasha clings to her illusions and longs to piece them together in new and fanciful ways. Yet of the gigolo's concentration on technique, she thinks, "—it sounds quite meaningless. It probably is meaningless. He's just trying to shock me or excite me or something . . ." (*Midnight*, p. 157). Sasha is terrified of the cost of such play. She fears that, at bottom, the improvisations and innovations of style—including her attempts at renewal—will be exposed as mere tricks, artificial and deceptive. As Girard has stated, "The very essence of modern society might be said to be its ability to sustain the possibility for new discoveries in the midst of an ever-worsening sacrificial crisis—not, to be sure, without many signs of anxiety and stress."[32]

The paradox of style that troubles Sasha—its power to effect new discoveries in the midst of crisis and the threat it presents of empty but controlling mechanical form—is inscribed in the formal strategies of the text in ways that help to explain the ambiguity and unease created by its conclusion. Two narrative methods continually vie with one another to create a complex and contradictory style; they also parallel the dual aspects of ritual that engage Sasha. Through one strategy, Rhys presents Sasha in varying degrees of split consciousness. Isolating and fracturing Sasha's perceptions, this strategy begins with abrupt shifts from first-person narration to direct interior monologues and back again. In the following passage, for example, we plunge directly into an interior monologue associating Sasha's memories of washrooms; just as suddenly, we switch to the present and first-person narration:

The lavabo in Florence and the very pretty, fantastically-dressed girl
who rushed in, hugged and kissed the old dame tenderly and fed her
with cakes out of a paper bag. The dancer-daughter? . . . That cosy
little Paris lavabo, where the attendant peddled drugs—something to
heal a wounded heart.

When I got upstairs the American and his friend had gone. "It was
something I remembered," I told the waiter, and he looked at me
blankly, not even bothering to laugh at me. (*Midnight*, p. 11)

The narrative fracturing of time and voice portrays Sasha at her most
desperate moments, in this case humiliated in a public bar where
she breaks into tears. The abrupt shifts from present to past portray
her struggles to revive, through memory, an identity now violently
disordered.

The second formal strategy, which perhaps builds on this fragmentation but also competes with it, is that of a poetic logic that
combines, condenses, and potentially transforms Sasha's fragmented
perceptions into newly unified acts and symbols. The most potentially renewing images resulting from this strategy appear in the visions she experiences in Serge's studio. The peaceful, empty room
with its opening door is transformed by its connection to the Caribbean Sea, Sasha's first and only, though imaginary, successful attempt at changing her room. In Part I, frightened by her dream and
threatened by her ghostly neighbor, she hopes to change everything
by changing her room. She decides she must have number 219—
"Who says you can't escape from your fate? I'll escape from mine,
into room number 219. Just try me, just give me a chance" (*Midnight*, p. 37). However, the hotel receptionist will not cooperate
with her request, and she returns to her old room:

A room? . . . But never tell the truth about this business of rooms,
because it would bust the roof off everything and undermine the
whole social system. All rooms are the same. . . .
The room welcomes me back. (*Midnight*, pp. 38, 39)

Through the recollection of particular rooms, Sasha attempts
to construct her memories. Part III of the novel consists entirely
of these memories; the passages begin typically with lines like
". . . *The room at the Steens'*" (*Midnight*, p. 113) or ". . . *The room
in the hotel in Amsterdam that night*" (*Midnight*, p. 116)—solitary,
introductory lines each marked by italics as if presenting a play-
wright's stage instructions. These rooms introduce Sasha and the

reader to her past and, as memories, become the connecting scenes in her search for an identity more solid and consistent than the scattered and improvised roles she now invents. But in each one of these rooms she meets barriers she must circumvent: desperate poverty, her pregnancy and the death of her child, Enno's faithlessness, and, finally, his abandonment, leaving her once again in a room: "A room? A nice room? A beautiful room with a bath? Swing high, swing low, swing to and fro . . . This happened and that happened . . ." (*Midnight*, p. 142). Unable to consolidate her self by placing it in rooms of the past, Sasha turns back to the narrative requirements of realist chronology. She also relies on irony, typical of the social criticism and self-criticism expressed in Anna's "voices" in *Voyage in the Dark*. In both novels, this voice indicates a resistant yet despairing effort to sustain multivocality in the absence or failure of carnival satire. Only in the community that she finds with Serge and Delmar and through the opening Serge gives her into another place and time can she fulfill her "self" and successfully change her room. The new room she envisions within the new room of Serge's studio and the exhibition he and Delmar set up provides the only possible exit from the Exhibition Internationale.

René, however, proves a poor understudy for Serge. He wants Sasha's money; he wants to use her sexually. As he begins to turn against her, the two formal strategies vie intensely with one another. Toward the novel's conclusion, Sasha parodies her own efforts at scriptwriting: "Thinking how funny a book would be, called 'Just a Cérébrale or You Can't Stop Me From Dreaming.' Only, of course, to be accepted as authentic, to carry any conviction, it would have to be written by a man" (*Midnight*, p. 161). She recognizes, with modernist female irony, that in this time and place, only a man's text, even dream text, appears authentic. The paradox of style is gender-coded, and in the misogynist Europe preceding World War II, her dreams of renewal through style will be dismissed as false.

Convinced by René that she is, "in fact, a monster," Sasha is ready to visit the exhibition. Here she finds "what I imagined," the Star of Peace. The place is "cold, empty, beautiful," and Sasha feels content, as if in the aftermath of another sacrificial transformation. One description of the 1937 exhibition in Paris refers to this emblem of peace:

Even without looking beyond the exhibition itself, those who visited
the international sector at the foot of the Trocadero hill must have
been gravely perturbed at the great pavilions of Germany and Russia,

challenging one another for dominance of the scene just as the nations themselves were soon to challenge one another for dominance
of the world, while the slim symbol of Peace, standing at the back of
the hill, seemed to be virtually crowded out of the picture.³³

The symbol could only have presented to Sasha another false promise. But false or not, "This is what I wanted—the cold fountains, the
cold rainbow lights on the water . . ." (*Midnight*, p. 164). Sasha's
willing acceptance of the exhibition's cold, empty beauty and its
false peace indicates her now willing sacrifice.

The gigolo accuses Sasha, this time of the crime committed by
them both: "You love playing a comedy, don't you?" Only her part in
the crime as a woman, however, makes her guilty and punishable. It
is as if the power exercised by Mr. Blank has not been sufficient to
silence Sasha's critical and parodic plays with style and language.
Now sexual violence erupts to forcefully purge her of such multivocality. In the struggle that follows, René pins Sasha to the bed,
threatening her with stories about gang rapes " 'for women like you,
who pretend and lie and play an idiotic comedy all the time . . . Je te
ferai mal, he says. 'It's your fault'" (*Midnight*, p. 182).

René demands that Sasha give "the ritual answer" to his commands and that she change her voice, "I don't like it . . . that voice."
Sasha tells him where she hides her money and begs him to leave a
little. When he finally departs, Sasha's voice does change. The narrative strategy of fragmentation takes over as she splits into another
kind of monster—a Dr. Jekyll and Mr. Hyde with two voices, first-
person "I" and third-person "she":

> Who is this crying? The same one who laughed on the landing,
> kissed him and was happy. This is me, this is myself, who is crying.
> The other one—how do I know who the other is? She isn't me.
>   Her voice in my head: "Well, well, well, just think of that now.
> What an amusing ten days! Positively packed with thrills. The last
> performance of What's-her-name And Her Boys or It Was All Due To
> An Old Fur Coat." (*Midnight*, p. 184)

"She" continues a sarcastic commentary alongside Sasha's "own"
voice. It seems this real self is only alive in pain—"My mouth hurts,
my breasts hurt, because it hurts, when you have been dead, to come
alive . . ." (*Midnight*, p. 182). Sasha believes that the voice who says
"I" resembles most the Sasha who was happy with Serge and who

felt for a moment that youthful romance was still possible with the gigolo; the second voice speaks for the Sasha who continually rewrites her script as a cynical parody. That the second voice has become "Other" to the "I" who speaks suggests perhaps that Sasha may have identified her "real self." However, the discovery exacts the price of pain and the death of her playful, parodic voice. Its greatest sacrifice is that of the multivocality that has rendered Sasha's consciousness so vital and critically perceptive.

Girard argues that the victim in ritual sacrifice becomes a "monstrous double," a doubling characterized by the individual's capacity to partake of "all possible differences within the community, particularly the difference between within and without . . ."[34] This doubling now severs Sasha in two. "She" departs, leaving Sasha with a mutilated, one-dimensional "I."

Then suddenly a new image appears, one that combines and condenses, creating formally the possibility of unity. The image expresses the results of her isolation and fragmentation, and it also portrays the artificiality and deception that Sasha has feared to discover and that René claims to have exposed in her gestures of style:

All that is left in the world is an enormous machine, made of white steel. It has innumerable flexible arms, made of steel. Long, thin arms. At the end of each arm is an eye, the eyelashes stiff with mascara. When I look more closely I see that only some of the arms have these eyes—others have lights. The arms that carry the eyes and the arms that carry the lights are all extraordinarily flexible and very beautiful. But the grey sky, which is the background, terrifies me. . . . And the arms wave to an accompaniment of music and of song. Like this: "Hotcha—hotcha—hotcha. . . ." And I know the music; I can sing the song. (*Midnight*, p. 187)

While the image itself expresses a futurist vision of mechanical fragmentation, the formal process of dream logic and metaphor creates this vision through a movement of condensation and unification.

The machine in Sasha's vision gains its meaning from associations with artificial limbs she has glimpsed in a shop window, the makeup she wears, the steel hand in her dream that points the way to the exhibition, and the stage lights that expose the crudity of a song that she knows well. In an earlier passage, Sasha has quoted a line from a poem in Heinrich Heine's "Lyrical Intermezzo": "aus meinen grossen Schmerzen mach ich die kleinen Lieder" (out of my great pains I make the little songs). The vision now exposes her songs as the dance-hall rhythms of mass culture, not the poetry she might have hoped for.

Here she recognizes herself as part of a feminized mass culture that she dreads for its mechanical artificiality. Yet its beauty attracts. Describing the great European exhibitions, Walter Benjamin wrote: "The world exhibitions glorify the exchange value of commodities. They create a framework in which commodities' intrinsic value is eclipsed. They open up a phantasmagoria that people enter to be amused. The entertainment industry facilitates this by elevating people to the level of commodities. They submit to being manipulated while enjoying their alienation from themselves and others."[35] Benjamin and Rhys, I would argue, see such deceitful and inauthentic pleasure in mass culture, not because of an elitest philosophy of individualism, but because of the totalitarian ideologies swaying masses of people during the 1930s. Associations among "the masses," "the primitive" or "the savage," and "the feminine" take a new turn in this era as masses of Europeans acquire more truly savage characteristics in paradoxically ordered and orderly ways. Rhys's novels are also, as we have seen, particularly sensitive to the commodification of women that mass culture makes so visible, and in *Good Morning, Midnight* Sasha fears the ordered sane existence that makes her "a bit of an automaton."

Yet in creating the machine vision, Sasha potentially transforms the fragmentation that has compelled her to improvise and borrow identities through commodified gestures into something whole. When she then begins to will the gigolo back into her room and finds that the man who does enter is wearing the white dressing gown of her nightmare, again the metaphorical process combines and condenses fragments of her consciousness; it must be the white nightgown because only that gown will crystallize the process, only then can she make a gesture that, as most readers believe, indicates triumph, union, rebirth: "I think: 'Is it the blue dressing-gown, or the white one? That's very important. I must find that out—it's very important.' I take my arm away from my eyes. It is the white dressing-gown" (*Midnight*, p. 190). The recurrence of the white dressing-gown—on the wounded figure in Sasha's dream who claims to be her father and screams "murder!"; on the priestlike *commis* whom Sasha compares to a skeleton and a ghost, who haunts the hallway of her rooming house and once tries to push his way into her room; and, finally, on the figure who enters her room in the concluding passage, "his mean eyes flickering"—becomes a symbol of all that Sasha has feared, of death itself. But the formal process that gives the image its power combines into the final, intense moment all of the previously fragmented elements of that image.

If this conclusion does indicate a way out of Sasha's "impasse," the sense of potential comes from the formal ambiguity of the passage. The ambiguity operates on several levels to become intensely disturbing to readers. First, the dream logic that creates these final metaphors vies with the narrative portrayals of fragmentation and mutilation that culminate in the split into first- and third-person voices. Second, the constitution of the symbol formally opposes its thematic associations; this conflict generates an ambivalence that leads our readings in two directions at once: toward suggestions of death in the elements combined ("skeleton," "ghost," "damned," "priest," "wounded," "Murder!") and, conversely, toward the unifying implications of the formal process that lead us to sense the possibility of new meaning and perhaps a renewed "self."

Third, even within the formal logic of condensation resides an ambiguity that gives the process of metaphor its power. Sasha's "yes" welcomes a moment in which she has stripped herself of the artificial qualities of style (she rises purposefully to undress) and has created through her own will and active knowledge an image that does subvert the oppressive and chaotic clichés of conventional consciousness. By calling for the white nightgown, she creates her own fate and emphasizes the one element that will formally combine, condense, and unify the fragments of her life. She overrides René's exposure and her resulting split consciousness by making René, with his wounds, only one element in the formal process that associates those wounds with the father figure who wore the white dressing gown in her dream. In this scene, we might view Sasha as "acting" but no longer in the sense of bringing to her performance an interpretation. Rather, the passage bears the full ambiguity of an original *act*. Her act creates a metaphor for sexual oppression that gives formal order to her experience. By shaping the symbol, she undermines the image of the marginal victim it creates.

> He doesn't say anything. Thank God, he doesn't say anything. I look straight into his eyes and despise another poor devil of a human being for the last time. For the last time. . . . Then I put my arms around him and pull him down on to the bed, saying: "Yes—yes— yes." (*Midnight*, p. 190)

Sasha imagined the gigolo's return, knowing the *commis* was present, knowing it was he who entered her door. As if following her earlier vision in Serge's studio, she deliberately left the door open, got up a second time to undress before lying down again to wait "as still as if I were dead" (*Midnight*, p. 190). Yet Sasha believes her real self waits for him: "Now I am simple and not afraid; now I am myself. He can look at me if he wants to" (*Midnight*, p. 189).

Metaphor, like ritual, contains a liminal phase, that point in between the meaning of an old identity and the creation of a new one, the moment of emptiness that transformation requires. Hence the title of the novel greets the midnight hour, between morning and night and between systems of explanation. Sasha's actions in this scene create a ritual moment of suspension that parallels the formal liminal moment of metaphor: is it enough to suggest renewal or is it, like René's technique, "possibly quite meaningless"? This is the question posed, in terms of sexual relations, by the novel—a challenge posed to the modernism that it participates in and contributes to yet, through the perceptions of a marginalized woman, also writes against.

We might, returning to Wilson Harris's concern with overcoming the stasis of victim/victimizer that guided our interpretation of Antoinette's dream text in *Wide Sargasso Sea*, argue that such a transcendence occurs with Sasha's concluding "Yes—yes—yes." After all, in the dream that this scene realizes, the identity of victim and victimizer blurred when Sasha's screams of "Murder!" joined those of the wounded father. In this light, we could view the formal process of the final visionary scene in *Good Morning, Midnight* not as empty or meaningless, but as a moment leading toward metamorphosis and the renewal of identity with other "poor devils."[36] However, we must also read the scene in the context of the Exhibition Internationale and the political conflict represented there as well as the social chaos in which it takes place. Considering again the confrontation of the Soviet and Nazi buildings, Italy's monument to fascism and futurism, and the symbol of peace they nearly obscure, we have to recognize the impending social annihilation threatening Europe. The exhibition's cold beauty and emptiness present the loss of community that Sasha experienced personally with the loss of Serge's friendship. This is the crucial difference between the endings of the two novels: in *Wide Sargasso Sea*, the final dream text returns Antoinette to the community of Caribbean women through whom she multiplies and fulfills her identity; in *Good Morning, Midnight*, the same formal process has been emptied of such a possibility and requires instead the sacrifice of multivocality in an artificially contrived union. The false unity of the exhibition's attempt at internationalism parallels I think what we must see as a false union between the *commis* and Sasha. Unable to join with other creative and marginalized individuals in acts of generosity, Sasha has joined instead with her accuser and tormentor. Her "yes—yes—yes" repeats the earlier moment of submission to the role of fool/victim in which the fascistic authority of Mr. Blank casts her:

> "Just a hopeless, helpless little fool, aren't you" . . .
> "Well, aren't you?"
> "Yes, yes, yes, yes. Oh, yes." (*Midnight*, p. 28)

Like the order promised by fascism, her submission demands pain and sacrifice. It convinces Sasha of her own guilt ("it's your fault") and makes her a willing victim of anonymous patriarchal forces in an act of literal self-sacrifice. If this final scene suggests birth, it is that of a machine with mascaraed eyes, an artificial woman like the shop dummies Sasha has cynically admired, and an automaton who dances to a debasing tune. Following the zombie logic of Rhys's other novels, *Good Morning, Midnight* portrays in its final scene death-in-life and the political-psychological powers that work such evil magic.

In modern European society, the "self," unified and consolidated, gains the status of the sacred. The selves of Rhys's heroines, so tenuous and pluralized already, are sacrificeable. Though they stubbornly attempt to find, assert, and protect the voices of their multiplicitous selves, they are imbued with the violence of the society around them that, feeling itself threatened, requires victims. The victims appear to lose "self-respect," a loss substituting perhaps for that which members of society who constitute themselves as autonomous individuals fear from "the Other"—the masses of mass culture, of women, and of "foreigners" or Jews. What Sasha loses, however, is, first, the carnival community experienced with the Jewish Serge that awakens a new vision of self, and, second, the voice, characterized as "she," of irony and critical play that allows her to survive by analyzing her marginality. In light of Caribbean cultural pluralism and the concept of multiplicitous and fulfilled selves it makes possible, the goal of a stable and discrete identity appears as a delusion, yet one that governs.

The happy ending that might have closed this novel takes place in its middle, with a glimpse of "somewhere else" in a vision of the sea and an opening door. Sasha cannot reenact the scene later because it depended upon a spontaneous community of marginalized individuals, acting in carnivalesque concert. The terrifying grey background of Sasha's vision, modern Europe on the verge of a war in which six million "marginal" individuals will be deliberately put to death, su-percedes in the novel's ending the possibilities offered by its middle. The epiphany of the middle section, however, suggests the Third World modernist concept of the individual that Rhys later develops in *Wide Sargasso Sea;* in this novel of the late 1930s it becomes a means to explore the social and political limitations governing the formalism of European modernism.

Conclusion

"World's End and a Beginning"

*A*t the conclusion of *Abeng*, a novel of childhood by the Jamaican writer Michelle Cliff, its protagonist, Clare Savage, has a dream:

> That night Clare dreamed that she and Zoe were fist-fighting by the river in St. Elizabeth. That she picked up a stone and hit Zoe underneath the eye and a trickle of blood ran down her friend's face and onto the rock where she sat. The blood formed into a pool where the rock folded over on itself. And she went over to Zoe and told her she was sorry—making a compress of moss drenched in water to soothe the cut. Then squeezing an aloe leaf to close the wound.[1]

Clare, who descends from English slave owners on one side and Maroon guerilla fighters on the other, has been separated from her black friend Zoe. The fight and the blood in her dream prefigure her first menstrual period, but they also mirror the scene in *Wide Sargasso Sea* in which Tia strikes Antoinette with a rock, and their faces, one wet with tears and the other with blood, reflect one another "like in a looking glass." The final lines of Cliff's novel echo the dream logic of *Wide Sargasso Sea* and stress the doubling of the two separated girls' identities: "She was not ready to understand her dream. She had no idea that everyone we dream about we are."[2]

Abeng shares much with Rhys's novel, especially its exploration of cultural marginality through historical juxtapositions and the logic of dreams and of turnabout. Its epigraph on the title page informs us that "*Abeng* is an African word meaning conch shell. The blowing of the conch called the slaves to the canefields in the West Indies. The *abeng* had another use: it was the instrument used by the Maroon armies to pass their messages and reach one another." Turned about, the conch shell becomes a kind of *zemi* or magical object through which another world is reached. Yet its "magic" is a practical one and, we learn in the course of Cliff's novel, the other world is a real place: "A settlement in the Cockpit Country, the land of endless funnels in the earth, the land of look behind. At the heart of the limestone plateau which forms the center of the island."[3] From this elusive yet central "land of look behind," the Maroon leaders Nanny and Cudjoe launched their raids.

A literature in which magic is simultaneously historical reality is hard to place. The term "magical realism" might suffice, yet one critic has questioned the "magic" of its realism, preferring instead the term "critical realism" as a description of Caribbean writing.[4] Its aesthetic is a political one of resistance, and its highest principle, according to Wilson Harris, is that of endurance.[5] In the context of this tradition, the metaphor of "elsewhere" resonates with real historical meaning yet retains its magical and transcendent properties. It also becomes the structuring motive of a fiction in search of both social community and aesthetic form.

In this study, I have argued that Jean Rhys's novels explore the possibilities for new aesthetic form at the intersection of three kinds of modernism—mainstream European, female, and Third World. The tensions and conflicts among them shape each of her novels differently, yet each involves a search for community and place that results from colonial and sexual exile and that supersedes the European quest for identity in the form of discrete individual "character."

We are accustomed to discussions of West Indian literature that refer to and explain the influences upon it of canonical "British" works such as *The Tempest, The Waste Land,* or *Heart of Darkness.* However, as Peter Nazareth once remarked, "The ships go both ways." In these chapters, I have attempted to trace the crossings and recrossings in Rhys's novels of colonial literary interdependence: the shaping of what appears as European modernism by Caribbean cultural influences. These influences, along with experiences of sexual exile in modern urban Europe, result in formal alterations of conventional fictional patterns, alterations that may appear as silences, stutterings, interruptions, or inconsistencies. If we begin, as this study does, with the "inconsistency" of Antoinette's disembodied first-person narrative voice interrupting Rochester's narrated interior dialogue with Christophine in the middle section of *Wide Sargasso Sea,* we discern the cultural conflicts of marginality and sexual exploitation within the context that gives them meaning for Rhys's earlier novels as well as for *Wide Sargasso Sea.* In the Caribbean context of slavery and colonialism, Maroon warfare and betrayals, obeah magic and rebellion, this narrative inconsistency becomes, rather, an opening onto alternate fictional possibilities for conceiving character, not as successful overcoming of obstacles by an increasingly consolidated ego, but as the brutal loss of identity that necessitates new spiritual and political alliances in a dreamed-of, magically realized, and chosen community.

Reading *Voyage in the Dark* from this perspective, then, we need no longer be concerned with evaluating Anna Morgan's "character" in moral terms, defending or explaining or criticizing her "failure." Rather, we can read the novel from within the deliberate turnabout of the Caribbean carnival whose images and formal logic erupt in its concluding passages and also shape its entire text with the play of voices in Anna Morgan's multidimensional consciousness. This play of voices sets up a tense dialogue between a modernist female irony characterized by disillusionment and isolation and a more communal satiric carnival laughter, enabling again an imagined "elsewhere" and a deliberate choice.

Voyage in the Dark becomes a pivotal novel in exploring the tensions between cultures that Rhys's novels inscribe. In its setting on the verge of World War I in England, we find the signs of another war, one waged against working-class women by the Purity Crusades, the police, and newly established medical powers, attempting to regulate and control female sexuality in the midst of rapidly changing sex/gender systems. Examining this context for *Voyage in the Dark* alongside the Caribbean gives wider meaning to the inconclusivity of the novel's ending, an ambiguity wrought as much by the social instabilities to which Rhys's writing responds as by the original publisher's request for a different ending.

We find formal alterations of fictional patterns brought by Rhys's Caribbean background to European modernism in the other early novels even when they do not explicitly refer to the West Indies. In *Quartet, After Leaving Mr. Mackenzie,* and *Good Morning, Midnight,* themes of possession and dispossession, of zombie life-in-death and death-in-life appear as metaphors for characterization but also as tropes for understanding features of style and structure such as the shifting and dissolving narrative point of view in *Quartet* and the ghostly circularity and repetition of *After Leaving Mr. Mackenzie.* In *Quartet, After Leaving Mr. Mackenzie,* and *Good Morning, Midnight,* carnival masks signify a conflict between social masking and subversive masquerade in the construction of feminine identity.

In these novels, Caribbean influences are felt as emergent shapes, shadow forms wrestling with the concrete experiential reality of Europe between the wars. A misogynist backlash in the 1920s and 1930s against the perceived independence of women during World War I, the tendency in psychoanalysis and sexology to pathologize women's sexual "nature," and the rise of fascism in the 1930s are important social subtexts of these novels, limiting the possibilities for plot and characterization in either European or Caribbean terms. In the early novels, attempts at community or alliance with other marginalized individuals ultimately fail but not without great effort exerted on the part of the protagonists, who seek to retain culturally plural identities in the face of constraining and reductive social pressures. Their efforts tear the fabric of realism—even of European modernism, with its illusions of a self to be fragmented—by rupturing sequences of beginning-middle-end and by exploring the possibilities for consciousness when a unified, discrete self has never been a possibility. Their sexual marginality exposes the conventions of marriage and romance within fiction as coercive institutions through which feminine identity is constructed while female subjectivity is denied.

Attempting to bring closer attention to Rhys's writing as Caribbean literature invokes the danger of romanticizing or exoticizing the West Indies. The islands have long suffered from such objectification. Rhys alludes to this kind of appropriation, disguised as benevolent interest, when Rochester turns to a book called *The Glittering Coronet of Isles* in search of information to help him manage his fears and his wife. Appreciating the beauty of the West Indies, the author also pretends to an insider's knowledge of its cultures and presents information about obeah and zombies for the purposes of colonial and psychological government. I cannot pretend to any insider's knowledge of the Caribbean, nor do I wish to romanticize West Indian cultures by arguing that Rhys's fiction takes on new and subversive meanings when read in their contexts. However, I do hope to shift critical attention away from the European aesthetic, moral, and psychological standards which I believe have operated to misread and at times to devalue Rhys's writing—writing that, in fact, challenges those standards. I wish also to complicate the feminist perspectives on Rhys that view her works in terms of sexual difference only and to suggest ways in which European systems of sexual and social control intersect in Rhys's writing with the history of colonialism and resistance to it to give voice to otherwise silenced "obscure persons." The intersection is not always one of parallel or analogous systems of oppression but one which invites a reconsideration of and movement beyond what Wilson Harris calls the "victim-victimizer stasis."

Discussing African literature, Abdul JanMohamed refers to a similar relationship in colonial literatures with the term "manichean aesthetics." Writing of both the colonizer and the colonized, JanMohamed states: "In fact, the colonial mentality is dominated by a manichean allegory of white and black, good and evil, salvation and damnation, civilization and savagery, superiority and inferiority, intelligence and emotion, self and other, subject and object."[6] It is precisely these opposing dualisms that *Wide Sargasso Sea* disrupts by incorporating within it the text of the "victimizing" culture, *Jane Eyre,* and rescripting its myths through Antoinette's "victimized" dream text. Dualisms of white and black are disrupted, too, in the creation of a character who is both or perhaps neither, "not *béké* like you, but . . . *béké,* and not like us either." We find in Rhys's earlier novels similar though perhaps fainter subversions of biological notions of race through explorations of the cultural constructions of both racial and sexual otherness. All of Rhys's novels take on one other manichean allegory—the good woman and the bad—and by exposing it as a cultural construct, complicit with colonial constructs, join fictions of decolonization with what might be termed fictions of demasculinization. The latter emerge in the context of modernist Europe undergoing a series of sex/gender crises as perceived by displaced women, and they render scripts of romantic thralldom impotent. Though we may expect or hope that male characters in Rhys's novels will become romantic heroes, they do not. Nor do men such as Horsfield, Serge, or even Rochester act as villains. Sometimes they seem simply indifferent to the script of romance. Often we perceive their vulnerability, victimization, and feminization. As the literary consciousness traces and retraces its route from colony to metropole and back again, the European sex/gender crises are refigured in Caribbean terms so that in the multiple contexts of an emergent Caribbean literature and European female modernism, female "heroines" who seem weak and victimized glimpse means of transformation and fulfillment in ways that reconceptualize the individual. The catastrophes that befall Rhys's characters take on historical scope and meanings that "look behind" to the islands located where "our habitable earth ends" in order to re-envision the sexual trespasses of women marginalized in the in-between spaces of European cities. In this turn of vision and values emerges the potential for new beginnings.

Rhys's writing is not only enhanced by its position at the intersection of these three modernisms; it is limited as well. The voices of black and native women, for instance, speak only through the consciousnesses of the English and Euro-Creole characters. Native voices and the islands to which they belong are, in a sense, appropriated in the protagonists' quests for relocated identities and communities. I have argued that by enduring sexual slaveries and identifying with native and black peoples, the protagonists of Rhys's novels share their histories and occupy their places or places similar to theirs. Yet we might question the full implications of such occupation and explore its literary politics by considering Rhys's work in comparison with that of other women writers of European descent born in the colonies and in contrast to the fiction of black and native women writers. A critical study of "colonial encounters"[7] between writers such as Olive Shreiner, Jean Rhys, and Doris Lessing on the one hand and Bessie Head, Buchi Emecheta, and Joan Riley or Beryl Gilroy on the other has yet to be written and would give us a new framework in which to consider all of these writers. To what extent do their writings reflect one another "like in a looking-glass"; to what extent and in what ways do they remain separate? Cliff's *Abeng*, published eighteen years after *Wide Sargasso Sea*, whose themes it echoes and extends, marks the route of another literary voyage on which we might also find the writings of Bessie Head and Paule Marshall—a female Third World modernism that explores the crossings and recrossings of cultural, racial, and sexual boundaries, mapping them in the psyches of exiled women. This grouping suggests another more contemporary framework for assessing the political, moral, and spiritual scope and limitations of Rhys's fiction.

Jean Rhys's writing challenges the Old World even in its modernist guise and seeks an alternate "New World" of an aesthetic form and social community that is still to be charted. In the later "postmodern" decades of the twentieth century, when European and North American concepts of history and society are discarded by their own cultures, violence against women and colonized peoples continues in historically conditioned and socially institutionalized practices. Occluded by definitions of our century that divide it into the modern and the "postmodern," female and Third World modernisms develop, nevertheless, their strategies of redefinition and transformation. In the "beginnings" that they dare, we can learn much about complicity, resistance, magic, and beauty.

Notes

Introduction

1. Kenneth Ramchand, "An Introduction to this Novel," in *The Lonely Londoners*, by Sam Selvon, p. 3.

2. Nancy R. Harrison points to this description of the lover talking and Rhys feeling as indicative of the sexual difference Rhys's narrative style inscribes (*Jean Rhys and the Novel as Women's Text*).

3. Pierre d'Ailly, Cardinal of Cambria, *Imago Mundi* (1410–1480), quoted by Christopher Columbus in marginal notes on his own copy. The passage describes a land near the Orient that Columbus later thought he had rediscovered from the West when he arrived in what he named the West Indies. See *Journals and Other Documents on the Life and Voyages of Christopher Columbus*, trans. and ed. Samuel Eliot Morison.

4. Teresa O'Connor adopts this term in *Jean Rhys: The West Indian Novels* to divide Rhys's novels into two groups according to their settings, rather than the history of the literary movements to which they contribute.

5. I have depended upon the following sources for chronological information. Where sources differ, I have made decisions based on the evidence brought to bear and agreements among most reliable or most recent sources. In some instances, exact dates, especially for periods of composition, were not available, and I have indicated the general period or most likely dates: Diana Athill, "Foreword," in *Smile Please: An Unfinished Autobiography*, by Jean Rhys, pp. 10–15; Arnold E. Davidson, *Jean Rhys*, pp. ix–x; Jean Rhys Collection, Rare Books and Special Collections, McFarlin Library, University of Tulsa; Jean Rhys, *The Letters of Jean Rhys*, ed. Francis Wyndham and Diana Melly, pp. 13–16; Jean Rhys, *Smile Please: An Unfinished Autobiography*; Thomas F. Staley, *Jean Rhys: A Critical Study*, chap. 1.

1. Modernist Crosscurrents

1. Bruce King, *The New English Literatures: Cultural Nationalism in a Changing World,* p. 107.

2. According to the chronology presented by Diana Athill in *Smile Please* and to other sources as well, Rhys was born Ella Gwendolen Rees Williams. In the chapter titled "Chorus Girls" (*Smile Please,* p. 107), Rhys mentions that "Gray was the name I was using then." Carole Angier describes Rhys's use of Ella and Emma Gray during the time she worked on the stage (*Jean Rhys,* chap. 2). According to Wyndham and Melly, Rhys took the stage name of Vivien Gray; her daughter Maryvonne preferred that she use her given name, Ella, long after she had been calling herself Jean (*The Letters of Jean Rhys,* pp. 13, 90, and 93n).

3. Elizabeth Burns discusses the social marginality of the theater throughout European history in *Theatricality.* Julie Holledge describes how women in the Edwardian theater recognized their subversive potential and began to use the stage for political purposes (*Innocent Flowers: Women in the Edwardian Theater*). See Albert Auster's *Actresses and Suffragists: Women in the American Theater, 1890–1920* for discussions of the feminization of the American theater and of feminist theater at the turn of the century.

4. Rhys, *Smile Please,* p. 52.

5. Roger D. Abrahams and John F. Szwed emphasize these qualities of the Caribbean carnival and their potential for catalyzing revolt: ". . . we do have considerable evidence that many rebellions which occurred did begin during one or another season of license. . . . at least 35% of the rebellions in the British Caribbean were planned or executed in late December" (*After Africa,* p. 226). Such evidence goes against the theory that carnival celebrations only reversed power hierarchies in order to reaffirm and sustain them. Discussion of the literary and "real" effects of carnival rebellion appears in recent literary criticism, including Terry Castle, "The Carnivalization of Eighteenth-Century English Narrative," *PMLA* 99 (1984): 903–991; and Natalie Davis, "Women on Top," in *Society and Culture in Early Modern France.*

6. In *After Africa,* Abrahams and Szwed describe the history of Jamaican set dances, which they state began as peasant dances in Europe, then spread to the upper classes, only to be changed, then carried to the West Indies by European planters whose slaves took them up and again changed them (p. 227).

7. Mikhail Bakhtin, "Introduction," *Rabelais and His World.*

8. For brief introductory discussions of the theme of masks in Rhys's fiction, see Judith Thurman, "The Mistress and the Mask," *Ms.* 4, no. 7 (January 1976): 50–53; and Helen Tiffin, "Colonial Motifs in the Novels of Jean Rhys," *World Literature Written in English* 17 (April 1978): 328–341.

9. Jean Rhys, *Good Morning, Midnight* (New York: Random House, Vintage Books, 1974), pp. 108–109. Subsequent references to this edition will be cited in the text.

10. Teresa de Lauretis discusses these two terms and their implications for feminist theory in "Issues, Terms, and Contexts," in *Feminist Studies/Critical Studies*, ed. Teresa de Lauretis, p. 17. The metaphor of the mask is also important to theories of colonization and its psychological effects on the colonized person. See Frantz Fanon, *Black Skin, White Masks*.

11. With the term "carnivalesque," I am referring to Mikhail Bakhtin's influential discussion of the role of the European medieval carnival in literature and especially the novel. See his "Introduction," in *Rabelais and His World*. For feminist perspectives on Bakhtin's theory, see Dale M. Bauer, *Feminist Dialogics: A Theory of Failed Community*; Davis, "Women on Top"; and Mary Russo, "Female Grotesques: Carnival and Theory," in *Feminist Studies/Critical Studies*, ed. Teresa de Lauretis.

12. Russo, "Female Grotesques," p. 214.

13. Ibid., p. 217.

14. Ibid. The portrayals of the carnival as "historical performance" place Rhys's novels in a tradition of West Indian literature in which Carnival figures as a climactic turning point. Some examples include Paule Marshall, *The Chosen Place, The Timeless People*; Sam Selvon, *Moses Migrating*; Earl Lovelace, *The Dragon Can't Dance*; and Wilson Harris, *Carnival*.

15. Cheryl M. L. Dash, "Jean Rhys," in *West Indian Literature*, ed. Bruce King, p. 197.

16. Such rearrangement and the implied, if not explicit, conflation of author and character appear in many critical discussions, including Elgin Mellown, "Character and Themes in the Novels of Jean Rhys," *Wisconsin Studies in Contemporary Literature* 13, no. 4 (Autumn 1972): 459–475; Peter Wolfe, *Jean Rhys*; Harrison, *Jean Rhys and the Novel as Woman's Text*; and Dash, "Jean Rhys." Though Harrison takes the single protagonist line, her study represents a partial exception to the fiction-as-autobiography argument since she redefines autobiography to give it a collective import—that is, the women Rhys writes about and for include herself but others, her readers, as well. Harrison still, however, conforms to biographical methods by citing Rhys's personal and autobiographical writings as evidence for interpretations of the novels. The most flagrant identification of author with character appears in the undocumented study by Angier, *Jean Rhys*.

17. Veronica Marie Gregg, "Jean Rhys and Modernism: A Different Voice," *Jean Rhys Review* 1, no. 2 (Spring 1987): 30–46.

18. Rhys, *The Letters of Jean Rhys*, ed. Wyndham and Melly, and the various manuscripts in the Jean Rhys Collection, including the original version of *Voyage in the Dark*, a radio script of *Good Morning, Midnight*, early drafts of short stories, and unpublished short stories and essays, which were often reworked into the published fiction. See Gregg, "Jean Rhys and Modernism," for a detailed account of the many drafts and the changes they underwent in Rhys's writing.

19. O'Connor, *Jean Rhys*.

20. For a summary of Rhys's life that includes a description of her relationship with Ford, see Staley, *Jean Rhys*, chap. 1.

21. King, *The New English Literatures*, chaps. 6 and 7.

22. Shari Benstock, *Women of the Left Bank: Paris, 1900–1940*, p. 448.

23. Wolfe (*Jean Rhys*) states that Rhys disguised herself in her characters, but he sees this disguise as a means of autobiography and does not consider the subversive nature of masquerade.

24. Andreas Huyssen, "Mass Culture as Woman: Modernism's Other," *After the Great Divide*, pp. 44–64.

25. Virginia Woolf, *Street Haunting*, p. 35.

26. Both O'Connor (*Jean Rhys*) and Harrison (*Jean Rhys and the Novel as Women's Text*) treat only *Wide Sargasso Sea* and *Voyage in the Dark*.

27. These are the reasons given by Harrison (*Jean Rhys and the Novel as Women's Text*) for her exclusive focus on these two novels. O'Connor does stress the importance of the West Indies as a place in a governing fictional myth. However, her study brings their history to bear as evidence for a psychological thesis concerning Rhys's relation to her mother and the trajectory of Rhys's career.

28. Elizabeth Nunez-Harrell, "The Paradoxes of Belonging: The White West Indian Woman in Fiction," *Modern Fiction Studies* 31, no. 2 (Summer 1985): 1–2.

29. Ramchand, "An Introduction to this Novel," p. 3. Ramchand's description may also take into account the questions Anna's aunt raises concerning her lineage as possibly racially mixed.

30. Derek Walcott, "A Far Cry from Africa," in *The Penguin Book of Caribbean Verse in English*, ed. Paula Burnett, p. 243.

31. Louis James, "Introduction," in *The Islands in Between*, ed. Louis James, p. 8.

32. Everett V. Stonequist, *The Marginal Man*, p. 8.

33. Tiffin, "Mirror and Mask," p. 328.

34. Jean Rhys, "How I Became a Novelist," unpub. ms., Jean Rhys Collection, quoted in Gregg, "Jean Rhys and Modernism," p. 32.

35. V. S. Naipaul uses these phrases to describe what must have been the European attitude toward the Caribbean in the 1920s. Quoted in Gregg, "Jean Rhys and Modernism," pp. 32–33.

36. Trevor James, *English Literature from the Third World*, p. 17. See also Bruce King, "Introduction," in *West Indian Literature*, ed. Bruce King, p. 6.

37. See Sandra M. Gilbert and Susan Gubar, *The Madwoman in the Attic: The Woman Writer and the Nineteenth-Century Literary Imagination*, for a post–*Wide Sargasso Sea* discussion of *Jane Eyre* that views Bertha Rochester as symbolic of Jane's repressed rage. Elizabeth Baer traces the parallels between Jane and Antoinette in both novels, arguing that in *Wide Sargasso Sea* Jean Rhys presents them as "sisters" ("The Sisterhood of Jane Eyre and Antoinette Cosway Mason," in *The Voyage In: Fictions of Female Development*, ed. Elizabeth Abel, Marianne Hirsch, and Elizabeth Langland).

38. The exceptions usually appear in essays by critics of Third World literature who address the implications of womanhood as presented in Rhys's novels. They tend not to draw on feminist theory or criticism to do so. These include, most notably, Tiffin, "Mirror and Mask"; Nunez-Harrell,

"The Paradoxes of Belonging"; and Erika Smilowitz, "Childlike Women and Paternal Men: Colonialism in Jean Rhys's Fiction," *Ariel* 17, no. 4 (October 1986): 93–104. Their analyses also tend to make analogous the social hierarchies of colonial and sexual oppression so that the protagonists are seen as all the more victimized. Selma James (*The Ladies and the Mammies*) identifies Rhys as a West Indian writer in sensibility and style. James, nevertheless, bases her discussion of Rhys's work on a comparison with that of Jane Austen. O'Connor's study (*Jean Rhys*) examines the "West Indian" novels within their Caribbean setting, but their location is important to her more for a psychological than a literary, cultural, or historical reading of Jean Rhys's vision. Bev E. L. Brown's essay, "Mansong and Matrix: A Radical Experiment," *Kunapipi* 7, nos. 2 and 3 (1985): 68–80, is exceptional in its analysis of specifically female Creole patterns in Rhys's writing.

39. Gayatri Chakravorty Spivak, "Three Women's Texts and a Critique of Imperialism," in *"Race," Writing, and Difference*, ed. Henry Louis Gates, Jr., pp. 262–280.

40. Judith Kegan Gardiner and Susan Squier have written about the ways in which *Good Morning, Midnight* suggests a critique of modernism through ironical allusions to works of Rhys's contemporaries. See Susan Squier, "'Yes—Yes': Sasha Jansen as a Critique of Molly Bloom" (Paper presented at the annual meeting of the Modern Language Association, Houston, Texas, 1980); and Judith Kegan Gardiner, "Good Morning, Midnight; Good Night, Modernism," *Boundary* 2 11, no. 2 (Fall/Winter 1982–83): 233–252. My point here, however, is that the very structure of Rhys's novels alters as a result of a Third World perspective that disrupts that of European modernism.

41. See Jean Rhys to Selma Vaz Dias, January 23, 1950, and the Green Exercise Book, Jean Rhys Collection.

42. Luce Irigaray writes, "It is therefore useless to trap women into giving an exact definition of what they mean, to make them repeat (themselves) so the meaning will be clear. They are already elsewhere than in this discursive machinery where you claim to take them by surprise." See Luce Irigaray, "This Sex Which Is Not One," trans. Claudia Reeder, in *New French Feminisms*, ed. Elaine Marks and Isabelle de Courtivron, p. 103.

43. Sandra Drake, *Wilson Harris and the Modern Tradition: A New Architecture of the World*, p. 175.

44. Drake identifies Third World modernism in her book on Wilson Harris (ibid.). I am aware of the problems in using the term "Third World"; it can become, as Régis Debray has charged, a dumping ground or "shapeless sack" that obscures whole peoples and continents and the differences among them. I use it here to call attention to emerging literatures that are ignored or marginalized in English departments and also to set up a view of Jean Rhys's writing as working in between problematic categories such as "British," "English," and "Third World." For a history of the term "Third World," see Barbara Harlow, *Resistance Literature*, pp. 5–6.

45. Perry Anderson identifies the social, political, and economic conditions of literary modernism in "Modernity and Revolution," in *Marxism and*

the Interpretation of Culture, ed. Cary Nelson and Lawrence Grossberg. He describes a triad of factors—persisting dominance by the aristocratic land-owning classes; emergence of novel and key technologies; and the imaginative proximity of social revolution—as present in Europe in the late nineteenth and early twentieth centuries and in "developing" Third World countries in the 1960s and 1970s.

46. Rhys's personal feelings about the history of slavery were quite mixed, for she wished to believe that her slave-owning grandfather might not have been a cruel man; yet she also identified closely with the blacks and their sufferings. See the Black Exercise Book, Jean Rhys Collection; and O'Connor, *Jean Rhys,* especially chap. 1. Writing about the struggles for independence, however, Rhys stated that it served the white people of the West Indies right to be no longer on top (Black Exercise Book).

47. Staley, *Jean Rhys,* p. 16; and O'Connor, *Jean Rhys,* p. 70.

48. Rhonda Cobham, "The Background," in *West Indian Literature,* ed. Bruce King; Bruce King, "Introduction," in ibid.; and Trevor James, "The Caribbean," in *English Literature from the Third World.*

49. Elaine Campbell, "Introduction," in *The Orchid House,* by Phyllis Shand Allfrey; and "From Dominica to Devonshire, A Momento of Jean Rhys," *Kunapipi* 1, no. 2 (1979): 13; Nunez-Harrell, "The Paradox of Belonging." In a letter dated December 6, 1960, Rhys describes her attempts to write "patois" and says that she has not read "any of the 'West Indian' people" (*The Letters of Jean Rhys,* p. 197). She may not have read them but she clearly knew about them and shared their project of representing in literature the folk dialects of the Caribbean.

50. Edward Brathwaite, quoted in Campbell, "Introduction," p. xv.

51. Simone Schwarz-Bart, *The Bridge of Beyond,* trans. Barbara Bray.

2. Countertexts, Countercommunities

1. Wilson Harris, "The Writer and Society," in *Tradition, the Writer and Society,* p. 48.

2. Ibid.

3. Harris, "Tradition and the West Indian Novel," in *Tradition, the Writer and Society,* p. 28.

4. Mary Louise Pratt, "Scratches on the Face of the Country; or, What Mr. Barrow Saw in the Land of the Bushmen," in *"Race," Writing, and Difference,* ed. Henry Louis Gates, Jr., pp. 138–162. See also Chandra Talpade Mohanty, "Under Western Eyes: Feminist Scholarship and Colonial Discourses," *Boundary 2* 12, no. 3 / 13, no. 1 (Spring–Fall 1984): 333–353, on the ways a similar dynamic operates in the discourse of Western feminism so that it constitutes its subject—the secular, mobile, independent woman—by positing Third World women as an undifferentiated mass, different only in respect to European and North American women.

5. Anne McClintock, "Maidens, Maps, and Mines: The Reinvention of

Patriarchy in Colonial South Africa," *South Atlantic Quarterly* 87 (Winter 1988): 163.

6. According to McClintock, scientists positioned the white prostitute on the threshold between white and black races. However, comparing the iconography of modern painting with that of medical texts, Sander Gilman finds that the white prostitute and the female "Hottentot" were identified with one another at the very bottom of the scale. See McClintock, "Maidens, Maps, and Mines"; and Sander Gilman, "Black Bodies, White Bodies: Toward an Iconography of Female Sexuality in Late Nineteenth-Century Art, Medicine, and Literature," in *"Race," Writing, and Difference*, ed. Henry Louis Gates, Jr., pp. 223–261.

7. Huyssen, "Introduction," p. vii.

8. Huyssen, "Mass Culture as Woman," p. 52.

9. Joseph Conrad, "A Familiar Preface," in *A Personal Record*, p. 10.

10. See Judith Walkowitz's account of the campaign to defeat the Contagious Diseases Acts in *Prostitution and Victorian Society: Women, Class, and the State*; and, for a first-hand account of the repeal campaign, see Josephine Butler, *Personal Reminiscences of a Great Crusade*.

11. Sandra M. Gilbert and Susan Gubar open the first volume of *No Man's Land: The Place of the Woman Writer in the Twentieth Century* with an epigraph from *The Education of Henry Adams* in which Henry Adams describes the "myriads of new types" of women "created since 1840" that "had been set free . . . running into millions on millions."

12. See Walkowitz, *Prostitution and Victorian Society*; and Mary Poovey, "'Scenes of an Indelicate Character': The Medical 'Treatment' of Victorian Women," *Representations* 14 (Spring 1986): 137–168.

13. Michelle Zimbalist Rosaldo, "The Uses and Abuses of Anthropology," *Signs* 5, no. 3 (Spring 1980): 389–417.

14. Sandra M. Gilbert, "Soldier's Heart: Literary Men, Literary Women, and the Great War," *Signs* 8, no. 3 (Spring 1983): 422–450; and *No Man's Land*, vol. 2, *Sexchanges*, chap. 7.

15. Paul Ricoeur, "Hermeneutics: The Approaches to Symbol," in *Freud and Philosophy*, pp. 494–552.

16. Anthony Layng, "Dominica, An Island in Need of an Historian," *Caribbean Quarterly* 19, no. 4 (December 1973): 36–41.

17. Raymond Meyer helped me to identify and translate this passage.

18. Elizabeth Abel, "Women and Schizophrenia: The Fiction of Jean Rhys," *Contemporary Literature* 20, no. 2 (1979): 155–177.

19. Robert Park, "Human Migration and the Marginal Man," in *Classic Essays on the Culture of Cities*, ed. Richard Sennett, pp. 131–142; Stonequist, *The Marginal Man*.

20. Fredric Jameson, "Cognitive Mapping," in *Marxism and the Interpretation of Culture*, ed. Cary Nelson and Lawrence Grossberg, p. 349.

21. Ibid.

3. Wide Sargasso Sea: *Obeah Nights*

1. Jean Rhys, *Wide Sargasso Sea* (New York and London: Norton, 1982), p. 102. Subsequent references to this edition will be cited in the text.
2. Wilson Harris, *Palace of the Peacock*, pp. 13–14.
3. Drake defines Third World modernism in *Wilson Harris and the Modern Tradition*.
4. Ibid., p. 4.
5. Wilson Harris, "The Whirling Stone," in *The Womb of Space: The Cross-Cultural Imagination*, p. 55.
6. Richard Price, "Introduction: Maroons and Their Communities," in *Maroon Societies: Rebel Slave Communities in the Americas*, pp. 1–30; Selwyn R. Cudjoe, *Resistance and Caribbean Literature*, chap. 1.
7. Florence Harris, quoted in *Ancestral Voices 4: Ancient Caribbean Music, Ritual and Dance* (London: Arts Center, Commonwealth Institute, 1986), p. 11. For a discussion of Maroon Nanny as an ancestor of Christophine in *Wide Sargasso Sea*, see Angelita Reyes, "Maroon Nanny and Creole Difference: Reconsidering Jean Rhys's West Indian Landscape and *Wide Sargasso Sea*."
8. See especially Nancy K. Miller, "Emphasis Added: Plots and Plausibilities in Women's Fiction," in *The New Feminist Criticism*, ed. Elaine Showalter, pp. 339–360.
9. Elizabeth Baer, "The Sisterhood of Jane Eyre and Antoinette Cosway."
10. Williams, *From Columbus to Castro*, p. 199.
11. Drake, *Wilson Harris and the Modern Tradition*, p. 23.
12. Williams, *From Columbus to Castro*, p. 199.
13. Ivor Morrish, *Obeah, Christ and Rastaman: Jamaica and Its Religions*, p. 40.
14. Abrahams and Szwed, *After Africa*, p. 182.
15. Sandra Drake has discussed the importance of the zombie motif in *Wide Sargasso Sea* in "'All That Foolishness': The Zombi and Afro-Caribbean Culture in Jean Rhys's *Wide Sargasso Sea*." In *Smile Please* (p. 30), Rhys defines *soucriant* ("women . . . who came at night and sucked your blood. During the day they looked like ordinary women but you could tell them by their red eyes") and *zombie* ("black shapeless things . . . you didn't see them . . .").
16. For descriptions of obeah practices and their social functions, see Morrish, *Obeah, Christ and Rastaman*; Abrahams and Szwed, *After Africa*; and Orlando Patterson, *The Sociology of Slavery*.
17. Peter Wolfe describes Antoinette in this scene as "beyond the purviews of reason" (*Jean Rhys*, p. 146). Helen Nebeker writes of Antoinette's "unreasoning fear and essential dependency," concluding that Antoinette (and "woman" in Rhys's novels) is "ultimately the victim, not of man but of herself" (*Jean Rhys: Woman in Passage*, p. 155). Teresa O'Connor states that Antoinette visits Christophine because she is "sexually obsessed, tor-

mented by . . . desire" and that "the desire to please the man" is "the first step in the cycle of descent of Rhys's women" (*Jean Rhys*, pp. 191, 164).

18. Wolfe does state that, while Antoinette's voice in Part II "breaks narrative consistency" (a flaw in his view), it does so at a time "when she reveals her true worth." He finds her worth, however, in the love for Rochester he sees expressed in her demand for an aphrodisiac (*Jean Rhys*, p. 146). This "love" is exactly the quality that O'Connor, in line with Thomas Staley, sees as "sexual obsession." Staley also faults Antoinette for her "assumption that sexual passion can evoke and redeem love" (*Jean Rhys*, p. 112).

19. Rachel Blau DuPlessis, *Writing Beyond the Ending: Narrative Strategies of Twentieth-Century Women Writers*, pp. 2, 5.

20. Staley discusses both Rochester's and Antoinette's character flaws as responsible for their inability to form "a vital union" (*Jean Rhys*, p. 116). Wolfe, faulting Rochester, describes the "excellent prospects for happiness" that he and Antoinette might have enjoyed (*Jean Rhys*, p. 114). O'Connor states, "With their union, the dissolution and resolution of the opposites symbolized by their respective homes might have been possible" (*Jean Rhys*, p. 157).

21. Harris, *Tradition, the Writer and Society*, pp. 28–30, quoted in Drake, *Wilson Harris and the Modern Tradition*, p. 7. Harris's critique of the self-sufficient and consolidated character contrasts strongly with the assumption made in O'Connor's critical study of *Wide Sargasso Sea* and *Voyage in the Dark* that the normal healthy ego is centered psychologically through a positive mother-child relationship.

22. For discussions of Anancy folktales and their social functions, see Abrahams and Szwed, *After Africa*; Wilson Harris, "The Whirling Stone"; and Patterson, *The Sociology of Slavery*.

23. Gordon Lewis, *The Growth of the Modern West Indies*, chap. 7.

24. Sigmund Freud, *The Interpretation of Dreams*, trans. and ed. James Strachey, especially chap. 6. Nancy Harrison also discusses Antoinette's dreams from a Freudian perspective, but her interest lies in their expression of a female, rather than a more specifically Third World or Caribbean female, text. In line with current emphases on mother-daughter relations in Rhys's writing, she describes Antoinette's dreams as a "mother text" (*Jean Rhys and the Novel as Women's Text*, chap. 7).

25. Jacques Lacan, "The Insistence of the Letter in the Unconscious," in *The Structuralists from Marx to Lévi-Strauss*, ed. Richard and Fernande De George.

26. Charlotte Brontë, *Jane Eyre*, p. 279.

27. Baer discusses textual parallels that link Jane and Antoinette in "The Sisterhood of Jane Eyre and Antoinette Cosway."

28. Harris, "The Whirling Stone," p. 58.

29. Wilson Harris, "Carnival of the Psyche: *Wide Sargasso Sea*," *Kunapipi* 2, no. 2 (1980): 143–144.

30. Wilson Harris identifies this voice as coming from ancient endangered peoples in "Jean Rhys's 'Tree of Life,'" *Review of Contemporary Fiction* 5, no. 2 (Summer 1985): 114–117.

31. Tiffin, in "Mirror and Mask," makes the point that Rochester's treatment of Antoinette allows her to overcome historical and racial barriers separating her from the island's blacks. Edward Brathwaite has argued to the contrary in "Contradictory Omens: Cultural Diversity and Integration in the Caribbean," in *Savacou, Monograph 1.* He states that "no matter what Jean Rhys might have made Antoinette think, Tia was historically separated from her" by racist ideologies and by the gulf, imposed by white Creoles as a group, between themselves and black West Indians (pp. 36–38). Brathwaite makes a valid point concerning actual historical events and ideologies as well as concerning *Wide Sargasso Sea* if one considers literature as obligated to reflect historical "reality." He does not consider, however, the novel as a creative response to that history and to its eclipse in nineteenth-century English fiction, a response written in another historical period of West Indian and colonial histories. Thus, he does not consider the ways in which the novel exposes Antoinette's racism as partly responsible for her dilemma nor the myth-making strategies of Rhys's writing that link Antoinette's consciousness to other groups of Caribbean peoples; nor does he consider her marriage as a kind of slavery, despite explicit portrayals of Rochester's legal possession and confinement of Antoinette and the rituals of slavery enacted in their relationship.

32. Ronnie Scharfman compares Antoinette to Simone Schwarz-Bart's character Telumee and states that Telumee keeps her "self" intact by joining female history because of early successful bonding with her grandmother. In contrast, she argues, Antoinette's inability to bond with her mother leads her to simply repeat her mother's madness and self-destruction. This interpretation denies the transformative power of Antoinette's vision and ignores the specifically Caribbean elements that enable Antoinette to overcome her alienation. See Ronnie Scharfman, "Mirroring and Mothering in Simone Schwarz-Bart's *Pluie et vent sur Télumée Miracle* and Jean Rhys's *Wide Sargasso Sea,*" *Yale French Studies* 62 (1982): 88–106. Scharfman, Harrison (*Jean Rhys and the Novel as Women's Text*), and Nancy J. Leigh emphasize sexual difference and focus on mother-daughter relations, neglecting the racial and cultural differences determining Antoinette's situation. Leigh even takes the European perspective that associates colonial natives with children by referring to native religion as a "childhood belief" in her discussion of the importance to Antoinette of her name. See Nancy J. Leigh, "Mirror, Mirror: The Development of Female Identity in Jean Rhys's Fiction," *World Literature Written in English* 25, no. 2 (1985): 270–285.

The predominance of analysis of the mother-daughter relationship in Rhys's life and writing testifies, I think, to its currency in feminist criticism and its ability to illuminate writing by women. However, while illuminating, it limits interpretation to an emphasis on sexual difference or flattens other kinds of difference to analogy with the sexual. It also encourages an ahistorical approach, or one that assumes twentieth-century European psychological norms to be representative. Rhys's novels remain compelling to us perhaps in part because they exceed our current categories of feminist analysis and call for a more complex theoretical accounting of social and textual difference.

33. Deborah Kelly Kloepfer argues that Rhys's characters are silenced or misunderstood "as the novels turn into schizophrenic monologues" and that such censorship is concurrent with maternal loss. See *"Voyage in the Dark:* Jean Rhys's Masquerade for the Mother," *Contemporary Literature* 26, no. 4 (1985): 443–459; and *The Unspeakable Mother: Forbidden Discourse in Jean Rhys and H. D.* I disagree that the narrative monologues are schizophrenic and see in them instead, as argued in Chapter 1, a strategy for identifying and engaging in dialogue with other marginalized people. Harrison (*Jean Rhys and the Novel as Women's Text*) also discusses the silencing of Rhys's characters and argues that in *Voyage in the Dark* and *Wide Sargasso Sea,* the silenced woman speaks through actions and words given to her by men. In these two novels, Rhys "speaks out loud what is left unsaid" in dialogues between men and women, thus retrieving the woman's voice. Harrison states that only in *Wide Sargasso Sea* does the female voice displace the dominant masculine discourse that suppresses it. Her analysis, however, is largely based on sexual difference. In contrast to both, Brown ("Mansong and Matrix") has demonstrated the ways in which Rhys's characters speak, not only against the suppression of masculine discourse, but through specifically female Creole patterns. By addressing the masculine bias in Edward Brathwaite's theory of creolization, Brown positions Rhys's characters as women within a specifically Caribbean context.

34. Toril Moi, *Sexual/Textual Politics.*

35. Nancy Chodorow, *The Reproduction of Mothering;* Elizabeth Abel, "(E)Merging Identities: The Dynamics of Female Friendship in Contemporary Fiction by Women," *Signs* 6, no. 3 (1981): 413–435; Judith Kegan Gardiner, "On Female Identity and Writing by Women," in *Writing and Sexual Difference,* ed. Elizabeth Abel, pp. 177–191.

36. See, for examples, the essays by Julia Kristeva, Hélène Cixous, and Luce Irigaray presented with helpful introductions in the French Feminist Theory issue of *Signs* 7, no. 1 (1981); and Jane Gallop, *The Daughter's Seduction: Feminism and Psychoanalysis.*

37. Margaret Homans, "'Her Very Own Howl': The Ambiguities of Representation in Recent Women's Fiction," *Signs* 9, no. 2 (1983): 200.

4. Voyage in the Dark: *Carnival/Consciousness*

1. Jean Rhys, *Voyage in the Dark* (1934; New York: Popular Library, n.d.), p. 63. Subsequent references to this edition will be included in the text.

2. DuPlessis, *Writing Beyond the Ending,* p. 4.

3. O'Connor describes the ending lines as expressing Anna's "false hope of starting again." Commenting on Anna's "yearning and nostalgia," O'Connor states that "she becomes more and more childlike" (*Jean Rhys,* p. 103). Staley

refers to "Anna's failure" and her "inability . . . to fit the experiences of both worlds together into her life" (*Jean Rhys*, p. 61). Nancy Casey, "Study in the Alienation of a Creole Woman—Jean Rhys's *Voyage in the Dark*," *Caribbean Quarterly* 19, no. 3 (September 1972): 96, states that Anna suffers from an "innate weakness" and "a lack of will, an absence of energy."

4. For the original version of the ending to *Voyage in the Dark*, see Nancy Hemond Brown, "Jean Rhys and *Voyage in the Dark*," *London Magazine* 25, nos. 1 and 2 (April/May 1985): 40–59.

5. Kloepfer argues that the changed ending forced Rhys to "mask the text," to censor the lost mother that Kloepfer believes Anna's death recalls ("*Voyage in the Dark*," p. 455). O'Connor states, on the other hand, that "the published version contributes more brilliantly to the structure Rhys has developed in the rest of the book" (*Jean Rhys*, p. 129).

6. See Mikhail Bakhtin, *The Dialogic Imagination*, ed. Michael Holquist, especially the fourth essay, "Discourse in the Novel."

7. Ibid., p. 273.

8. Abrahams and Szwed, *After Africa*, p. 227; and chap. 1, note 6. Edward Brathwaite describes more general social parallels between West Indian planter society and medieval European society in *The Development of Creole Society in Jamaica 1770–1820*.

9. Paul Fussell, *The Great War and Modern Memory*, pp. 7–8.

10. Stonequist, *The Marginal Man*, p. 145.

11. Georg Lukàcs, *The Theory of the Novel*, trans. Anna Bostock.

12. Bakhtin, *Rabelais and His World*, p. 47.

13. Rhys, *Smile Please*, p. 31.

14. See chap. 1, note 5.

15. Wilson Harris, quoted in Drake, *Wilson Harris and the Modern Tradition*, p. 37.

16. Kloepfer, "*Voyage in the Dark*." Harrison, *Jean Rhys and the Novel as Women's Text*, also interprets the meaning of the masks as reflections of power differences between men and women, differences which she argues remain even though racial difference is parodied. She does not consider the possibility that the masks may parody the condition of white women in European culture. Harrison consequently sees Anna's vision of the carnival as one of brutal injustice and does not find in the novel or its conclusion in either version any liberating or even illuminating moments.

17. Abrahams and Szwed, *After Africa*, Figure 18.

18. Etching reproduced in Ruth Perry, *The Celebrated Mary Astell*, p. 38.

19. Brown, "Jean Rhys and *Voyage in the Dark*," p. 52.

20. Bakhtin, *Rabelais and His World*, p. 53.

21. Ibid., p. 21.

22. In *The Politics and Poetics of Transgression*, Peter Stallybrass and Allon White cite the passage in *Smile Please* in which Rhys describes watching the Dominican carnival with mixed feelings of envy and fear. They refer to it as an example of "bourgeois hysteria" or "the phobic fascination afflicting bourgeois women in their exclusion from the carnivalesque" (p. 182). This clinical diagnosis does not take sufficiently into ac-

count the sexual subordination of women within the bourgeois class and the political dimensions of Rhys's wish to be part of the masquerade. Nor does it account for the cultural differences between Caribbean carnivals and those taking place in Europe. Even if such a diagnosis were valid in the case of the author, it becomes contradictory if applied to her novel, for it is the very excess or "hysteria" of Anna's hallucinations that allows her to resolve, through a politicized understanding of the carnival masks, her "neurotic" conflict.

23. We should also remember that Jean Rhys remained faced with a conflict between her preference for the more closed and conventional ending that an explicitly conveyed death would have given the novel and her publisher's demand for a less depressing ending. The ray of light Anna sees under the door in the final paragraph is "like the last thrust of remembering before everything is blotted out." We cannot be certain, even in the published version, that Anna actually lives.

5. Voyage in the Dark: *The Other Great War*

1. Jean Rhys, *Voyage in the Dark* (1934; New York: Popular Library, n.d.), p. 160. Subsequent references to this edition will be included in the text.

2. Fredric Jameson, "Imaginary and Symbolic in Lacan: Marxism, Psychoanalytic Criticism, and the Problem of the Subject," *Yale French Studies*, nos. 55/56 (1977): 338–395, discusses the ways in which the use of pronouns divides the subject.

3. I owe to a conversation with Katherine Hayles the idea of the mistress as a destabilizing third term.

4. I am alluding to the "French" feminists such as Julia Kristeva, Luce Irigaray, and Hélène Cixous. See the 1981 *Signs* issue (vol. 7, no. 1) on French Feminist Theory for excerpts from their work, accompanied by helpful introductions. See also Moi, *Sexual/Textual Politics*, for a critical introduction to their theories.

5. The original version appears in Brown, "Jean Rhys and *Voyage in the Dark*," p. 52.

6. Jean Rhys, Black Exercise Book, Jean Rhys Collection.

7. Wolfe, *Jean Rhys*, p. 117.

8. Ibid., "Preface."

9. Claude Lévi-Strauss, *The Elementary Structures of Kinship*.

10. Michelle Zimbalist Rosaldo, "Woman, Culture, and Society: A Theoretical Overview," in *Woman, Culture, and Society*, ed. Michelle Zimbalist Rosaldo and Louise Lamphere, pp. 17–42, develops the implications of Lévi-Strauss's analysis, arguing that the confinement of women to a domestic realm in virtually every culture maintains an asymmetrical opposition between domestic and public lives. Her later article, "The Uses and Abuses of Anthropology," reconsiders her earlier position, noting that the categories "domestic" and "public" in social analysis derive from Victorian social science with its implicit interest in developing an ideology of the family.

11. Jane Lewis, *Women in England 1870–1950: Sexual Divisions and Social Change*, pp. 147, 156.

12. Sheila Rowbotham, *Hidden from History*, chaps. 17 and 19.

13. Lewis, *Women in England 1870–1950*, p. 16.

14. René Girard, *Violence and the Sacred*, p. 231.

15. President of the Board of Trade to Parliament, *Statistical Abstract for the United Kingdom, 1935–1946*, no. 84 (February 1935).

16. Samuel Hynes, *The Edwardian Turn of Mind*, p. 200.

17. Ibid., p. 211.

18. Poovey, "'Scenes of Indelicate Character.'"

19. Ibid., p. 146.

20. Ibid., p. 153.

21. Josephine Butler, quoted in Walkowitz's detailed description and analysis of the Contagious Diseases Acts and the campaign for their repeal (*Prostitution and Victorian Society*, p. 114).

22. Quoted in ibid., p. 80.

23. Quoted in ibid., p. 81.

24. Quoted in ibid., pp. 45–46.

25. Quoted in ibid., p. 87.

26. Ibid., p. 87.

27. Lewis, *Women in England 1870–1950*, p. 133.

28. Walkowitz, *Prostitution and Victorian Society*, p. 244.

29. Erving Goffman has analyzed the significance of chance encounters in solidifying other kinds of group identity. Goffman suggests, for instance, that encounters with strangers present a contrast to and reinforce the solidarity of a group that the participants already belong to. A few strangers invited to a party, for example, reinforce the group's sense of itself and marks the occasion as memorable. The chance encounter with Anna and Maudie then reinforces the class, gender, and kinship ties between Walter and his male friend, the only participants in the encounter who belong to solid social groups. See Erving Goffman, "Preface," *Encounters*.

30. Lyn Hebert Lofland, *A World of Strangers: Order and Action in Urban Places*, examines the kinds of codes enacted by strangers in urban milieus and ways of learning them. Richard Sennett, *The Fall of Public Man*, describes the history of changes in dress and their significance for expressing and identifying personality and social position in urban environments.

31. Girard, *Violence and the Sacred*, p. 231.

32. As both Karl Marx and Georg Lukàcs have pointed out, in a society based on exchange of commodities, the workers must exchange their labor for wages, they become estranged from their productive activity, and their own labor power becomes a commodity: "*Subjectively*—where the market economy has been fully developed—a man's activity becomes estranged from himself, it turns into a commodity which, subject to nonhuman objectivity of the natural laws of society, must go its own way independently of man just like any consumer article" (Lukàcs, "Reification and the Consciousness of the Proletariat," *History and Class Consciousness*, p. 87).

33. "The direct barter of products attains the elementary form of the relative expression of value in one respect, but not in another. That form is x Commodity A = y Commodity B. The form of direct barter is x use-value A = use-value B. The Articles A and B in this case are not as yet commodities, but become so only by the act of barter" (Karl Marx, *Capital*, vol. 1, p. 87). Urban environments intensify this reduction of human life and experience to quantitative values of exchange, as noted by George Simmel, "The Metropolis and Mental Life," *Classic Essays on the Culture of Cities*, ed. Richard Sennett, pp. 47–60.

34. Marx's commodities speak, saying, "In the eyes of each other, we are nothing but exchange-values" (*Capital*, vol. 1, p. 87).

35. Marx analyzed the alienation felt by workers whose labor power becomes a commodity, which he called "estranged labor" or "alienated labor": "It [alienated labor] alienates from man his own body, external nature, his mental life and his human life . . . This is self-alienation . . ." (Karl Marx, "The Economic and Philosophical Manuscripts," in *Karl Marx, Early Writings*, trans. and ed. T. B. Bottomore, pp. 129, 126).

36. Fernando Henriques discusses the history of prostitution and attitudes toward it in the Caribbean in his book *Children of Caliban*. Henriques describes the open systems of prostitution that operated on estates and the open acquisition of mistresses or concubines by white men. The men might set up private housekeeping with a black or colored woman but would never consider marrying her. A woman who became mistress to a white man might, however, expect to gain from the alliance either in status, wealth, or, during slavery, through the purchase of her freedom. On the other hand, such women who remained slaves were subject to gross mistreatment at the hands of their masters and often their masters' wives. In *Voyage in the Dark* Anna may hope at first to marry her lover, but mostly she expects improvements in her life. Though the system of exogamous exchange in marriage breaks down for women like Anna, class groups still adhere to norms of endogamy. Prostitution and the practice of keeping mistresses help maintain marriage alliances within class strata by protecting upper-class women from illicit sexual advances and, at the same time, allowing men of their class extramarital sexual relations. Anna's situation is thus not atypical, but her déclassé position, intensified by the anomic urban environment, casts her unprepared into this unexpected state of affairs.

37. Marcel Mauss, *The Gift: Forms and Functions of Exchange in Archaic Societies*, trans. Ian Cunnison. Gayle Rubin discusses both Mauss's theory and its significance for Lévi-Strauss's analysis of kinship and marriage in "The Traffic in Women," in *Towards an Anthropology of Women*, ed. Rayna Reiter, pp. 157–210.

38. From a review contained in the Jean Rhys Collection.

39. Michel Foucault, *The Birth of the Clinic*, trans. A. M. Sheridan-Smith, p. 34.

40. Ibid., pp. 34–35.

41. I owe to Katherine Hayles a suggestion concerning some of the im-

plications of the man's occluded role in circulating venereal disease that the discourse and enactment of the Contagious Diseases Acts institutionalized.

42. Girard, in *Violence and the Sacred*, describes the social victim as a marginal individual sacrificed for the sake of public calm and order.

6. Quartet: *"Postures," Possession, and Point of View*

1. Wolfe considers all of Rhys's protagonists to be examples of a psychological type characterized by "her readiness to subjugate herself" (*Jean Rhys*, p. 25). Wolfe places all responsibility on the character's personality, argues that she "perpetuates male tyranny," and states that "Jean Rhys does not study the dynamics of dominance and dependence" (pp. 28–29). Mellown, "Character and Themes in the Novels of Jean Rhys," p. 464, claims that Marya "increasingly debases herself . . . a victim of love because she is at the mercy of her uncontrollable desires." Thurman, "The Mistress and the Mask," compares Marya with the character in *The Story of O*, who no longer wishes to remove the mask her sadistic master forces her to wear. Staley perceives that "the exploration of [Marya's] passivity lies at the heart of the novel" and describes Marya as unable "to assume postures which would require decisiveness and direction" ("The Emergence of a Form: Style and Consciousness in Jean Rhys's *Quartet*," *Twentieth Century Literature* 24, no. 2 [Summer 1978]: 206–207). He states that these negative qualities are "in her nature" and thus he, too, concentrates on Marya, the psychological type, rather than the social relations and institutions that involve her.

2. Jean Rhys, *Quartet* (New York: Random House, Vintage Books, 1974), p. 34. Subsequent references to this edition are cited in the text.

3. Mellown writes of Rhys's "failure to control the point of view" in her first two novels and states that in *Quartet* "Rhys's point of view is so patently that of the main female character and so biased in her favor" ("Character and Themes in the Novels of Jean Rhys," p. 470). Staley defends Rhys's technique in *Quartet* but also remarks that "she may occasionally appear to hover too closely over her heroine's misfortunes" (*Jean Rhys*, p. 204). Arnold E. Davidson sums up the general critical view: *Quartet* is "too close to . . . the writer's life to allow her the total dispassion and control that we expect in a major work of modernist fiction" (*Jean Rhys*, p. 61). His statement reveals the aesthetic values (of dispassion and control) behind such critical judgments, which we might question for their cultural and sexual biases.

4. Staley has described their affair in *Jean Rhys*, chap. 1. Davidson's chapter on *Quartet* in *Jean Rhys* continually compares the real-life individuals involved in Rhys's affair with Ford to the characters in the novel. To my mind the best criticism of *Quartet* compares, not Rhys's life to her novel, but the text to another text—that is, to Ford's *The Good Soldier*, elaborating his literary influence on Rhys's writing and her transformation of his artistic precepts to suit her own purposes. See Judith Kegan Gardiner, "Rhys Recalls Ford: *Quartet* and *The Good Soldier*," *Tulsa Studies in*

Women's Literature 1 (Spring 1982): 67–81; and Todd K. Bender, "Jean Rhys and the Genius of Impressionism," *Studies in the Literary Imagination* 11, no. 2 (Fall 1968): 43–54.

5. Rhys first titled the novel *Masquerade,* then changed it to *Quartet,* but the publishers encouraged her to call it *Postures.* At first she thought this title was meaningless but, in retrospect, believed it conveyed the sense of pretense she originally intended. See Jean Rhys to Selma Vaz Dias, January 23, 1950, and the Green Exercise Book, Jean Rhys Collection.

6. Mellown, "Character and Themes in the Novels of Jean Rhys," p. 470.

7. Bakhtin, *Rabelais and His World,* p. 9.

8. Dee Garrison describes Horney's debate with Freud in "Karen Horney and Feminism," *Signs* 6, no. 4 (1981): 672–691. Other voices participated in the debate, including those of Joan Riviere, Marie Bonaparte, and Clara Thompson. For an introduction to their work, see the collection *Psychoanalysis and Female Sexuality,* ed. Hendrik M. Ruitenbeek. For an account of these debates that defends Freud's radical notion of the unconscious from a feminist perspective, see Juliet Mitchell, "Introduction—I," in *Feminine Sexuality: Jacques Lacan and the Ecole Freudienne,* by Jacques Lacan.

9. Karen Horney, "The Flight from Womanhood," in *Feminine Psychology,* ed. Harold Kelman, pp. 54–70. This paper is discussed by Garrison, "Karen Horney and Feminism," p. 679.

10. Karen Horney, "Inhibited Femininity," in *Feminine Psychology,* p. 82.

11. See also Karen Horney, "The Overvaluation of Love," in *Feminine Psychology,* pp. 182–213; and "The Problem of the Monogamous Ideal," in *Feminine Psychology,* pp. 84–98.

12. Garrison discusses Deutsch's views in "Karen Horney and Feminism," p. 681.

13. Karen Horney, "The Problem of Feminine Masochism," in *Feminine Psychology,* p. 230.

14. Ibid., p. 226.

15. Mellown, "Characters and Themes in the Novels of Jean Rhys."

16. Horney, "The Flight from Womanhood," p. 57.

17. Sigmund Freud, "Feminine Sexuality," in *Psychoanalysis and Female Sexuality,* ed. Hendrik M. Ruitenbeek, p. 93.

18. Mitchell, "Introduction—I."

19. Rhys has deliberately departed from autobiographical fact in portraying the Heidlers as legally married since Ford and Stella Bowen were not. Her fictional experiment—in narrative point of view and analysis of the social construction of feminine character—requires the marriage.

20. Tiffin's excellent article, "Mirror and Mask," makes similar analogies, discussing Marya's postures in relation to Stephan, Lois, and Heidler as reflections of colonial relations between captives, victims, and underdogs, the ruler and the ruled.

21. Havelock Ellis, *Studies in the Psychology of Sex,* vol. I, p. 89.

22. Ibid., p. 42.

23. Bakhtin, *Rabelais and His World,* p. 39.

24. Ibid., p. 40.

7. After Leaving Mr. Mackenzie: *Repetition and Counterromance*

1. Jean Rhys, *After Leaving Mr. Mackenzie* (1930; New York: Random House, Vintage Books, 1974), p. 53. Subsequent references to this edition will be cited in the text.
2. Susan Gubar, "'The Blank Page' and Female Creativity," in *Writing and Sexual Difference*, ed. Elizabeth Abel, pp. 73–94.
3. John Berger, *Ways of Seeing*, p. 47.
4. O'Connor, *Jean Rhys*. Kloepfer also mentions *After Leaving Mr. Mackenzie* in connection with this theme in "*Voyage in the Dark.*"
5. Mary Ann Doane, "Veiling Over Desire: Close-Ups of the Woman," pp. 6–7.
6. Ibid., p. 4.
7. Elaine Showalter, *The Female Malady: Women, Madness, and English Culture, 1830–1980*. See also Alex Zwerdling, *Virginia Woolf and the Real World*, pp. 29–31.
8. Gilbert, "Soldier's Heart"; and Gilbert and Gubar, *No Man's Land*, vol. 2, chap. 7.
9. Gilbert, "Soldier's Heart."
10. Virginia Woolf, *Three Guineas*. Woolf quotes a British editorial of the 1930s: "Homes are the real places of the women who are now compelling men to be idle. It is time the Government insisted upon employers giving work to more men, thus enabling them to marry the women they cannot now approach" (p. 53). Woolf compares the argument to Hitler's philosophy that "the woman's world is her family, her husband, her children, and her home," stating that both represent the interrelated dictatorial impulses of fascism and patriarchy.
11. Ellis, *Studies in the Psychology of Sex*, vol. 2. Ellis writes, for example, "first of all, women must claim their right to their own womanhood as mothers of the race and thereby the supreme lawgivers in the sphere of sex and the large part of life dependent on sex" (p. 411). See Margaret Jackson, "Sexual Liberation or Social Control?" *Women's Studies International Forum* 6, no. 1 (1983): 1–17, for an analysis of Ellis's work as a reaction against feminists' efforts toward women's sexual autonomy.

8. Good Morning, Midnight: *The Paris Exhibition and the Paradox of Style*

1. John Allwood, *The Great Exhibitions*. The Champs de Mars, as Lucio Ruotolo has reminded me, was traditionally a parade ground for the French military, so the location both joins and opposes the Soviet and Nazi exhibition buildings through a symbol of France's own military aggression.
2. Jean Rhys, *Good Morning, Midnight* (1939; New York: Random House, Vintage Books, 1974), p. 13. Subsequent references to this edition will be cited in the text.

3. Staley, *Jean Rhys*, p. 84. Following Staley's insistence on viewing Rhys's writing exclusively as an expression of interiority, Helen Nebeker, for instance, analyzes the dream from a Jungian perspective as presenting the "warring mythologies of time" in Sasha's psyche (*Jean Rhys*, pp. 95–96). Peter Wolfe comments briefly that Sasha dreams "about her father being shot through the head in a London tube station" (*Jean Rhys*, p. 124). He also describes what he sees as Rhys's "indifference to the writing of social criticism" (p. 122). Jan Curtis interprets Sasha's dream metaphorically, stating that the Paris Exhibition is all exhibitions, displays, and "sketches of . . . illusions." She also reads *Good Morning, Midnight* as a social critique, but one critical of "the social system" and the "conventional regularity of the world" rather than of any historically specific time or place. See Jan Curtis, "The Room and the Black Background: A Re-interpretation of Jean Rhys's *Good Morning, Midnight*," *World Literature Written in English* 25, no. 2 (1985): 264–270.

4. Both Gardiner ("Good Morning, Midnight; Good Night, Modernism") and Squier ("'Yes—Yes'") have discussed the allusion to Molly Bloom in this final line.

5. Rosalind Miles, *The Fiction of Sex*, pp. 96–106.

6. Wolfe, *Jean Rhys*, p. 133; Nebeker, *Jean Rhys*.

7. Abel, "Women and Schizophrenia," p. 167.

8. Staley, *Jean Rhys*, p. 98.

9. Thurman, in "The Mistress and the Mask," describes ambiguity as the ending's important quality. She does not, however, develop her conclusion beyond attributing ambiguity to modern tragedy. Nebeker (*Jean Rhys*) also discusses an exhilarating ambivalence felt by the reader at the conclusion to the novel. Her archetypal analysis, however, leads her to stress themes of rebirth even while acknowledging this ambivalence.

10. Squier, "'Yes—Yes.'"

11. In this scene's interior monologue, Sasha quotes Heine's "Lyrical Intermezzo": "aus meinen grossen Schmerzen mach ich die kleinen Lieder" (out of my great pains, I make the little songs) (*Midnight*, p. 24). Raymond Meyer helped me to identify and translate this passage. See Chapter 1 for a full discussion of the paragraph's textual dynamics and significance.

12. Allwood describes the Italian exhibit as "the most extensive of the foreign pavilions . . . [showing] every aspect of life under Mussolini" (*The Great Exhibitions*, p. 141).

13. Gertrude Stein, quoted in Benstock, *Women of the Left Bank*, p. 130.

14. Woolf, *Three Guineas*, p. 142.

15. Ibid., p. 141.

16. Ibid., p. 142.

17. " . . . situations of danger, of birth and death, of suicide and homicide . . . are indicated by ritual, taboo and forbidden language." R. H. Grathoff, *The Structure of Social Inconsistencies* (The Hague: Nighoff, 1970), p. 147, quoted in Burns, *Theatricality*, p. 131.

18. Jean-Paul Sartre has stated that in a consumer society the labor pro-

cess itself is not as significant as the product, reified as an object and ritualistically consumed. Nevertheless, the claim to labor (property) lends that ritual authenticity. Neither thieves nor monks, he says, produce; their consumption is a stolen illusion, a fake participation in society's most meaningful activity. The female derelict also gains her money obliquely and spends it in a false world of appearances that negates, as through a distorted mirror, the authentic, real world. An inability or refusal to use the world as it defines itself renders its categories of morality and reason useless. Jean-Paul Sartre, *Saint Genet, Actor and Martyr,* pp. 361–363.

19. Ibid.

20. Staley, *Jean Rhys,* p. 91.

21. Girard, *Violence and the Sacred,* p. 12. Though Girard often conflates myth, literature, and more empirical social reality, he does convincingly describe the pattern of victimization and sacrifice in cultural and symbolic systems.

22. Benstock, *The Left Bank,* p. 134.

23. Marshall Dill, Jr., *Paris in Time,* p. 195.

24. Harold Ettlinger, *Fair Fantastic Paris,* pp. 129–145.

25. Dill, *Paris in Time,* pp. 297–300; Ettlinger, *Fair Fantastic Paris,* chaps. 13 and 17.

26. Bakhtin, *Rabelais and His World,* p. 40.

27. Thurman, "The Mistress and the Mask."

28. Printed in "Leaving Dominica," in *Smile Please,* by Jean Rhys, and contained in the Jean Rhys Collection.

29. Orin T. Klapp has said about the role of the fool: "Chiefly, the social type of the fool functions as a device of status reduction and social control. . . ." See "The Fool as Social Type," *American Journal of Sociology* 4 (1949): 162, quoted in Burns, *Theatricality,* pp. 123–124. And Girard has commented, "The fool is eminently 'sacrificeable'" (*Violence and the Sacred,* p. 12).

30. Allwood, *The Great Exhibitions,* p. 144.

31. Michel Foucault has traced through the theater a theme common to the subversive powers of appearance and madness. He refers to the plays of Georges de Scudery, in which illusion becomes the equivalent of madness: "One group of actors takes the part of spectators, another that of actors. The former must pretend to take the decor for reality, the play for life, while in reality these actors are performing in a real decor; on the other hand, the latter must pretend to play the part of actor, while in fact, quite simply, they are actors acting. . . . In this extravaganza, the theater develops its truth which is illusion. Which is, in the strict sense, madness." See Michel Foucault, *Madness and Civilization,* trans. Richard Howard, p. 35.

32. Girard, *Violence and the Sacred,* p. 238.

33. Kenneth W. Luckhurst, *The Story of Exhibitions,* p. 162.

34. Girard, *Violence and the Sacred,* p. 271.

35. Walter Benjamin, "Paris, Capital of the Nineteenth Century," in *Reflections,* p. 152.

36. Gardiner, for instance, has argued that the ending presents a culmination of the novel's textual collapsing of oppositions ("Good Morning, Midnight; Good Night, Modernism").

Conclusion

1. Michelle Cliff, *Abeng*, p. 21.
2. Ibid., p. 166.
3. Ibid., p. 21.
4. Selwyn R. Cudjoe, *Resistance and Caribbean Literature.*
5. Wilson Harris, cited in ibid., p. 266.
6. Abdul R. JanMohamed, *Manichean Aesthetics: The Politics of Literature in Colonial Africa*, p. 4.
7. I am modeling this suggestion on the title of the study by M. M. Mahood, *The Colonial Encounter: A Reading of Six Novels*, which treats novels by Conrad, Forster, and Greene and by Achebe, Narayan, and Naipaul.

Selected Bibliography

Works by Jean Rhys

Novels

Rhys, Jean. *After Leaving Mr. Mackenzie.* London: Jonathan Cape, 1930;
New York: Alfred Knopf, 1931; New York: Random House, Vintage
Books, 1974.
———. *Good Morning, Midnight.* London: Constable, 1939; New York: Har-
per and Row, 1939; New York: Random House, Vintage Books, 1974.
———. *Quartet.* London: Chatto and Windus, 1928 (as *Postures*); New
York: Simon and Schuster, 1929; New York: Random House, Vintage
Books, 1974.
———. *Voyage in the Dark.* London: Constable, 1934; New York: William
Morrow, 1934; New York: Popular Library, n.d.
———. *Wide Sargasso Sea.* London: André Deutsch, 1966; New York: W. W.
Dutton, 1966; New York: Popular Library, 1966.

Short Stories and Essays

Rhys, Jean. *The Left Bank and Other Stories.* Preface by Ford Madox Ford.
London: Jonathan Cape, 1927.
———. *My Day.* New York: Frank Hallman, 1975.
———. *Sleep It Off, Lady.* London: André Deutsch, 1976; New York: Harper
and Row, 1976.
———. *Tigers Are Better-Looking.* Includes a selection from *The Left Bank.*
London: André Deutsch, 1968; New York: Harper and Row, 1968.

Autobiography and Letters

Rhys, Jean. *Smile Please: An Unfinished Autobiography.* Foreword by
Diana Athill. London: André Deutsch, 1979.
———. *The Letters of Jean Rhys.* Edited by Francis Wyndham and Diana
Melly. New York: Elisabeth Sifton Books—Viking, 1984; Published in
Great Britain as *Jean Rhys Letters 1931–1966.*

Manuscripts, Notebooks, and Correspondence

Rhys, Jean. Jean Rhys Collection. Rare Books and Special Collections, McFarlin Library, University of Tulsa, Tulsa, Oklahoma.

Works about Jean Rhys and Her Fiction

Abel, Elizabeth. "Women and Schizophrenia: The Fiction of Jean Rhys."
Contemporary Literature 20, no. 2 (1979): 155–177.
Alvarez, A. "The Best Living English Novelist." *New York Times Book Review,* March 17, 1974, pp. 6–8.
Angier, Carole. *Jean Rhys.* Middlesex, England: Penguin, 1985.
Athill, Diana. Foreword to *Smile Please,* by Jean Rhys. London: André
Deutsch, 1979.
Baer, Elizabeth. "The Sisterhood of Jane Eyre and Antoinette Cosway Mason." In *The Voyage In: Fictions of Female Development,* edited by
Elizabeth Abel, Marianne Hirsch, and Elizabeth Langland. New Hampshire: University Press of New England, 1983.
Bender, Todd K. "Jean Rhys and the Genius of Impressionism." *Studies in
the Literary Imagination* 11, no. 2 (Fall 1968): 43–54.
Brown, Bev E. L. "Mansong and Matrix: A Radical Experiment." *Kunapipi* 7,
nos. 2 and 3 (1985): 68–80.
Brown, Nancy Hemond. "Jean Rhys and *Voyage in the Dark.*" *London
Magazine* 25, nos. 1 and 2 (April/May 1985): 40–59.
Campbell, Elaine. "From Dominica to Devonshire, A Momento of Jean
Rhys." *Kunapipi* 1, no. 2 (1979): 6–22.
———. Introduction to *The Orchid House,* by Phyllis Shand Allfrey. London: Virago Press, 1982.
Casey, Nancy. "Study in the Alienation of a Creole Woman—Jean Rhys's
Voyage in the Dark." *Caribbean Quarterly* 19, no. 3 (September 1973):
95–102.
Curtis, Jan. "The Room and the Black Background: A Reinterpretation of
Jean Rhys's *Good Morning, Midnight.*" *World Literature Written in English* 25, no. 2 (1985): 264–270.
Dash, Cheryl M. L. "Jean Rhys." In *West Indian Literature,* edited by Bruce
King. Hamden, Connecticut: Archon Books, 1979.
Davidson, Arnold E. *Jean Rhys.* New York: Frederick Ungar, 1985.

Drake, Sandra. "'All That Foolishness': The Zombi and Afro-Caribbean Culture in Jean Rhys's *Wide Sargasso Sea*." Unpublished manuscript.

Emery, Mary Lou. "The Paradox of Style: Metaphor and Ritual in *Good Morning, Midnight*" *Review of Contemporary Fiction* 5, no. 2 (Summer 1985): 145–150.

———. "The Politics of Form: Jean Rhys's Social Vision in *Voyage in the Dark* and *Wide Sargasso Sea*." *Twentieth Century Literature* 28, no. 4 (Winter 1982): 418–430.

Ford, Ford Madox. "Preface to a Selection of Stories from *The Left Bank*." In *Tigers Are Better-Looking*, by Jean Rhys, pp. 159–162. New York: Popular Library, 1976.

Gardiner, Judith Kegan. "Good Morning, Midnight; Good Night, Modernism." *Boundary* 2 11, no. 2 (Fall/Winter 1982–83): 233–253.

———. "Rhys Recalls Ford: *Quartet* and *The Good Soldier*." *Tulsa Studies in Women's Literature* 1 (Spring 1982): 67–81.

Gregg, Veronica Marie. "Jean Rhys and Modernism: A Different Voice." *Jean Rhys Review* 1, no. 2 (Spring 1987): 30–46.

Harrison, Nancy. *Jean Rhys and the Novel as Women's Text*. Chapel Hill: University of North Carolina Press, 1988.

James, Louis. *Jean Rhys*. London: Longman Group, Ltd., 1978.

———. "Sun-Fire—Painted Fire: Jean Rhys as a Caribbean Novelist." *Ariel* 8, no. 3 (July 1977): 111.

———. "Unconquerable Spirit." In *Essays in West Indian Literature*, pp. 11–23. London: Oxford University Press, 1968.

Harris, Wilson. "Carnival of the Psyche: *Wide Sargasso Sea*." *Kunapipi* 2, no. 2 (1980): 143–144.

———. "Jean Rhys's 'Tree of Life.'" *Review of Contemporary Fiction* 5, no. 2 (Summer 1985): 114–117.

James, Selma. *The Ladies and the Mammies*. Bristol, England: Falling Wall Press, 1983.

Kloepfer, Deborah Kelly. "*Voyage in the Dark*: Jean Rhys's Masquerade for the Mother." *Contemporary Literature* 26, no. 4 (1985): 443–459.

———. *The Unspeakable Mother: Forbidden Discourse in Jean Rhys and H. D.* Ithaca, New York: Cornell University Press, 1989.

Leigh, Nancy J. "Mirror, Mirror: The Development of Female Identity in Jean Rhys's Fiction." *World Literature Written in English* 25, no. 2 (1985): 270–285.

Look Lai, Wally. "The Road to Thornfield Hall." In *New Beacon Reviews: Collection One*, edited by John La Rose, pp. 38–52. London: New Beacon Books, 1968.

Luengo, Anthony. "*Wide Sargasso Sea* and the Gothic Mode." *World Literature Written in English* 15 (April 1976): 230–245.

Mellown, Elgin. "Character and Themes in the Novels of Jean Rhys." *Wisconsin Studies in Contemporary Literature* 13, no. 4 (Autumn 1972): 458–475.

Miles, Rosalind. *The Fiction of Sex*. New York: Barnes and Noble, 1974.

Nebeker, Helen. *Jean Rhys: Woman in Passage*. Montreal: Eden Press, 1981.

Nunez-Harrell, Elizabeth. "The Paradoxes of Belonging: The White West Indian in Fiction." *Modern Fiction Studies* 31, no. 2 (Summer 1985): 281–293.

O'Connor, Teresa. *Jean Rhys: The West Indian Novels.* New York and London: New York University Press, 1979.

Porter, Dennis. "Of Heroines and Victims: Jean Rhys and Jane Eyre." *Massachusetts Review* 17, no. 3 (Autumn 1976): 540–552.

Ramchand, Kenneth. "Terrified Consciousness." In *The West Indian Novel and Its Background*, pp. 230–236. London: Faber and Faber, 1970.

Scharfman, Ronnie. "Mirroring and Mothering in Simone Schwarz-Bart's *Pluie et vent sur Télumée Miracle* and Jean Rhys's *Wide Sargasso Sea.*" *Yale French Studies* 62 (1982): 88–106.

Schwartz, Lynne Sharon. "Between Dog and Wolf: The Fiction of Jean Rhys." *San Francisco Review of Books* 3, no. 8 (December 1977): 17–20.

Smilowitz, Erika. "Childlike Women and Paternal Men: Colonialism in Jean Rhys's Fiction." *Ariel* 17, no. 4 (October 1986): 93–104.

Spivak, Gayatri Chakravorty. "Three Women's Texts and a Critique of Imperialism." In *"Race," Writing, and Difference*, edited by Henry Louis Gates, Jr., pp. 262–280. Chicago: University of Chicago Press, 1986.

Squier, Susan. "'Yes, Yes': Sasha Jansen as a Critique of Molly Bloom." Paper presented at the 1980 annual meeting of the Modern Language Association, in Houston, Texas.

Staley, Thomas F. "The Emergence of a Form: Style and Consciousness in Jean Rhys's *Quartet.*" *Twentieth Century Literature* 24, no. 2 (Summer 1978): 202–224.

———. *Jean Rhys: A Critical Study.* Austin: University of Texas Press, 1979.

Thomas, Clara. "Mr. Rochester's First Marriage: *Wide Sargasso Sea* by Jean Rhys." *World Literature Written in English* 17 (April 1978): 342–357.

Thurman, Judith. "The Mistress and the Mask." *Ms.* 4, no. 7 (January 1976): 50–53.

Tiffin, Helen. "Mirror and Mask: Colonial Motifs in the Novels of Jean Rhys." *World Literature Written in English* 17 (April 1978): 328–341.

Wolfe, Peter. *Jean Rhys.* Twayne English Author Series. Boston: Twayne, 1980.

Wyndham, Francis. Introduction to *Wide Sargasso Sea*, by Jean Rhys. New York: Popular Library, 1966.

Additional Works Cited

Abel, Elizabeth. "(E)Merging Identities: The Dynamics of Female Friendship in Contemporary Fiction by Women." *Signs* 6, no. 3 (1981): 413–435.

Abrahams, Roger D., and John F. Szwed. *After Africa.* New Haven: Yale University Press, 1985.

Allwood, John. *The Great Exhibitions.* London: Studio Vista Books, 1977.

Ancestral Voices 4: Ancient Caribbean Music, Ritual and Dance. London: Arts Center, Commonwealth Institute, 1986.

Anderson, Perry. "Modernity and Revolution." In *Marxism and the Interpretation of Culture,* edited by Cary Nelson and Lawrence Grossberg. Urbana and Chicago: University of Illinois Press, 1988.

Auster, Albert. *Actresses and Suffragists: Women in the American Theater, 1890–1920.* New York: Praeger, 1984.

Bakhtin, Mikhail. *The Dialogic Imagination.* Edited by Michael Holquist. Translated by Caryl Emerson and Michael Holquist. Austin: University of Texas Press, 1981.

———. *Rabelais and His World.* Translated by Hélène Iswolsky. Cambridge, Massachusetts: M.I.T. Press, 1965.

Bauer, Dale M. *Feminist Dialogics: A Theory of Failed Community.* Albany: State University of New York Press, 1988.

Benjamin, Walter. "Paris, Capital of the Nineteenth Century." In *Reflections.* New York and London: Harcourt Brace Jovanovich, 1978.

Benstock, Shari. *Women of the Left Bank: Paris, 1900–1940.* Austin: University of Texas Press, 1986.

Berger, John. *Ways of Seeing.* London: BBC and Penguin Books, 1972.

Brathwaite, Edward. "Contradictory Omens: Cultural Diversity and Integration in the Caribbean." In *Savacou, Monograph 1.* Kingston, Jamaica: Savacou Publications, 1974.

———. *The Development of Creole Society in Jamaica 1770–1820.* Oxford: Clarendon Press, 1971.

Brontë, Charlotte. *Jane Eyre.* 1847. Reprint. New York: Bantam Books, 1981.

Burns, Elizabeth. *Theatricality.* New York: Harper and Row, 1972.

Butler, Josephine. *Personal Reminiscences of a Great Crusade.* London: Horace Marshall & Son, 1911.

Castle, Terry. "The Carnivalization of Eighteenth-Century English Narrative." *PMLA* 99 (1984): 903–916.

Chodorow, Nancy. *The Reproduction of Mothering.* Berkeley: University of California Press, 1978.

Cixous, Hélène. "Castration or Decapitation?" Translated and introduced by Annette Kuhn. *Signs* 7, no. 1 (Autumn 1981): 36–55.

Cliff, Michelle. *Abeng.* New York: Crossing Press, 1984.

Cobham, Rhonda. "The Background." In *West Indian Literature,* edited by Bruce King, pp. 9–29. Hamden, Connecticut: Archon Books, 1979.

Conrad, Joseph. "A Familiar Preface." In *A Personal Record.* New York and London: Harper Brothers, 1912.

Cudjoe, Selwyn R. *Resistance and Caribbean Literature.* Athens: Ohio University Press, 1980.

Davis, Natalie. "Women on Top." In *Society and Culture in Early Modern France.* Stanford, California: Stanford University Press, 1975.

Dill, Marshall, Jr. *Paris in Time.* New York: G. P. Putnam's Sons, 1975.

Doane, Mary Ann. "Veiling Over Desire: Close-Ups of the Woman." Unpublished manuscript.

Drake, Sandra. *Wilson Harris and the Modern Tradition: A New Architecture of the World.* New York: Greenwood Press, 1986.

DuPlessis, Rachel Blau. *Writing Beyond the Ending: Narrative Strategies of*

Twentieth-Century Women Writers. Bloomington: Indiana University Press, 1985.

Ellis, Havelock. *Studies in the Psychology of Sex*. 4 vols. New York: Random House, 1936.

Ettlinger, Harold. *Fair Fantastic Paris*. Indianapolis and New York: Bobbs-Merrill Co., 1944.

Fanon, Frantz. *Black Skin, White Masks*. Translated by Charles Lam Markham. New York: Grove Press, 1967.

Foucault, Michel. *The Birth of the Clinic*. Translated by A. M. Sheridan-Smith. New York: Vintage Books, 1975.

————. *Madness and Civilization*. Translated by Richard Howard. New York: Vintage Books, 1973.

Freud, Sigmund. *The Interpretation of Dreams*. 1900. Reprint. Translated and edited by James Strachey. New York: Avon Books and Basic Books, 1965.

Fussell, Paul. *The Great War and Modern Memory*. New York and London: Oxford University Press, 1975.

Gallop, Jane. *The Daughter's Seduction: Feminism and Psychoanalysis*. Ithaca, New York: Cornell University Press, 1982.

Gardiner, Judith Kegan. "On Female Identity and Writing by Women." In *Writing and Sexual Difference*, edited by Elizabeth Abel, pp. 177–191. Chicago: University of Chicago Press, 1982.

Garrison, Dee. "Karen Horney and Feminism." *Signs* 6, no. 4 (1981): 672–691.

Gilbert, Sandra M., and Susan Gubar. *The Madwoman in the Attic: The Woman Writer and the Nineteenth-Century Literary Imagination*. New Haven and London: Yale University Press, 1979.

————. *No Man's Land: The Place of the Woman Writer in the Twentieth Century*. Vol. 1, *The War of the Words*. Vol. 2, *Sexchanges*. New Haven and London: Yale University Press, 1988 and 1989.

Gilbert, Sandra M. "Soldier's Heart: Literary Men, Literary Women, and the Great War." *Signs* 8, no. 3 (Spring 1983): 422–450.

Gilman, Sander. "Black Bodies, White Bodies: Toward an Iconography of Female Sexuality in Late Nineteenth-Century Art, Medicine, and Literature." In *"Race," Writing, and Difference*, edited by Henry Louis Gates, Jr., pp. 223–261. Chicago: Chicago University Press, 1986.

Girard, René. *Violence and the Sacred*. Baltimore and London: Johns Hopkins University Press, 1977.

Goffman, Erving. *Encounters*. Indianapolis: Bobbs-Merrill, 1961.

Gubar, Susan. "'The Blank Page' and Female Creativity." In *Writing and Sexual Difference*, edited by Elizabeth Abel, pp. 73–94. Chicago: University of Chicago Press, 1982.

Harlow, Barbara. *Resistance Literature*. New York and London: Methuen, 1987.

Harris, Wilson. *Carnival*. London: Faber and Faber, 1985.

————. *Palace of the Peacock*. London and Boston: Faber and Faber, 1960.

————. *Tradition, the Writer and Society.* London and Port of Spain: New Beacon Publications, 1967.

————. *The Womb of Space: The Cross-Cultural Imagination.* Westport, Connecticut: Greenwood Press, 1983.

Henriques, Fernando. *Children of Caliban.* London: Secker and Warburg, 1974.

Holledge, Julie. *Innocent Flowers: Women in the Edwardian Theater.* London: Virago Press, 1981.

Homans, Margaret. "'Her Very Own Howl': The Ambiguities of Representation in Recent Women's Fiction." *Signs* 9, no. 2 (1983): 186–205.

Horney, Karen. "The Flight from Womanhood." In *Feminine Psychology.* Edited by Harold Kelman. New York: W. W. Norton, 1967.

————. "Inhibited Femininity." In *Feminine Psychology.* Edited by Harold Kelman. New York: W. W. Norton, 1967.

————. "The Overvaluation of Love." In *Feminine Psychology.* Edited by Harold Kelman. New York: W. W. Norton, 1967.

————. "The Problem of Feminine Masochism." In *Feminine Psychology.* Edited by Harold Kelman. New York: W. W. Norton, 1967.

————. "The Problem of the Monogamous Ideal." In *Feminine Psychology.* Edited by Harold Kelman. New York: W. W. Norton, 1967.

Huyssen, Andreas. "Introduction," and "Mass Culture as Woman: Modernism's Other." *After the Great Divide.* Bloomington: Indiana University Press, 1986.

Hynes, Samuel. *The Edwardian Turn of Mind.* Princeton: Princeton University Press, 1968.

Irigaray, Luce. "And the One Doesn't Stir without the Other." Translated and introduced by Hélène Vivienne Wenzel. *Signs* 7, no. 1 (Autumn 1981): 56–67.

————. "This Sex Which Is Not One." Translated by Claudia Reeder. In *New French Feminisms,* edited by Elaine Marks and Isabelle de Courtivron. New York: Schocken Books, 1981.

Jackson, Margaret. "Sexual Liberation or Social Control?" *Women's Studies International Forum* 6, no. 1 (1983): 1–17.

James, Louis. Introduction to *The Islands in Between.* Edited by Louis James. London: Oxford University Press, 1968.

James, Trevor. *English Literature from the Third World.* Beirut and England: York Press, Longman Group, Ltd., 1986.

Jameson, Fredric. "Cognitive Mapping." In *Marxism and the Interpretation of Culture,* edited by Cary Nelson and Lawrence Grossberg. Urbana and Chicago: University of Illinois Press, 1988.

————. "Imaginary and Symbolic in Lacan: Marxism, Psychoanalytic Criticism, and the Problem of the Subject." *Yale French Studies,* nos. 55/56 (1977): 338–395.

JanMohamed, Abdul R. *Manichean Aesthetics: The Politics of Literature in Colonial Africa.* Amherst: University of Massachusetts Press, 1983.

King, Bruce. *The New English Literatures: Cultural Nationalism in a Changing World.* New York: St. Martin's Press, 1980.

————, ed. *West Indian Literature*. Hamden, Connecticut: Archon Books, 1979.

Kristeva, Julia. "Women's Time." Translated by Alice Jardine and Harry Blake. *Signs* 7, no. 1 (Autumn 1981): 5–35.

Lacan, Jacques. "The Insistence of the Letter in the Unconscious." In *The Structuralists from Marx to Lévi-Strauss*, edited by Richard De George and Fernande De George. New York: Doubleday, 1972.

Lauretis, Teresa de. "Issues, Terms, and Contexts." In *Feminist Studies/Critical Studies*, edited by Teresa de Lauretis. Bloomington: Indiana University Press, 1986.

Layng, Anthony. "Dominica, An Island in Need of an Historian." *Caribbean Quarterly* 19, no. 4 (December 1973): 36–41.

Lévi-Strauss, Claude. *The Elementary Structures of Kinship*. 1949. Reprint. Boston: Beacon Press, 1969.

Lewis, Gordon. *The Growth of the Modern West Indies*. New York and London: Monthly Review Press, 1968.

Lewis, Jane. *Women in England 1870–1950: Sexual Divisions and Social Change*. Bloomington: Indiana University Press, 1984.

Lofland, Lyn Hebert. *A World of Strangers: Order and Action in Urban Places*. New York: Basic Books, 1973.

Lovelace, Earl. *The Dragon Can't Dance*. England: Longman Group, Ltd., 1979.

Luckhurst, Kenneth W. *The Story of Exhibitions*. New York and London: Studio Publications, 1951.

Lukàcs, Georg. *History and Class Consciousness*. Translated by Rodney Livingstone. Cambridge, Massachusetts: M.I.T. Press, 1971.

————. *The Theory of the Novel*. Translated by Anna Bostock. Cambridge, Massachusetts: M.I.T. Press, 1965.

Mahood, M. M. *The Colonial Encounter: A Reading of Six Novels*. New Jersey: Rowman and Littlefield, 1977.

Marshall, Paule. *The Chosen Place, The Timeless People*. 1969. Reprint. New York: Avon, 1976.

Marx, Karl. *Capital*. Vol. 1, 1887. Reprint. New York: International Publishers, 1967.

————. *Karl Marx, Early Writings*. Translated and edited by T. B. Bottomore. Foreword by Erich Fromm. New York: McGraw-Hill, 1964.

Mauss, Marcel. *The Gift: Forms and Functions of Exchange in Archaic Societies*. Translated by Ian Cunnison. Introduction by E. E. Evans Pritchard. New York: Norton, 1967.

McClintock, Anne. "Maidens, Maps, and Mines: The Reinvention of Patriarchy in Colonial South Africa." *South Atlantic Quarterly* 87 (Winter 1988): 147–192.

Meisel, Perry. *The Myth of the Modern: A Study in British Literature and Criticism after 1850*. New Haven: Yale University Press, 1987.

Miller, Nancy K. "Emphasis Added: Plots and Plausibilities in Women's Fiction." In *The New Feminist Criticism*, edited by Elaine Showalter, pp. 339–360. New York: Pantheon, 1985.

Mitchell, Juliet. "Introduction—I." In *Feminine Sexuality: Jacques Lacan and the École Freudienne*, by Jacques Lacan. New York: W. W. Norton, 1985.

Mohanty, Chandra Talpade. "Under Western Eyes: Feminist Scholarship and Colonial Discourses." *Boundary 2* 12, no. 3 / 13, no. 1 (Spring–Fall 1984): 333–353.

Moi, Toril. *Sexual/Textual Politics*. London: Methuen, 1985.

Morison, Samuel Eliot, trans. and ed. *Journals and Other Documents on the Life and Voyages of Christopher Columbus*. New York: Heritage Press, 1963.

Morrish, Ivor. *Obeah, Christ and Rastaman: Jamaica and Its Religions*. Cambridge, England: James Clarke and Co., 1982.

Park, Robert. "Human Migration and the Marginal Man." In *Classic Essays on the Culture of Cities*, edited by Richard Sennett, pp. 131–142. New York: Appleton-Century-Crofts, 1969.

Patterson, Orlando. *The Sociology of Slavery*. London: Associated University Press, 1969.

Perry, Ruth. *The Celebrated Mary Astell: An Early English Feminist*. Chicago and London: Chicago University Press, 1986.

Poovey, Mary. "'Scenes of an Indelicate Character': The Medical 'Treatment' of Victorian Women." *Representations* 14 (Spring 1986): 137–168.

Pratt, Mary Louise. "Scratches on the Face of the Country; or, What Mr. Barrow Saw in the Land of the Bushmen." In *"Race," Writing, and Difference*, edited by Henry Louis Gates, Jr., pp. 138–162. Chicago: Chicago University Press, 1986.

President of the Board of Trade to Parliament. *Statistical Abstract for the United Kingdom, 1935–1946*. No. 84. London: His Majesty's Stationery Office, February 1935.

Price, Richard. "Introduction: Maroons and Their Communities." In *Maroon Societies: Rebel Slave Communities in the Americas*, edited by Richard Price, pp. 1–30. 2d ed. Baltimore and London: Johns Hopkins University Press, 1979.

Ramchand, Kenneth. "An Introduction to this Novel." In *The Lonely Londoners*, by Sam Selvon. 1957. Reprint. Essex: Longman Group, Ltd., 1987.

Ricoeur, Paul. "Hermeneutics: The Approaches to Symbol." In *Freud and Philosophy*. New Haven: Yale University Press, 1970.

Rosaldo, Michelle Zimbalist. "The Uses and Abuses of Anthropology: Reflections on Feminism and Cross-Cultural Understanding." *Signs* 5, no. 3 (Spring 1980): 389–417.

———. "Woman, Culture, and Society: A Theoretical Overview." In *Woman, Culture, and Society*, edited by Michelle Zimbalist Rosaldo and Louise Lamphere. Stanford, California: Stanford University Press, 1974.

Rowbotham, Sheila. *Hidden from History*. London: Pluto Press, 1973.

Reyes, Angelita. "Maroon Nanny and Creole Difference: Reconsidering Jean Rhys's West Indian Landscape and *Wide Sargasso Sea*." Unpublished manuscript.

Ruitenbeek, Hendrik M., ed. *Psychoanalysis and Female Sexuality.* New Haven: College and University Press, 1966.

Russo, Mary. "Female Grotesques: Carnival and Theory." In *Feminist Studies/Critical Studies,* edited by Teresa de Lauretis. Bloomington: Indiana University Press, 1986.

Rubin, Gayle. "The Traffic in Women." In *Towards an Anthropology of Women,* edited by Rayna Reiter. New York and London: Monthly Review Press, 1975.

Sartre, Jean-Paul. *Saint Genet, Actor and Martyr.* New York: New American Library, 1971.

Schwarz-Bart, Simone. *The Bridge of Beyond.* Translated by Barbara Bray. 1972. Reprint. London and Kingston: Heinemann Educational Books, Ltd., 1982.

Selvon, Sam. *Moses Migrating.* England: Longman, 1983.

Sennett, Richard. *The Fall of Public Man.* New York: Vintage Books, 1978.

Showalter, Elaine. *The Female Malady: Women, Madness, and English Culture, 1830–1980.* New York: Pantheon, 1985.

Simmel, George. "The Metropolis and Mental Life." In *Classic Essays on the Culture of Cities,* edited by Richard Sennett. New York: Appleton-Century-Crofts, 1969.

Stallybrass, Peter, and Allon White. *The Politics and Poetics of Transgression.* London: Methuen, 1986.

Stonequist, Everett V. *The Marginal Man.* New York: Charles Scribners, 1937.

Walcott, Derek. "A Far Cry from Africa." In *The Penguin Book of Caribbean Verse in English,* edited by Paula Burnett. Middlesex: Penguin Books, 1986.

Walkowitz, Judith. *Prostitution and Victorian Society: Women, Class, and the State.* Cambridge and New York: Cambridge University Press, 1980.

Williams, Eric. *From Columbus to Castro: The History of the Caribbean, 1492–1969.* London: André Deutsch, Ltd., 1970.

Woolf, Virginia. *Street Haunting.* San Francisco: Westgate Press, 1930.

———. *Three Guineas.* New York: Harcourt Brace Jovanovich, 1938.

Zwerdling, Alex. *Virginia Woolf and the Real World.* Berkeley: University of California Press, 1986.

Index